Intimate Distance

Michelle Bigenho

Intimate Distance

ANDEAN MUSIC IN JAPAN

Duke University Press

Durham and London

2012

© 2012 Duke University Press
All rights reserved
Printed in the United States of America
on acid-free paper ♾
Designed by C. H. Westmoreland
Typeset in Charis with Lato display
by Tseng Information Systems, Inc.
Library of Congress Cataloging-
in-Publication Data appear on the
last printed page of this book.

*Frontispiece art based on photograph
from the author's collection*

FOR PAUL,

MÚSICA DE MAESTROS,

AND THE GREENFIELD IRISH SESSION

Contents

Acknowledgments

The myth of the single-authored book lives on in spite of the fact we are all in on the secret. The book in your hands would not be possible without the cooperation and contribution of many different individuals, many of whom I am sure I will forget as I make my way through the genealogy of this text.

The project emerged in the realm of music performance and friendships developed over the last seventeen years. I give my heartfelt thanks to Rolando Encinas, the director of Música de Maestros, who over the years has tolerated my itinerant comings and goings from his Bolivian orchestra and has always welcomed me with rehearsals, recording sessions, new pieces to learn, and other compelling reasons to practice my violin. The names of the members of Música de Maestros are too numerous to list here, but they all deserve recognition for their roles in keeping me connected to Bolivian music. These shared musical moments always pull me away from the textual realms that usually dominate the day-to-day activities of an academic. They remind me of the importance of *doing* music, even if I don't make a living at it. I am grateful to those musicians with whom I toured Japan and shared an intense three months on the road: Rolando Encinas, Yuliano Encinas, Victor Hugo Gironda, Claudia Gozalves, Koji Hishimoto, and Edwing Pantoja.

Many musicians in Japan and Bolivia shared with me their musical histories. Special thanks go to Koji Hishimoto and Takaatsu Kinoshita for helping me make contacts in Japan and for sharing the stories of their extensive work in Bolivian music. Ernesto Cavour generously allowed me to interview him three times over a period of several years. Additionally, conversations and interviews with the following people were key to the unpacking of this project: Virginia Benavides, Alejandro Cámara, Juan Carlos Cordero, Donato Espinoza, Daiji Fukuda, Luis Guillén, Jiro Hamada, Hitoshi Hashimoto, Kenichi Inazawa, Suyoku Ito, Ernesto Kawamoto, Zenobia Mamani, Shizue Shimada, Kaiya Yoshihiro, and members of the groups Los Borrachos and Los Vientos.

On my annual visits to Bolivia, many people have welcomed me with their generous hospitality and with their intellectual exchanges about

Bolivian politics and/or music: Rossana Barragán, Julio Calla, Pamela Calla, Martha Cajías, Juan Carlos Cordero, Rolando Encinas, Elizabeth Jiménez, Yolanda Mazuelos, Iris Mendizábal, Ramiro Molina, Alvaro Montenegro, Julieta Paredes, and Cecilia Rocabado.

Members of a writers group in which I participate (Julie Hemment, Beth Notar, Joshua Roth, and Barbara Yngvesson) saw different chapters of this book at different stages of its writing. Key ideas, like the focus on "intimate distance" emerged from these readings and conversations, all conducted around delicious home-cooked meals. Participation in this group has sustained my writing process in a community of reciprocal exchanges, commentary, and constructive critique.

Hampshire College, an innovative liberal arts institution, has provided me with a professional context in which to develop fully this ethnographic project. Hampshire's support of my research—over several years of summer and extra faculty development grants—has made possible annual visits to Bolivia. Under Hampshire's sabbatical policy I was able to conduct the original fieldwork "on the road" as a Bolivian musician in Japan, and a Whiting Foundation Grant made possible part of my fieldwork in both Bolivia and Japan. The intellectual curiosity of Hampshire students and the incredible engagement of my colleagues have inspired me, showing me exactly what it means to combine scholarship and teaching. Within this context, I presented parts of this book to and subsequently benefited from exchanges with Margaret Cerullo, Jennifer Hamilton, Frank Holmquist, Kay Johnson, and Barbara Yngvesson. In the Five Colleges I have also presented this work at the University of Massachusetts, Amherst, receiving crucial comments from Sonia Alvarez, Gloria Bernabe-Ramos, and Millie Thayer. To other friends and colleagues in the Five Colleges and elsewhere I am thankful for dialogues that motivate continued intellectual engagements: Steffan Igor Ayora Diaz, Carollee Bengelsdorf, Maggie Bolton, John Borneman, Ilana Gershon, Karen Graubart, Billie Jean Isbell, Amy Jordan, Lili Kim, Liz Miller, Valentina Napolitano, Bethany Ogdon, Falguni Sheth, Jutta Sperling, Gabriela Vargas Cetina, and Helena Wulff.

In other venues I have had an opportunity to present initial ideas related to this work. To Sarah Radcliffe I owe special thanks for encouraging me to submit a chapter for her edited volume, *Culture and Development in a Globalizing World*. Conferences about Bolivia organized at Northwestern University and about Andean Music at University of California, Riverside, gave me the opportunity to continue exchanges with specialists working in the Andes—Heidi Feldman, Nicole Fabricant, Daniel Goldstein, Bret Gustafson, Zoila Mendoza, Jonathan Ritter, and Henry Stobart, among others.

I greatly appreciate Marisol de la Cadena and Orin Starn's invitation to participate in a Wenner-Gren symposium they organized on "Indigenous Experience Today." I benefited tremendously from exchanges with fellow symposium participants: Amita Baviskar, Claudia Briones, Michael Brown, James Clifford, Julie Cruikshank, Kregg Hetherington, Valerie Lambert, Francesca Merlan, Franics Nyamnjoh, Mary Louise Pratt, Louisa Schein, Paul Chaat Smith, Linda Tuhiwai Smith, Anna Tsing, and Emily Yeh.

A fellowship at the Humanities Institute of the University of Connecticut (Storrs) allowed me to begin the difficult work of moving from fieldwork to the conceptualization of the book. I greatly appreciate the insights gained from conversations with fellows and other members of the UCONN community: Guillermo Irizarry, Rosa Helena Chinchilla, Anke Finger, Robin Adèle Greeley, Michael Lynch, Sally O'Driscoll, Mark Overmeyer-Velázquez, Karen Spalding, Guanhua Wang, and Richard Wilson.

In the final stages of the project I was welcomed at Colgate University as an NEH Visiting Associate Professor of Humanities in Native American Studies and Sociology and Anthropology. Native American studies professors and students read a few chapters of this work and generously provided me with their ideas as I was finishing up the manuscript: Liza Bakewell, Helen Balut, Melissa Kagle, Jordan Kerber, Jenna Reinbold, Starr Kelly, Chris Vecsey, and Sarah Wider. At Colgate I further benefited from conversations with Michelle Stephens as we discussed parallel projects that addressed music and race.

Andrew Canessa, Paul Lopes, and Joshua Roth gave me invaluable feedback after reading the entire manuscript at different points of its elaboration; to each of them I am tremendously grateful for these readings of a work in progress. While this book has almost nothing to do with Irish music, as I was writing it, the Greenfield Irish session fed an important part of my life beyond the academic, bringing me countless pleasures: shared Sunday dinners and hours of playing music with friends. Sessioners have been extremely patient with my obvious lack of practice over long periods of time, with my engagement with another Other music, and with my extended absences as I traveled to Bolivia and other far-flung places like Cazenovia.

Valerie Millholland at Duke University Press showed enthusiasm in this project from its early stages and guided me through the review process. Thoughtful comments made by three anonymous reviewers helped me sharpen key points of the manuscript. Gisela Fosado at Duke also assisted with multiple queries as the book moved into production.

I am incredibly fortunate to have as parents Caryl and Edward Bigenho, who among so many other things, made sure music had a central place in my life. Finally, throughout the writing of this book, my compañero, Paul Lopes always had just the right recipe for the right moment, whether that was feedback, patience, encouragement, debate, humor, or a good *cataplana*.

At the completion of this project, however, I assume the myth of single authorship, and therefore the responsibility for what follows in these pages.

Parts of chapter 2 were first published as "Bolivian Indigeneity in Japan: Folklorized Music Performance," in *Indigenous Experience Today*, edited by Marisol de la Cadena and Orin Starn, 247–72 (Oxford: Berg Publishers, an imprint of A&C Black Publishers Ltd., 2007).

Parts of chapter 3 were first published as "Laboring in the Transnational Culture Mines: The Work of Bolivian Music in Japan," in *Culture and Development in a Globalizing World: Geographies, Actors, and Paradigms*, edited by Sarah A. Radcliffe, 107–25 (New York: Routledge, 2006).

Parts of chapter 6 were first published as "Inter-area Ethnography: A Latin Americanist in Japan," in *Anthropological Quarterly* 79, no. 4 (2006): 667–90.

1 Setting the Transnational Stage

"What are we going to do with your hair?" was the band director's worried comment when he met me at the airport in La Paz. He added this problem to his lengthy list of concerns that would have to be addressed before the band left to tour Japan. My shortly cropped hair thwarted any possibility that I might be asked to wear fake braids, a standard accessory in Bolivia's world of women's folklore costumes. Many women use these hair extensions to complete their look in an entrance parade like Gran Poder, a ritual in which numerous dance and music troupes take over the streets of La Paz, displaying colorful, kinesthetic, and sonorous splendor, as well as demonstrating religious faith and social power.[1] When I danced in Gran Poder in the early 1990s, I had spent hours combing the outdoor shopping booths for blonde braids, definitely a rarity in La Paz. Wearing fake braids for an annual ritual dance in La Paz seemed quite different from the possibility of wearing them as part of a performance costume on a transnational music tour. The thought of putting them in and taking them out before and after each performance already had me exhausted, particularly since I've never had a knack for "doing things with my hair." Short hair meant freedom from this rather time-consuming aspect of dressing up as an indigenous or urban indigenous Bolivian woman.

I also felt somewhat strange about putting on costumes that in Bolivia were not part of our performances. In Bolivia we wore a uniform of black pants, black vests, white shirts, and black fedora hats, a more mestizo look even if our repertoire always included indigenous genres as well. The term "mestizo" might be glossed as a reference to mixed Spanish and indigenous heritage, but it often refers to a non-indigenous person,[2] and thus it sets up a racialized binary that has deeply marked Bolivian history and to which I will return. Sometimes women in the group would exchange the pants for a skirt, but all other details of the outfits remained the same. It was when we traveled internationally that costume changes became an important part of the music performance, when women were asked to dress like women and everyone had to pack indigenous clothes. The Bolivian musicians on the tour took great pride in the different outfits they wore. Although most of them did not themselves identify as indigenous, the indigenous costumes as well as the mestizo ones were fully incorporated into their own nationalist sentiments about the project. While I was fully committed to the musical project of the group, as a US citizen my Bolivian nationalist sentiments were decidedly lacking. I also carried with me my white middle-class gringa reservations about representing indigenous peoples on stage, a process that, if transposed to my own country, could be heavily critiqued as something akin to the minstrelsy use of blackface or the scouts playing Indians.[3] I asked myself, why couldn't we just play great music? I often had to remind myself that mimicry might be as easily an expression of admiration as one of disrespect.[4]

In this book, I follow Bolivian and Japanese performances of Andean music—participating myself in these activities—in order to unpack the meanings behind playing what might be called "someone else's music." In different ways, Bolivians, Japanese, and I were all performing someone else's music, even though we all had strategies of making it our own. Bolivians played indigenous music as nationally identifying mestizos. The Japanese played Bolivian music as foreigners who claimed a closeness with Bolivia's indigenous peoples. And I played Bolivian music as a gringa anthropologist trying to make sense of this country's multicultural and indigenous politics. The story about my short hair indexes a myriad of issues about playing someone else's music. It points to the bodies that produce musical sounds of Others, the labor involved in the visual transformations of those bodies for the sake of performance, the perceived limitations of bodies that play the music of Others, the audiences' expectations for staged otherness, and the distinct racialized ideologies that shape interpretations of these shows. Short hair both marks the impossibility of using fake braids and reminds one of the fuzzy boundaries between the supposed interiorities of bodies—what is assumed to be there already in material form—and what is put on the outside of the body—the clothes, the dress, the costume. Short hair marked the contrast between my reluctance to dress indigenous on a transnational stage and Bolivian and Japanese expectations for precisely such costumed performances. The international presentation of Bolivian music was about the staging of an indigenous world, and the fascination with indigeneity had different meanings for all involved.

The experience of playing someone else's music points to a key theme of the book: that pull of desire toward difference and the contrasting distance that one still maintains while taking on the cultural trappings of an Other, about the multiple and contrasting stories of *intimate distance*—a key idea about which I will say more below. Here, I look at the staging of Bolivian music for Japanese audiences, as well as the Japanese fascination with Andean music. The Bolivian musicians, however, do not merely respond to exoticizing demands of foreign audiences. Nor do the Japanese simply appropriate this music for economic ends. Economies of affect are present in the playing of someone else's music, and in this work these affective exchanges revealed racialized narratives in which Japanese and Bolivians described a closeness to each other through an imagined common indigenous ancestor. What do these narratives mean for Bolivians and Japanese? While studies of transnational music and culture often draw attention to exoticism, commodification, appropriation, and tourism, I want to set aside these predominant interpretive frames, giving a more prominent place instead to the motivating factors of transcultural affect, the material effects of transnational cultural labor, and the racialized narratives of culture that reveal both new and old perspectives on questions of nationalism and transnationalism.

The "problem" of my short hair underscored the distinct performance demands of the international context. If for nine years I had performed with the Bolivian orchestra Música de Maestros (Music of the Masters) in a black vest, white shirt, and black fedora hat, now I was being asked to dress in indigenous clothes, and preferably in accordance with my gender. As part of my doctoral fieldwork, I had performed with this ensemble between 1993 and 1995, and since that time, annual return research trips to Bolivia have been coordinated with the ongoing performance and recording schedules of this group.

A week before our departure to Japan, the director of Música de Maestros, Rolando Encinas, had held a meeting to discuss the details of the trip and to make final decisions about costumes. In his apartment that doubled as his rehearsal space in the lower middle-class La Paz neighborhood of San Pedro, we sat on the low seats assembled from wooden crates and homemade cushions, the furniture of the ensemble's meeting space since the end of 1993 when I first began playing with them as a violinist. The other five musicians who would travel to Japan had completed a similar tour the previous year. Although I knew these musicians from previous performance work in Bolivia, I was the new one on board for the Japan tour. We had been rehearsing music every evening, and I felt quite comfortable with the repertoire, but costume issues represented a different kind of challenge. The director told me that we would all carry two costumes, an indigenous one for the first half of the program and, for the second half, our usual mestizo look—"as a *maestrito*" they would say in reference to our ensemble's name. To distinguish the group that toured Japan, we would wear burgundy colored suits rather than our usual black attire (see figure 1). The director made arrangements for me to visit the tailor who was making all the pants and vests. In La Paz, tailors do much more than alter clothing, and they often provide the least expensive option for anyone trying to uniform a group of performers. For the Japan tour, adding a burgundy skirt to the vested mestizo image was not an option. To dress as a woman, I would have to match the *cholita paceña* costume of the only other woman on the tour who was also a violinist, Claudia Gozalves.

The term "cholita" can refer to an indigenous mestiza woman, but comes from the term *"chola"*—a loaded reference in many Andean contexts. In her study of cholas throughout the Andes, Mary Weismantel calls attention to the fact that this imagined and real social figure is often described in sartorial terms—with reference to her "typical" dress—in spite of the fact that the term's referent is also heavy with meanings of both race and sex—what is imagined to be in the body and underneath the clothes.[5] The typical dress of the cholita paceña includes a wide gathered skirt (*pollera*) over at least three petticoats that are seen below the skirt hem like a lacy white border, a fringed shawl pinned together with a broach, and a bowler hat worn over hair parted into two long braids—the requisite hair style for anyone wanting to approximate a Bolivian woman's indigenous dress. The clothes of a cholita from La Paz, including a skirt from a colonial Spanish wardrobe and a hat from British railway workers, today may index an urbanized indian, but ultimately they reflect a complex history of European and indigenous aesthetics.[6] The aesthetic mix continues to shift and turn. The shoes of a contemporary cholita paceña are flat elegant slippers that look something like ballet shoes. But for our performances, the director had opted for a period look, taking inspiration from photographic images of the 1920s; with this costume, the other violinist, Claudia Gozalves, had to wear high-heeled lace-up boots (see figure 2). For this half of the program, I thankfully wore the pants in which I felt comfortable performing.

My short hair posed the most problems for the first half of the show, the indigenous section; I could not simply slip into a woman's pollera and fake braids. Actually, no one ever "slips" into these costumes. In folklore tours of France, I had seen Bolivian dancers set aside over an hour just for costume preparation. In theatrical work there is nothing unusual about spending this amount of time for costume and makeup preparation, but on this tour, in which everyone was a performing musician, there would be expectations about both costumes and musical preparation. It was something akin to the idea that an opera company's orchestra members would do their hair, apply their makeup, and change elaborate costumes as they also warmed up on their instruments. I had foreseen this possi-

1. Música de Maestros poses in Kyoto Japan wearing "mestizo" costumes.

2. Claudia Gozalves and Rolando Encinas dance the *cueca* in Japan. Claudia wears a "period" *cholita* costume with high-heeled boots.

Both photographs from the author's collection.

bility, and short hair seemed like my best defense, the best way of keeping an extra hour for practicing music rather than parting and braiding hair.

In the end, my costume problem was not insurmountable. After Encinas reviewed his vast knowledge about different forms of women's indigenous dress—a mental archive that came from performing folklore and traveling throughout the country since he was a young boy—he found the solution in a head veil that covered a woman's hair completely, and that was then topped off with a white wool hat. Gozalves and I would wear these headpieces, gathered wool skirts, and colorfully woven belts. For this part of the program the men on the tour wore white cloth pants, white peasant shirts, wide woven belts, *lluch'us* (men's woven hats with ear flaps), the same white wool hats, and an *aguayo* (woven cloths) folded and tied diagonally across their chests. The *abarcas* or indigenous sandals went with these costumes, while dress shoes were combined with the mestizo suits of the program's second half. For the second part of the program, I abandoned the feminine look, dressed like the men, and was thus spared any further clothing changes. But Gozalves changed costumes a total of four times—representing in turn a highland indigenous woman, an African Bolivian woman, a cholita paceña, and a woman from Bolivia's southern region of the Chaco. All her costumes fit in a huge bag that she herself had difficulty lifting.

Since the 1970s, Bolivian musicians have been touring Japan, often coming to rely heavily on these short-term jobs to sustain their economic and artistic goals at home. Those who earn a living in Bolivian music struggle at home with underemployment and general employment insecurity. A one-to-three-month tour of Japan is ephemeral in the long term, and a sure thing in the short term, a guarantee of significant income that might finance the next eight months of living in La Paz, and also allow for small capital investments that help move musicians out of their usually precarious economic position. When viewed in relation to other music employment opportunities at home or abroad, a tour of Japan is one of the best remunerated gigs that a Bolivian musician can secure. These jobs have shaped significantly the economic lives of Bolivian musicians, and to grasp ethnographically their significance, the interpretive frame must move beyond a predominant focus on transnational exoticism.

For these coveted contracts, musicians do their best to guard their reputations, trying to avoid or at least dissimulate the personal frictions that inevitably emerge from the extended close contact of on-the-road employment. Work relations on the tour may determine whether or not musicians receive another invitation. Juan,[7] a musician in La Paz who was worried about not getting another contract, speculated that his own music group might no longer fit what the Japanese wanted because his ensemble did not include any women, even as dancers. He surmised that the Japanese sponsors probably wanted both masculine and feminine representations of Bolivian folklore. Then he complained about how problematic it is to complete these tours with women, a comment that was repeated to me by other musicians as well. "Look at Ximena!" he said, referring to a woman who allegedly had been stealing and using up the phone cards of other tour members to call her boyfriend back in Bolivia. But stories of dishonesty among tour members cross all genders. With these close working conditions, a single experience of this kind was enough for a director to say "never again" to a tour with that person. Too much was at stake: the group's chemistry, performance moods, and ultimately future work.

Juan extended his discussion about the problems of women on the road, alluding to concerns about romantic entanglements. He mentioned Bolivian women who had married Japanese men and the "problems" that ensued. Their decisions about where they would live (Bolivia or Japan) and whether or not they stayed together often affected the complex and fragile social relations through which Bolivians either received a contract offer or continued waiting for a call. This musician was not alone in his opinion that feminine presence brought risk to this predominantly male performance space. Other fellow musicians made similar statements in my presence. Following comments like these, the person would quickly add, speaking to me, "of course you are different." They never elaborated on the ways that I was different. I surmised that as a gringa who worked as a professor of anthropology in the United States, I was already in a different economic position from other women who have performed Bolivian music in Japan. Or at least I had a certain license to behave differently through the privileges of being a gringa.[8] In spite of these general sentiments about the dangers of female presence, many Bolivian tours of Japan included women through dance. Although Gozalves played the violin, her presence was also used to feature four different typical costumes and dances. Three years after this tour, she married a Japanese man who had lived for six years in Bolivia, learned Bolivian music, and returned home to perform his own compositions of Bolivian music in Japan. But I'm getting ahead of myself in the story. Suffice it to say that love, intimacy, and sometimes marriage are also part of these Bolivian-Japanese encounters.

While this book is about Bolivian musicians who tour Japan, it is also about a significant Japanese presence in the Bolivian music scene. Through the 1970s and 1980s, Japan experienced an economic bubble that would burst by the early 1990s; Bolivian music touring patterns were established during this economic upswing. Japanese audiences have been far from passive in their reception of these Bolivian cultural performances; they have taken up these musical forms as hobbyists and professional musicians, often residing in Bolivia for extended periods of time. These Japanese who travel to Bolivia are not immigrants or diasporic populations but rather sojourners who, somewhat like tourists, seek temporarily an Othered experience that takes them away from what John Urry called tourism's opposite, the routines of organized work.[9] Urry's early tourism study framework, however, with its focus on the visually driven "gaze," the consumption of goods, and the clear us/them distinctions, seems inadequate to interpret the ethnography at hand, where Japanese are learning to perform their own Bolivian music, some of them even becoming professional "Bolivian" musicians.[10] Studies of tourism and exoticism read these transcultural encounters through models in which cultural commodities (or Others as commodities) are consumed.[11] While commodification and consumption of culture have formed common anthropological themes,[12] I find these approaches insufficient to address the affective economies of desire and imitation that rest at the heart of "playing someone else's music." While we had to tailor our performance presentations for the Japanese listeners, these audiences varied widely in their expectations and background knowledge, ranging from the uninformed school children who were watching a multicultural spectacle to the extremely well-informed avid hobbyist who might even join the musicians on stage. Understanding these phenomena requires going beyond a framework of staged exoticism as passively consumed by an audience of tourists.

The meeting of Bolivians and Japanese around the performance of Bolivian music shapes what I call an intercultural nexus, a cross-cultural intersection that is not necessarily shaped by direct colonial or imperial ties between the parties involved, and through which one can reflect on grounded practices that are often elusively termed "global flows." The metaphor of "flow," as Mary Louise Pratt points out, is a legitimizing and official language of globalization that tends to naturalize a social world, neutralize political differences, and evade the question of who benefits and who loses in this nebulous global tide.[13] Bolivians and Japanese are not directly connected by their respective colonial and imperial histories, and these distinct national contexts shape very different conditions under which Bolivian musicians seek temporary employment in Japan and Japanese musicians become sojourners to Bolivia. As an unusual space of connection, the intercultural nexus differs slightly from Renato Rosaldo's border theorizing or Pratt's "contact zones," because these authors' concepts are developed to grasp the intercultural politics in social landscapes that have been shaped by colonialism over hundreds of years.[14] Here, I heed Aihwa Ong's caveats about blanket applications of postcolonial theory to understand contemporary relations of inequality. Ong points to postcolonial theory's limitations for interpreting Asian contexts because it is built on a model of "the West and the Rest" and particularly on the historical foundations of European colonialisms.[15] A Japanese fascination with Bolivian music cannot be read simply through the usual interpretive frame of white Westerners' fascination with the dark-skinned exotic Other. Standard postcolonial interpretations are thrown off balance within the fieldwork of this study, which is contextualized neither fully within Bolivia nor fully within Japan, but somewhere in between. Bolivia and Japan have their own respective colonial and imperial histories, but they are decidedly not intertwined with each other. Nevertheless, the Japanese-Bolivian nexus still bears certain similarities with a contact zone or a border in that it is still permeated by unequal relations of power and saturated with feelings of desire and fear, intimacy and distance. Indigeneity may provide a point of emotional and affective connection, but in these stories, the travel of Bolivians and the travel of Japanese reflect a differentiated balance of power. The particular nexus I examine here is further complicated by my presence that triangulated imagined otherness across multiple cultural boundaries.

Why do I use the term "intercultural" rather than "transcultural"? Language and representation tend to force me into the use of a single word, but this project ultimately calls for flexibility around these terminologies. If the intercultural assumes the possibility that cultural forms—or in this case cultural performances—can be separated from the people who produce them (indigenous peoples and/or mestizos) and can enter into another kind of circulation as cultural commodities, this seems to fit the processes whereby Bolivian musicians are contracted to perform their national folk music in Japan. Reference to the intercultural tends to highlight ideologies of cultural ownership, copyright, and concepts of authentic and unchanging cultural expressions. On the other hand, Ong has argued, "Trans denotes moving through space or across lines, as well as the changing nature of something." Ong is particularly interested in the term "transnational" as a way to signal not disappearing nation-states, but new global articulations of capital within persistent nation-state forms.[16] My ethnography delves into the economy of transnational music work that is still driven, on the one hand, by nationalist sentiments and, on the other hand, by globally circulating imaginings of an Andean world. Terms like "transcultural" and "transnational" can capture these oblique movements across national borders, as well as the ways Bolivians, Japanese, and I are all changed through our performance of Bolivian music. In this case, people and culture hardly seem to be breaking apart, as we come to understandings, as well as misunderstandings, of our similarities and differences. But in the middle of this messier world of the transcultural, the transnational, and the transformational, our performances were ultimately straitjacketed into certain narrow expectations about proper Andean music expressions—the ideologies profiled within an intercultural view. Rather than fixing the intercultural and the transcultural to particular ethnographic moments, I find it more productive to let the interpretations slide between them, between the idea of culture as something that can be separated from persons and sold in a capitalist economy and something that is read through embodied practices, affective experiences, racially identified persons, and the performativity of everyday life. As Peter Wade has suggested, to understand the politics of culture, one needs to grasp the "contradictory coexistence" of "culture as a unity" and "culture as object and commodity."[17] This book highlights seemingly unexpected intersections in the politics of culture—ones I contend are happening more frequently within a globalized world. Music making becomes the lens through which to examine transnational music work, and the desires that bring Japanese, as well as myself, to dedicate ourselves to performing what is literally a foreign national music. The Bolivians, the Japanese, and I are *all* performing "someone else's music," and the draw to those cultural performances is highly associated with representations of indigenous worlds.

Staging Indians

In Bolivia's census of 2001, 62 percent of the population declared themselves as indigenous. This indigenous majority sits next to other significant statistics from the same census—that a majority of Bolivians speak Spanish as a first language and that many self-ascribed indigenous people live in cities. The census, always an imperfect instrument, has been critiqued because it did not include the category "mestizo," and also because it tends to frame indigeneity in rather singular terms.[18] Indigeneity in Bolivia is not about blood quantum. It does have something to do with colonial structures that shaped separate "Spanish" and "indian" republics, the hierarchical divide that continued after independence from Spain and that is viewed as one of the most debilitating legacies of the conquest.[19] At the base of this division rests a pernicious racism, the paradox of indigeneity in many Latin American contexts today. As Diane Nelson noted for the Guatemalan case, "hostile markings" imposed by others are reworked as indigenous identification and even as resistance.[20] Today, Bolivia's indigenous majority is composed of Aymaras and Quechuas in the western highlands and over thirty-three different ethnolinguistic groups who live in the eastern lowlands. The indigenous majority, however, can hardly be treated as a single unified block, and in some cases the differences between highland and lowland indigeneity have been manipulated by Bolivian state policies.[21] This book, however, is not about self-ascribing indigenous subjects. Nor is it about those who are pejoratively called "indians" by others. Rather, the book is about those who perform indigeneity for Japanese audiences, and about Japanese who come to relate to Bolivians and Bolivian music through their own racialized narratives of indigeneity.

During the time I conducted research on this project, the Bolivian political landscape underwent tumultuous shifts, and many of these transformations have been depicted to varying degrees as "indigenous," even though they often featured key alliances of different social movements — indigenous, leftist, middle class, and resource based.[22] The first shift came in 2000 with a Water War that put the brakes on the multinational privatization of water. Expressed through the popular ousting of President Gonzalo Sánchez de Lozada, the Gas War of 2003 set the "October agenda" that included demands for renegotiation of the international contracts by which Bolivia sells its hydrocarbon resources, an assembly to rewrite the constitution (this demand emerged first in the Water War), and the calling of special elections that in 2005 brought to power Evo Morales, Bolivia's first indigenous president. Unlike some recent Bolivian governments that have had to form postelection coalitions to assume the presidency, Morales was elected by a record majority. Within antiglobalization movements, Bolivia's indigenous majority has captured international attention. However, throughout my work with Bolivian musicians and Japanese enthusiasts of this music, the general silence — with a few exceptions — around these topics reflected the gulf between Bolivia's contemporary indigenous politics and the musical work of staging indigenous worlds.

Like many Latin American countries, since the early twentieth century, indigenous expressions have provided the raw materials for Bolivian *nationalist* performances, forming an *indigenista* sensibility through which indigenous things are represented, but often without the presence of indians themselves. Since the 1930s, a process of folklorization had slowly brought indigenous musical forms and instruments into the heart of the national project. Acceptance of these musical expressions in urban spaces, however, was still an uphill battle, fought first through the international popularization of Andean sounds. As I will show, Bolivian music's trajectory to Japan took several circuitous routes—through "gringo" associations, US popular music, and even through Bolivia's southern neighbor, Argentina.[23] Significant foreign presences and connections have shaped the historical trajectory of Bolivian folklore music. For example, a Swiss man, Gilbert Favre, loomed large on the horizon in the 1960s. Known by the nickname that also titles a song dedicated to him, "El gringo bandolero," Favre arrived in Bolivia via Chile, and is remembered for many things: for his purported romance with the Chilean protest singer Violeta Parra who eventually committed suicide, for his influence on how the *quena* (notched flute) was interpreted and viewed in Bolivia, and for his role in Los Jairas, one of the first Bolivian folklore bands that traveled to Europe during the Andean music boom of the late 1960s and early '70s. As Luis Carlos Severich, a Bolivian musician now residing in Japan, told me, "When El Gringo stepped out . . . it was something revolutionary. . . . The quena was dressed in gala clothes! A gringo played it! So the people said, 'Listen, if a gringo plays it we can play it.' That's how it was at that time." Severich referred to the racism of urban mestizos and elites in Bolivia that at the time was expressed through disparaging views about instruments or anything having to do with indians. When foreigners heard and began to desire and champion the sounds of the *charango* (small plucked stringed instrument), the quena, and the *zampoña* (panpipes)—the instrument trio that indexes a generic Andean indigenous world—Bolivian mestizos began to reassess their own appreciation for indigenous expressions, even as indigenous politics and indigenous subjects were still cordoned off in a separate world. Japanese listeners also fell under the spell of these Andean instruments.

"A Friendly Invasion"

Bolivian music is statistically insignificant when viewed in relation to Japan's multiple niche markets that feature fan organizations and entire concert circuits developed around foreign musical traditions that Japanese groups have made their own. As Bolivians and Japanese in this project were always quick to remind me, Bolivian music is a mere crumb in a musical smorgasbord in which Japanese have recreated tango, salsa, blue grass, jazz, Irish, hip-hop, reggae, and hula musics.[24] The quena, charango, and zampoña come to represent for a general Japanese audience what is glossed as "folklore." Only after several interviews in which I kept attaching a national modifier to the term "folklore," trying to clarify if they were talking about Bolivian, Peruvian, or even Mexican folklore, did I realize that Japanese fans of this music used the bare term "folklore" (*fokuroa*) interchangeably with "Andean music." In Japan, "folklore" refers to music with quena, zampoña, and charango.

What first piqued my interest in this project was the presence of Japanese within the music scene in Bolivia, a country with about nine million inhabitants. We have enjoyed the prominent participation of Koji Hishimoto as a first-rate quena player, zampoña player, and music arranger in the group with which I have played since the end of 1993. His orchestrations have shaped the sound of more than half of Música de Maestros's repertoire, and when he resided in Bolivia, other Bolivian ensembles also benefited from his musical contributions (Wara, Bolivian Jazz, and backup bands for Jaime Junaro, Enriqueta Ulloa, Jenny Cárdenas, Zulma Yugar, and Yayo Joffré). In seventeen years of working with Música de Maestros, I have seen at least five other Japanese perform with this ensemble at different times. Another Bolivian ensemble, Luz del Ande, has been led and directed by a Japanese man, Takaatsu Kinoshita, who lived in Bolivia for twelve years. When I first became aware of these facts, I didn't give them much thought until I heard that Los Kjarkas, probably one of the most commercially successful folklore bands within and outside Bolivia, had held a competition to replace their charango player. The winner of the competition was a young Japanese man, Makoto Shishido.

The contagious spirit of Bolivian music has attracted foreigners of other national origins, myself included. In a balanced assessment, I should add that during the years I have worked with Música de Maestros, three US, three German, one English, and one Swiss musician have participated at different times with this ensemble. Sometimes ignoring barely muffled critiques from Bolivians, the director of this ensemble has remained quite open to foreign participation, and the group's form—an orchestra that can number between seventeen and thirty members—expands and contracts according to those who are available for a performance.

While Japanese are not the only foreigners to mark the Bolivian music scene, their participation stands out like no other. As more than one Bolivian musician has told me, "It's like a friendly invasion." At the intersection of these two movements of people and artistic ideas—Bolivian musicians to Japan and Japanese to the Bolivian music scene—emerges a window into both the global political economy of Andean music and the more general question of how both Japanese and Bolivians at this musical intersection mutually imagine an exotic Other. The "friendly invasion" is usually carried out by young middle-class Japanese who may be taking time off between high school and university studies, putting off entering the Japanese workforce where jobs are difficult to find, volunteering their time for a year or two with the Japan International Cooperation Agency (JICA) in Bolivia, or traveling extensively as tourists before settling down into a work routine in their country. While a few Japanese women are part of this transnational process, most of the "invaders" of this music scene are men.

The Japanese who join the Bolivian music scene do not fit the general trends of Japanese immigration to South American countries. When I talked about this project with Bolivian musicians, two people strongly suggested I pack myself off to Santa Cruz, in the eastern lowlands of Bolivia, where significant Japanese immigrant communities can be found. However, while the nexus of Bolivian music in Japan intersects briefly with stories of Japanese immigration, in general these are two different storylines that run quite diverging courses, one about immigration and the other more akin to tourism. The summarized narrative of Japanese immigration to South America goes something like this. At the end of the nineteenth century and the beginning of the twentieth, Japanese companies facilitated contracts that brought immigrants to South American countries, and many Japanese left their country that, as it modernized and militarized, put increasing pressures on its citizens. The early immigrants went to Peru and Brazil to work in sugar and coffee. The Japanese had been immigrating to countries in North America, but by 1900, the opportunities were closing in these areas, and immigration shifted to South American countries. The first small group of Japanese immigrants to Bolivia arrived via Peru; they had abandoned work on Peruvian sugar plantations in search of better wages in rubber tapping, a business that declined by 1917. But the main flow of Japanese immigration to Bolivia did not occur until after World War II. After the war, the US occupation government in Japan planned large-scale emigration of Okinawans to Bolivia as a way to relieve the potential unrest on the war-torn Ryukyu Islands. The US Department of State sponsored Japanese colonies in Bolivia, and the Bolivian government responded with land grants to Japanese colonists. Thus Bolivia became the center of a plan for Japanese emigration that was only partially realized because Japan's postwar economy began to turn around.[25]

Taku Suzuki, who conducted ethnography in Colonia Okinawa in Bolivia, focused on the ambivalence felt by members of this diasporic community; they may emphasize Japanese-ness next to a fear of becoming Bolivian, but Okinawans, as historically colonial subjects within Japan,

3. Compact disc cover of Los Caballeros del Folklore, who toured Japan in 1973. *Image used with kind permission of Edgar Patiño.*

hardly have a straightforward relation to a Japanese "homeland."[26] According to Dale Olsen's ethnomusicological study, the communities of Japanese, and more specifically of Okinawans living in eastern Bolivia, are more involved in keeping alive Okinawan musical traditions than in becoming caught up in the Bolivian folklore scene.[27] Jeffrey Lesser's work on Japanese communities in Brazil highlights other concerns: the mixing of imagined nations of "Brazil" and "Japan" precisely in this community.[28] The Japanese who become involved in the Bolivian music scene do not generally enter these compound nationality equations. Rather, they remain "Japanese" as they imagine other prenational points of connection with Bolivians.

My angle into the Bolivian-Japanese connection is of course partial and decidedly *not* focused on Japanese immigrant communities.[29] However, in one ethnographic tip, that may or may not hint at other icebergs, I encountered an intersection of these two different transnational projects. Los Caballeros del Folklore (The Gentlemen of Folklore) is consistently remembered by Bolivian musicians as the first Bolivian group that toured Japan (see figure 3). When I interviewed René Masao Noda, one of the group's members who was born to a Peruvian mother and a Japanese father, he told me the story of how they received their contract. In Bolivia, they had performed for visiting Japanese businessmen, and the visitors were enthusiastic about Noda's presence in the ensemble. Not long after that concert in the 1970s, Los Caballeros received their invitation to tour Japan. On tour, Noda sensed he was treated like a lost son who was returning to his national home, even though he could not speak Japanese.

While Noda's story is connected to the larger overall narratives of Japanese diaspora to South America, most stories in this nexus go against prevailing immigration tales. Bolivians and Japanese in this transcultural nexus travel globally, but for the most part they are not immigrants. While a few Bolivians marry Japanese and end up residing in Japan, most Bolivian musicians with whom I talked enter Japan by invitation and under very specific and restrictive visas that their contracting company procured for them.[30] In contrast to the Bolivians who travel to work in Japan, Japanese who seek Bolivian musical experiences travel under very different circumstances. Unlike the flow of Japanese immigrants to communities throughout Latin America, these travelers have different reasons for leaving home and different expectations in the foreign country. Within the common narrative of Japanese immigration to Latin America, people think they will leave home temporarily, work hard, make money, and then return home; but they end up remaining permanently in the new country. I haven't met any Japanese in Bolivia's music scene who came with the intention of making money, at least not beyond what they needed to live during their sojourn in Bolivia. They come to learn about Bolivia, to experience cultural difference, and to apprentice themselves to master musicians. From the perspective of tourism scholarship, these travelers might resemble Valene Smith's "explorers," who are more like anthropologists than tourists.[31] Or they might look something like Nelson Graburn's "Nomads from Affluence" on a spirit quest.[32] Rather than the Japanese-to-Latin America immigration narrative, these travelers share more with Karen Kelsky's ethnographic subjects—Japanese women who seek international experiences and seem to "defect" from expected life courses.[33] The difference in my study is that more Japanese men become involved in this specific international nexus. Their narratives usually begin with an expectation of a short residency that is then extended as the travelers become enamored with the country and sometimes with a specific Bolivian. Even as they begin to imagine a possible life-long change of residency, their narratives more often than not, conclude with a return to Japan and ongoing longing and saving for the next trip to Bolivia. For those who go to Bolivia as volunteers, the sponsoring

Japanese agency limits their stays. A Japanese violinist who volunteered as a violin teacher at the national conservatory, and who played with Música de Maestros, attempted to extend her residency slightly beyond a two-year limit in order to accommodate performance activities in which she was involved. Her attempts failed, and she had to leave Bolivia according to schedule. These stories of travel to Bolivia are much more like those of the gringo student, tourist, researcher, or volunteer. Their motives for traveling—usually a desire to know and perhaps help a Bolivian Other—frame a different mode of interaction than those of an immigrant who wants to work, make money, and return home.

For the Japanese, being a fan of Bolivian music means *playing* that music—a messy melding of consumption and production that might call for a sojourn to the music's country of origin. Although I was taken with Bolivian music only *after* I was in Bolivia, I had much in common with the Japanese I encountered in this project. With them I shared the position of being a foreigner who was immersed in Bolivian music performance, and whose country of origin was thought by Bolivians to be rich, modern, and powerful. But I would discover that the Japanese and I also articulated quite different positions in relation to the foreign music we played.

Heart and Blood

When I perform with Música de Maestros, I am often asked to participate in public relations activities that promote an upcoming performance. At a rehearsal, Encinas tells us the times and places for interviews with specific radio and television programs, and we are asked to volunteer our time, play for the team, and do what we can to help publicize the concert. I've done my fair share of interviews and know the dreaded questions. Why are they so interested in my civil status when they rarely pose this question to my male counterparts? I know which DJs have to be approached like a minefield because they have a reputation for drawing out the negative tensions that might exist in the group. All radio DJs and television program heads must be approached with kid gloves. In Bolivia, noncommercialized musical endeavors—like Música de Maestros—that hope to draw crowds, depend on the goodwill of radio and television announcers to push their work and build up an audience. During these media encounters, I try to be as specific as possible in reiterating the upcoming events we are preparing, the new repertoire we are developing, and the distinct features of the programs. But one of the inevitable questions they ask is something along the lines of: "Why is a North American so interested in playing Bolivian music?"[34] In the early years of playing with the group, I answered the question by saying how I enjoyed playing the *cueca*, one of my favorite genres of Bolivian music. I also talked about the challenge of learning a different musical style, one that drew on my classical music training, but that had an entirely different character, *otro gusto*, another taste. Ten years later, in these interviews I also emphasized the friendships I have developed in this music-making process. But I never talk about feeling *Bolivian*. In fact, I have never reconciled the paradoxes of my own anthropological critiques of nationalism with the unapologetically nationalist current of Música de Maestros.

Quite separate from the pleasures of playing music with this group, my analytical work further develops interpretations that show how nationalism continues rather than breaks with colonial structures.[35] Bolivia's colonial and postcolonial contexts are not exceptions. Although the indian became championed within Bolivian national folklore music, socioeconomic structures have continued to produce unequal relations between indigenous and non-indigenous people, and dismantling those structures has become a major objective of more recent national politics. However, it is much easier to critique nationalism when you come from a powerful country that has bullied its way around the world, and perhaps it is more problematic to do so when you come from a country in which nationalism is one of few ideological tools that might tenuously tie together members of an impoverished country. Even as Thomas Abercrombie critiques the "Indian within" as danced by non-Indians in Oruro's carnival, he also recognizes the complexities of Bolivian nationalism that is "in sore need of an anti-imperialist and legitimating identity."[36] I still stand by my critiques of nationalism as an ideology—anti-imperialist or otherwise—and much of this book addresses how different nationalist ideologies play out in a music performance world. While I was on tour, Bolivian, Japanese, and US nationalisms intermingled and haunted this project in a peculiar way. My critiques of nationalism, nevertheless, are accompanied by an equally weighted engagement with the affective attachments to nationalist music performances and the material possibilities that emerge from these in terms of musicians' employment. I do not intend to reconcile the contradictions between the critiques of nationalism, the affective attachments to nationalist music, and the material potential of employment in this realm. Rather, I want to maintain these points in their inevitable tensions, proposing a different kind of understanding about all three.

When I perform with Música de Maestros, my dirty-blonde, blue-eyed appearance always draws attention to my non-Bolivian-ness. At one moment during a folklore tour of France in 1996, I was accused of being "a fake" (i.e., not Bolivian). I felt somewhat redeemed when the charango player came to my defense saying, "Oh, but she is Bolivian at heart."[37] My non-Bolivian-ness, however, was an issue for the Japanese tour organizers. In 2002, when my semester of paid leave from teaching at Hampshire College coincided with a three month tour of Japan with a reduced ensemble of Música de Maestros, I asked Encinas if I could join them, paying my own way and donating my musical performances to the group. My presence did not jeopardize the coveted contracted spaces that should be occupied by Bolivians. Explaining to Bolivians how I received a salary while not "working" at my academic institution was indeed complicated, and from their perspectives, rather incomprehensible. The director was thrilled to have me join the group. Everything seemed to be given *la luz verde*, the green light, until Encinas was told that my presence had to be approved by the Japanese company that sponsored the ensemble. Hishimoto asked me to send my "musical" CV, and we waited anxiously for the decision. I was not privy to the conversations that determined the outcome, but later Hishimoto told me the company had worried about having a North American in a Bolivian group that was supposed to be performing this nation's music. Hishimoto had faced similar personal struggles when he became a translator for the company. He had taken this job upon his return to Japan, after living several years in Bolivia. When Bolivian groups toured with the company, Hishimoto—seen by many Bolivians as a friend and accomplished Bolivian musician—wanted to join their staged performances. It took a few years, however, before this company accepted his presence beyond the capacity of translator. Since we had played music together with this same band in Bolivia, I suspect that Hishimoto was persuasive in getting the company to accept my presence there as well.

One might say my activity fell under the rubric of "playing Indian," but one also needs to consider who is making the "at heart" claim or defense. While Luke Lassiter began his personal journey among scouts and Native American hobbyists, he eventually developed a different relation to the native people with whom he worked—a relation in which his gifts as a singer were viewed above, or in spite of, his non-Indian subjectivity.[38] Bolivians accepted my place on this tour not because I played indian or performed Bolivianness, but rather because I played the violin and had established a trajectory with this group.

With Hishimoto and the other Japanese in this project, I shared the position of foreigner in relation to the music we performed. Both similarities and differences emerged, however, in the ways we imagined our relation to these Other musical traditions. When I turned the radio and television announcers' question on the Japanese, asking them why they felt an affinity for Bolivian music, I received an array of answers quite different from my own. When I interviewed a Japanese man I met in La Paz, a musician who went by the nickname "Apache," he drew connections between the Andean indigenous ritual world and a Japanese ritual world he perceived to be disappearing in post–World War II Japan. He said, "I think there is a little blood of the same race, from a long time ago, because if you look at the Japanese language and Quechua and Aymara [highland indigenous languages in Bolivia], some words even have the same pronunciation. They are the same Mongols."

Apache's statement was exemplary of many other responses I received when I asked that question. Japanese made references to similar musical instruments, pentatonic scales, and a world that sounded quite familiar to them.[39] But most of them alluded to a common "race," mentioning possible ancient ties with the indigenous peoples of Bolivia. These narratives that racialized culture were not ones I could share in locating my own position in relation to Bolivian music. I could accept the Other-ascribed "Bolivian at heart" narrative that referenced friendships and a desire to play a music that, when played well, gives me goose bumps. Here, similar bodily metaphors narrativize connectedness through interiorities, through heart and blood, but references to blood also signal race thinking. When I posed the question to Bolivians about why they thought Japanese liked their music, they repeated these narratives that racialized culture, referencing possible shared ancestry. Once again I was left out of this narrative of blood but implicitly included in one of friendship. Although most Bolivian musicians who tour Japan do not identify as indigenous, they often are required to perform indigeneity on Japanese stages. When Bolivians talk about an imagined shared ancestry with Japanese, they do so through an identification with these indigenous roots that are temporally shifted to a perceived prehistoric moment. In both the Japanese and Bolivian cases, intimacy is about narratives of shared blood traced to an imagined past that is safely distanced from contemporary nationalist narratives.

Bolivian musicians perform the indigenous Other of their own national narrative, the country's majority population that has been the nation's outside, the symbolic detour where non-indigenous Bolivians have constructed a national identification.[40] While I used friendship as a strategy of intimacy in the playing of someone else's music, the Japanese and Bolivians deployed imagined and temporally displaced genealogies. This ethnographic triangle leads to several questions about race, nationalism, and intimacy.

Hauntings

Eric Wolf reminded us of the "perilous ideas" about race that remain stubbornly present in the world.[41] He wrote in the 1990s, at a moment when academics began to reassess their own silences on race and the way "culture" and "ethnicity" seemed to leave race out of the analytic picture but viciously persistent in the racist one. For example, Walter Benn Michaels showed how contemporary politics of cultural identity in the United States continued rather than repudiated racial thought.[42] Anthropologists have been taken to task by those of their own tribe. If at the beginning of the twentieth century Franz Boas thought race could be separated from racism, leaving the former to the realm of biology while doing away with the latter, Kamala Visweswaran showed that such a separation is impossible, because the construing of race as biology needs to be recognized in itself as a cultural and ideological move.[43] The world of music is completely wrapped up in a racial imagination. As Ronald Radano and Philip Bohlman explain in their ghost-busting work, "A specter lurks in the house of music, and it goes by the name of race."[44] Following this line of work, I want to make explicit the multiple spaces where race thinking haunts the social constructs of this ethnography.

Race thinking haunts nationalism, as it also haunts the study of music, and the East-West dichotomy that conditions how one might play someone else's music. I call them hauntings because these ways of thinking are ever present yet often denied or attributed to others who are purportedly ill informed or not quite modern yet. As many authors have noted, race concepts have been not peripheral but central to a Eurocentric modernity, European colonialisms, and their emerging national projects.[45] Race thinking also laces discussions about who can most appropriately perform a specific genre of music. "It's in the blood," remains a common popular view, often seen in newspaper articles about musicians who are ethnicized and racialized in relation to the genres they play. In contrast, the classical musician is framed in terms of "talent"—a don of sorts—and perhaps in terms of the hard work she or he has completed to achieve a level of performance.[46] Discourses about music and about ethnomusicology, as Radano and Bohlman convincingly argue, emerge from racial categories.[47] Not unlike Boas's race/racism proposal in anthropology, ethnomusicology's focus on culture was supposed to respond to race theories that had prevailed in early twentieth-century musical thought.[48] Instead, ethnomusicology seemed to deny the racial foundations of its discourse by focusing on distinct musical *objects* rather than on diverse music-producing *subjects,* and by celebrating difference in a framework of cultural relativism that failed to question the construction of difference itself.[49] This ethnography focuses on music-producing subjects and pays attention to the nationalist and racialized thinking that frames the performance of "someone else's music."

While the question of imagining an exotic Other is often addressed through the dichotomy of East and West, of the Euro-American subject who imagines the non-Western Other as experienced in tourist, artistic, musical, or anthropological encounters,[50] the nexus of Japanese and Bolivians unsettles this angle. Postcolonial analyses often begin with Europe. When Europeans began to stage the world as an exhibition in the nineteenth century, non-Europeans became objects that could represent an "outside" or an "external reality."[51] However, contemporary "Latin America" does not fall easily into an East-West division of corresponding exotics and exoticizers, the West and the Rest. Fernando Coronil suggests that "the West" has maintained a shifting center of gravity, moving from Europe to the United States after 1945; he even entertains the idea of including Japan as "honorary European" in the Western construct.[52] Such a positioning for Japan would reflect the success of the Meiji government's nineteenth-century plan to "leave Asia" and get to know modern Western ways of wealth and power. Their campaign—as a strategy to eventually reframe unequal maritime treaties that were negotiated under European dominance—included sending students and government officials on study missions to the United States and European countries.[53] Within these missions, Japanese came to see themselves as "honorary whites."[54] Japan reversed this position in the 1990s, calling for "Asianization," a policy driven as much by a reaction against the United States as by Asian economic regionalism.[55]

As a construct, "the West" is indeed geographically slippery, following concentrated centers of economic and political power, and remaining haunted by its racialized trappings. In the Japanese-Bolivian transcultural nexus, race is more present than ever. If the reader will indulge me in the tongue twister—non-Western Others are getting together and imagining the otherness of the Other whom they see as not so other from themselves. While racialized attitudes within and between these groups can hardly be seen as uniform, race thinking remains key to these imagined connections.

Diverse geopolitical histories, colonialisms, and imperialisms still create a distance between the Bolivians and Japanese who meet around the performance of Bolivian music. Global inequalities still determine who needs to work in the transnational sphere and who is privileged enough to travel to Bolivia as a tourist, student, volunteer, or researcher.[56] In this project, Bolivians, Japanese, and I all made different kinds of attachments that worked within different racialized dynamics. My presence in this research as a musician who performs Bolivian music, and also as a white middle-class woman from the United States, triangulated the Japanese-Bolivian connections, sometimes putting me in new uncomfortable positions that ultimately unveiled different ways of viewing fieldwork attachments, area studies training, and critiques of nationalisms.

To give the reader a bare-bones introduction to my methods: this work is based on participant observation as a performing musician with a Bolivian band that toured Japan, interviews with Bolivian musicians who have toured Japan, interviews with Japanese hobbyists and enthusiasts of Bolivian music, interviews with Japanese who have become professional "Bolivian" musicians, and intermittent fieldwork in the music scene of La Paz since the end of 1993 (two years followed by annual month-long visits between 1997 and 2009). I have been working in Latin America since the 1980s, but I have no equivalent language or area training for Japan. Not only was I a *gaijin* (foreigner) in Japan but I was also a gringa. My work in Japan was shaped through a previous relation with Latin America, and my primary language in the field was Spanish. Rather than merely lamenting my lack of area and language studies training as appropriate to Japan, I conceptualize this work as a unique inter-area ethnography in which specific ethnographic insights emerged not in spite of, but because of the divergence in my area studies trainings. In chapter 6, I will examine more thoroughly these crucial methodological issues and their implications. This is a somewhat unusual textual location for the contemporary anthropologist's classic methodological discussion. I have preferred to present first the flow of stories about Bolivian music in Japan, and return to methodology, not as an appendix (as might be seen in a previous generation's ethnography), but as a chapter in which ethnographic innovations can be considered in relation to the main theoretical points that I develop throughout the book.

Intimacy with and Distance from the Indian

On the street of any major cosmopolitan city one might encounter poncho and sandal-clad musicians playing the quena, the breathy panpipes, the deep sounding drum, and the high-pitched charango. Although many Bolivian musicians resist this stereotypical representation of "Andean music," whenever I mentioned the topic of this book to friends in the

United States, many of them responded with reference to these street bands. Who has *not* heard one? The Andean street band may seem to represent the quintessential case through which the Other is exoticized for the pleasure of the Euro-American consumer—a process in which both performers and audiences participate. But what happens when the Andean sounds and performers go to Japan? What happens when non-Euro-American Others meet, and not simply as performers and passive listeners, but as musicians who sometimes come to share an intercultural stage?

When Hishimoto and I perform Bolivian music, we both draw on years of commitment to a particular musical project and on the friendships we have developed in that context. But when I dress up as a Bolivian, and particularly as an indigenous Bolivian, I have my own issues about embodying a historically subjugated Other. When Bolivian musicians dress indigenous, many of them are also embodying an Other—although they do not see it that way. For them, *not* to express the indigenous side of their Bolivian heritage would be tantamount to showing embarrassment about part of their national identity. For example, one musician critiqued other Bolivians who were unwilling to wear indigenous sandals in international performances, as if their refusal reflected both racism and an alienation from their own roots. For some musicians, wearing indigenous sandals on a Japanese stage is an embarrassment. For others, not wearing them represents a rejection of one's national indigenous heritage. The Bolivian musicians who decide whether or not to wear sandals are usually not indigenous themselves. These details resonate with what Michael Herzfeld called "cultural intimacy." Herzfeld coined this term to refer to a fundamental ideological apparatus of the everyday experiences of nationalism, grappling with the aspects of an identity that may be the source of embarrassment ("forms of rueful self-recognition") when facing outsiders, but that nevertheless give insiders common points of identification.[57] While "rueful self-recognition" captures part of what goes on in Bolivian nationalist sentiments in relation to indigeneity, it is necessary to engage the seemingly opposite feelings of pride in relation to indigenous things. While pride in and embarrassment about indigenous worlds mark a fundamental dynamic at the root of Bolivian nationalist sentiments, one can find in Japanese performances of Bolivian music similar issues about both closeness to and distance from the performed indigenous Other.

As Japanese performers embodied the Bolivian Other, they expressed no qualms about dressing up as indians, and they also drew on narratives of shared blood to express their closeness to an indigenous Bolivian world. Japanese who dress as Bolivian indians and perform Bolivian indigenous music, I will argue, reaffirm rather than challenge Japanese national narratives. In an essay titled "The Yellow Negro," the African American writer Joe Wood tried to make sense of Japanese youth who wore blackface in Japan; he came to see this phenomenon in relation to the specific Japanese national narrative of homogeneity that the "black-facers were poking fun at with their silly getups."[58] I suggest that Japa-nese have different reasons for dressing as Bolivian indians as they per-form Bolivian music—reasons that are more acquiescent with rather than critical of Japan's national narrative of homogeneity. In a study of the all-female Japanese revue Takarazuka, Jennifer Robertson drew parallels between staged cross-dressing and "cross-ethnicking"; the revue's cross-ethnic performances, during Japan's imperial moment, were part of offi-cial rhetoric about Japanization of colonized subjects; however, just as women performing as men in the revue did not become men, colonial subjects were not really expected to become Japanese.[59] Cross-ethnic per-formances of indigeneity are bound to have distinct meanings for Bolivian and Japanese musicians, as shaped by different nationalist histories and ways of deploying racial thinking. Ultimately, I will unpack both common and distinct roots of racial thinking that shape the Japan-Bolivia transcul-tural nexus.

The embodiment of the Other becomes a strategy for quite different claims of both intimacy and distance, ways of feeling simultaneously oh so close to and yet still so far from an Other. I use the term "intimate dis-tance" to focus on the desire across these boundaries, and to maintain the conceptual tension of those experiences through which one feels like and unlike others. Let me say a few things about intimacy. First, I am re-ferring to intimacy in its broadest sense, an understanding that allows for affect, desire, pleasure, and passion within and beyond sexual intimacy. I am following several authors who call for a conceptualization of inti-macy that extends outside the one handed to us by Western modernity. Lauren Berlant and Michael Warner suggest that the criminality of "non-standard intimacies" would not seem so criminal or fleeting if we still had a wider reading of normal intimacy, one that "included everything from consorts to courtiers, friends, amours, associates, and coconspira-tors."[60] Ann Stoler, who re-reads Foucault's *History of Sexuality* through the lens of European imperialism, also suggests moving to an understand-ing of "the education of desire" that is not already trapped in the narrow nineteenth-century discourses that "read all desires as sexual ones."[61] As I draw on Stoler's approach to intimacy, however, I must also add that her models, as well as Foucault's, are seen through the prism of a Eurocentric modernity and specifically through late European colonialisms. There do not appear to be direct historical or geographic connections between the colonial and imperial histories of Bolivia and Japan, although these countries indeed have their own colonial tales. In the sixteenth century, the Spanish colonized what is today called Bolivia. In the twentieth century, Japan had its Asian empire. While neither Bolivians nor Japanese are completely outside the Euro frame, imaginative ties between them disrupt the usual ways one talks about European colonizers imagining exotic colonized non-Western Others.

For thinking about this rather skewed connection of intimacy, I find useful parts of Svetlana Boym's concept of "diasporic intimacy," a reading of the intimate that shifts away from the sexual and the personal interiorities of the modern private Western subject, and instead takes up chance meetings, fleeting relations established in passing, and the belief that human beings just might be able to get along.[62] Stories about Japanese and Bolivians who connect through music speak to the "normative stranger-sociability" of the modern world,[63] even though globally determined unequal positions of Bolivians and Japanese enabled the encounter from the get-go. While many imagined intimacies form the basis for national communities, what we have here is an intimacy across nations, a "we" constructed through imagined genealogies, located at a point in time long before the existence of nation-states, and one that draws on a racialization of culture.[64] Of course, these central questions remain: How do these intimacies coexist with national projects? How are these intimacies doing different symbolic work for Bolivians and Japanese?

Diasporic intimacy allows for an interpretation of the seemingly oblique connections formed between Japanese and Bolivians who play Andean music. The Bolivians and Japanese I describe in this ethnography, however, are not part of diasporas. Furthermore, the intimacies of colonialisms and subsequent nationalisms also shape these tales. To examine this more power-laden side of intimacy, I find useful Elizabeth Povinelli's ideas on liberal subjectivities as formed within settler modernity. Povinelli argues that settler modernity produces and pits against each other two liberal subjectivities: the autological subject, whose life is imagined through the lenses of freedom and choice, and the genealogical subject, whose life is imagined as constrained by kinship and inheritances.[65] To develop her argument, Povinelli sets next to each other two ethnographic cases, US radical faeries and their references to Native American worlds, and her ongoing ethnography with Aboriginal Australians. Indigeneity, heavily referencing the genealogical subject, is a nodal point of connection between her two cases. She also frames her discussion of intimacy as "not about desire, pleasure, or sex per se, but about things like geography, history, culpability, and obligation."[66] When she writes about "love" she refers to geographically distributed processes that emerge from a dialectic between individual freedom and social bondage.[67] To summarize Povinelli: liberal subjects either have too much sociality or not enough; this oppositional framework is sustained within modernity; and geographies of colonialism tend to reflect this dichotomy. To consider the geography, history, culpability, and obligation between Japanese and Bolivians, I must look at the figure that anchors the point of their narrativized connection: the imagined indigenous ancestor.

Indirect "culpability" may be more relevant in the Japanese case, because the Japanese have no colonial history with Bolivians. The Japanese-Bolivian claim to indigenous intimacy, made through reference to blood and genetics, conveniently ignores the colonial and postcolonial formation of indigenous subjects within these respective countries. Since the Spanish colonial period, the area known today as Bolivia has been structured by a dual social system that classified people as indigenous or non-indigenous, even as complex social realities always challenged this simple dichotomy. The Spanish colonial apparatus designated two republics, one of indians and one of Spaniards. "Indians" paid tribute to the crown and were subject to a labor tax or *mita*; as such indians formed "an institutionalized identity" that served the colonial ends of organizing people, land, and resources for Spanish extraction of wealth.[68] "Mestizos," an expanding category not originally envisioned within the colonial apparatus, were included within the "republic of Spaniards."[69] Like many bureaucratic systems of categorization, these designations were indeed slippery and historians have dedicated detailed works to unpacking how colonial subjects navigated them.[70]

Upon independence from Spain, the new republics at first attempted to abolish the indigenous tribute, but as the new states needed revenue, the mode of extraction was reinstated through the euphemistically labeled "indigenous contribution."[71] By the end of the nineteenth century, and with the rise of liberalism, the category of "indian" was hardly determined by the tribute, and it had become more like a class designation, as states sought to reshape "indians" into individual land-holding peasants.[72] While the realm of Bolivian liberal politics included laws that attempted to de-link indigenous communities from communal land holdings (Disentailment Law of 1874, Ley de Exvinculación), some indigenous communities resisted these liberal moves, preferring to renegotiate their relations with the Bolivian state precisely by maintaining a special tribute status.[73]

In the first half of the twentieth century, several Latin American countries were once again reconsidering the categories of indian and mestizo. Within the idealized romanticized representation of the indian, intellectuals sought the roots of their nation—the indigenista sensibility mentioned earlier in this chapter. But *indigenismo*, as a nationalist discourse, went hand in hand with its fraternal twin: *mestizaje*. Between the beginning of the twentieth century and 1952, the mestizo went from being considered an abomination for all concerned, to being the positive center of a national project of inclusive citizenship.[74] In 1900, Bolivian intellectuals positioned mestizos as dangerous feudal overlords from whom indians needed to be rescued.[75] Indigenous rebellions also forced Bolivian elite to ponder more seriously what they referred to as "the problem of the indian" (*el problema del indio*) and the incorporation of this statistical majority into the nation-state's projects. Brooke Larson's work shows how, by the 1920s, the Bolivian state was burrowing into the homes of Aymaras through a rural indigenous school program that took family, hearth, and home as sites through which they aimed to reshape indians into productive peasants.[76] By midcentury and the revolution of 1952, Bolivian nationalism was characterized by an ideology of mestizaje that sought to incorporate indigenous subjects as homogeneous liberal citizens. Under this ideology, "indians" (*indios*) would become "peasants" (*campesinos*),[77] and indigenous expressions entered urban performance spaces as representations of the nation. The nationalist celebration of folklorized indigeneity, a form of indigenismo, worked in tandem with assimilationist politics of mestizaje.

In this reading of mestizaje and indigenismo I want to avoid the tendency to view these ideological discourses as uniform and directed only from above by a monolithic state toward its opposing popular and diverse sectors below.[78] I also want to avoid a mere dismissal of the resulting musical representations; dismissing them as performing the indian without indians does not get at the heart of the matter: how that intimacy of embodying an Other actually works symbolically, and how people come to make someone else's music their own. Here I want to look beyond the value-laden language of cultural theft and appropriation that closes off more thorough analyses of how cultural economies of desire and pleasure work. Under the discursive umbrella of mestizaje and indigenismo, music associated with indians becomes the center of Bolivian *national* folklore. Mestizo—or non-indigenous—musicians have often spearheaded these cultural-musical developments.[79] Bolivian politics of indigeneity have taken a new turn since the election of the first indigenous president in 2005, but initial assessments seem to show how musical indigenism persists within this new horizon.

When Japanese become enamored with Bolivian music and come to identify with an imagined indigenous ancestor, often referenced through the "Andean" region—their moves of intimacy and distance are similar to those of Bolivian mestizos who perform indian-ness as part of their nationalist repertoire. Like the Bolivian identifications with indigeneity, the Japanese ones also leave intact their own contemporary national narrative. In contrast with the Bolivian case, the claimed indigenous ancestry remains completely outside the dominant national narrative of homogeneity. Homogeneity is claimed in spite of the country's multicultural tensions around the indigenous peoples like the Ainu, the imperial incorporation of Okinawans, the return migrant Japanese, and the presence of foreign workers. In his study of Japanese Brazilian migrants in Japan, Joshua Roth indicated that Japanese can be quite enthusiastic about foreign cultures while showing decidedly less interest in engaging with foreign workers in their country.[80]

The realm of music might evoke ideas of pleasurable encounters with otherness or, in this case, with "Others who seem like us"—encounters where "global friction," as Anna Tsing calls it, may seem enjoyable rather than problematic.[81] However, perceptions of inconvenience, fear, and danger are always a possibility. South Americans' attitudes toward Japanese immigrants during World War II provide one clear example of the turn to fear. During the war, more than two thousand Japanese were deported from Latin American countries and sent to internment camps in the United States.[82] While the Bolivians and Japanese with whom I worked had mostly positive reports to make about their encounters in this nexus, the friction across these cultural boundaries is always about both desires and fears.

Love and Sweat in the Nexus

While on tour in Japan with Música de Maestros, we gave seventy-five performances in eighty-eight days. Each of us carried two white shirts for our staged performances. The problem we all faced was not being in one place long enough to wash and air dry these shirts. The heat and extreme humidity in Japan, so different from the cold dry highlands of La Paz, also seemed to work against attempts at keeping our costumes clean. When we heard that we were staying in the same place for two or three nights, energetic clothes washing began as each of us worked to remove the sweat that flowed from bodies to costumes in the process of extended daily cultural work.

Affective experiences emerge at this musical nexus, but so do relations of work. With the term "sweat" I want to dispel any preconceptions about music as some lightweight form of labor. Anyone who has watched a classical pianist perform a concerto will certainly see sweat. But I am also referring to the work of a tour, what occurs in addition to the moment of actual staged performance. Transnational music tours involve muscles (big and small), the disruption of regular eating and sleeping patterns, separation from family, and the usual job insecurity or "labor flexibility" that characterizes post-Fordist capitalism. I take seriously these realms of physical and emotional sweat, detailing the work of a three-month music tour and discussing how Bolivians secure these contracts in Japan. I also reference stories from Bolivian musicians who claim to have turned down the more physically taxing tours, preferring to wait for the one in which they might be treated "like an artist."

Here, I purposely combine concepts of music as work and music as pleasure, two perspectives that may seem contradictory and two approaches that have not been center stage in previous research. Music is often studied anthropologically in relation to the ritual and social reproduction of a community, as a vehicle of identity construction for migrants in a new context, or as a form of cultural resistance within a contested political or national space.[83] "Local" music in the global arena also becomes tied up in discussions of cultural appropriation, cultural borrowing, and marketing.[84] Once the folklore has been wrested from the "folk," so to speak, some analyses begin from an assumed level of alienation. The interpretations remain focused on cultural meaning, ethnic identities, nationalist projects, and political economy. My work on the Bolivian-Japanese nexus will address some of these previous war horses, but it must also encompass realms of both work and affective experience. To dismiss transnational folklore performances as fakelore is to make naïve assumptions about authenticity. To denounce them as mere cultural appropriation (i.e., Bolivian musicians representing indians without being indian or Japanese musicians representing Bolivians without being Bolivian) seems to miss the point of how these affective and cultural economies speak to the experiences of global cultural work, transnational pleasures, and the connections between these and nationalisms.

Bolivian musicians speak quite generously about Japanese participation in their music, even about ensembles that are comprised entirely of Japanese members. On the other hand, Bolivian musicians are likely to give you an earful about Chilean groups that, in their opinion, have stolen and commercialized their own national music. These Bolivian-Chilean relations are tainted by the histories of two bordering nations and by the nineteenth-century War of the Pacific in which Bolivians lost to Chile their access to the sea. Gripes about world-famous Chilean groups playing Bolivian music may sound like jingoistic nationalism, but they are also fundamentally about musicians competing for work in a global market. Cultural appropriation may be the surface issue in Bolivian complaints about Chileans playing Andean music, but such comments are absent in the case of Japanese playing the same kind of music. For Bolivian musicians, the Japanese connection has been key to opening up economic possibilities that counter their limited employment options at home. Along with pleasure and intimacy, this ethnography grapples with the work and symbolic economy of global Andean music. Through the staged ideas of indigenous dress and sounds, Bolivians and Japanese come to identify with each other by referencing a "hyperreal Indian,"[85] one that does not exist in real life but one that shapes real work contracts for Bolivians, motivates real journeys for Japanese, and fosters ways that Bolivians and Japanese imagine alternative paths of modernity. In the next chapter, I turn to stories about how Bolivian music traveled to Japan and examine how metropolitan manipulations and representations of indigeneity were central to this process.

2 "What's Up with You, Condor?"

PERFORMING INDIGENEITIES

¿Qué te pasa, condor? (What's up with you, condor?)
—Ironic expression used by Bolivian musicians
to refer to the composition "El condor pasa"

Around 1977, the sound of the quena "grabbed" Koji Hishimoto. "That year, Andean music was in fashion here in Japan," he told me. On a November evening of our tour, we were sitting on *tatami* mats in a traditional Japanese hotel or *ryokan*. My tape recorder was running. Yuliano Encinas, who shared a room that night with Hishimoto, didn't pay us much attention; he wore his headphones and his PlayStation was hooked up to the television. Thinking back on the 1970s, Hishimoto didn't remember exactly why Andean music was in fashion. Maybe because music groups arrived in Japan from Argentina. He mentioned the performances of Uña Ramos, an Argentine quena player who lived in France, and Antonio Pantoja, a Peruvian quena player who had toured with Yma Sumac and settled in Buenos Aires. He suggested that maybe Andean music was popular because Paul Simon and Art Garfunkel's "El condor pasa" was all the rage at that time:[1] "Sometime around the 1970s, I heard that song on the radio and in the street too." He admitted that in his earlier days of playing this music, he preferred Peruvian and Argentine forms of Andean music, those with which he was more familiar at the time. Only later did he come to like Bolivian music, live an extended period in Bolivia, and become a professional Bolivian folklore musician in Japan.

Hishimoto assumed three roles on our tour: guide, translator, and fellow performing musician. One afternoon, in the role of our guide, he announced "separate rooms tonight," and we all cheered. On the road, we were often paired off to share hotel rooms, and when you spend three months, 24/7, with nine people, the separate room is a dream. Separate rooms also meant we were staying in a "businessman's hotel," and this usually meant we were sleeping in beds rather than on the floor—another reason some of us cheered. With a few exceptions though, tour members still sought company at the dinner hour. We also spent a good deal of time together in three different shopping spaces: supermarkets, "one hundred yen" shops (*cien yen*, as Bolivians would call it in Spanish), and Book Off stores (a chain that sold used books, comic books, and CDs). As we all checked into our separate rooms in the late afternoon, one band member, Victor Hugo Gironda, asked if I would translate some songs on recordings he had just purchased at a Book Off. In his room, he put on Simon and Garfunkel's "El condor pasa," a song we knew all too well. As I did my best to translate the song, Gironda's comment about it was "Nada que ver"— that Simon's lyrics had "nothing to do" with this composition. "No, they don't," I agreed. I suggested that the singers had made it into a song that tangentially and ambivalently referenced unequal social relations: "I'd rather be a hammer than a nail." Although "El condor pasa" has become the calling card for Andean music, and although it was the second tune we played for *every* performance in Japan, many Bolivian musicians feel it has little to do with their country. But it has much to do with the shaping of Andean music for global consumption.

Bolivian music did not travel directly to Japan, but it went through several detours that structured the rubric of "the Andean" frame, resting on stereotypes of indigeneity and the exotic Other. If a performance of "El condor pasa" was required to get Bolivians to Japan, it was followed by a repertoire shaped with the explicit intention of showing the diverse musical genres of Bolivian music, a multicultural nationalist project. Our group's staged indigeneity, while distinct from the poncho-clad street band, still formed a nationalist proposal that stood in contrast with a different kind of indigenous performance that has taken center stage in Bolivia's contemporary politics. While Bolivia is considered a country with an indigenous majority, Bolivian folklore musicians have generally been mestizos. The ambiguities of the term "mestizo," as introduced in chapter 1, are further complicated by the question of whether or not anyone in Bolivia ever personally claims to be mestizo or if this is an identity assigned by others.[2] My point here is that, with a few exceptions, most internationally touring Bolivian musicians do not personally identify as indigenous, and some of them do claim a mestizo identity; however, they all claim indian-ness as part of their Bolivian *national* heritage, and they are expected to perform an essentialized indian, particularly for international audiences.

Indigenousness, like any identity, is relational and articulated around sameness and difference.[3] In addressing the global circulation of ideas about indigeneity, I find useful Anna Tsing's concept of "indigenous voice," by which she refers to genres through which public statements are made about indigeneity, and where the speaker's power is secondary to that of the genre's conventions.[4] Tsing develops this concept with reference to classic areas of indigenous struggles like sovereignty, autonomy, and the environment.[5] Generally speaking, these are not the areas that concern Bolivian music performers. Extending the framework of indigenous genre conventions, I suggest that the Bolivian-Japanese nexus is a window into representations of indigenous voice that become marketed to a global audience. Internationally touring Bolivian musicians are pulled between these indigeneities. They dance with the Andeanist and folklorized nationalist ones, but they remain distanced from social movements that currently shape a radical politics within Bolivia. Bolivian musicians compose and perform, for themselves and others, what they want to represent as distinct about their identity (local, regional, national), but this staging is also filtered through a set of audience expectations about the Other. The debated middle ground in folklorization of indigeneity is between performers' desires, audience expectations, and the different meanings that folklore performances acquire as they move between international, national, and local contexts.

Through a consideration of the Bolivian-Japanese nexus of Andean music, this chapter will unpack distinct but overlapping performances of indigeneity. If at first glance this nexus looks like a non-Western to non-Western point of intimacy, a closer look reveals that Andean music, before it arrives in Japan, is mediated through Western frameworks. In a general sense, both Bolivians and Japanese represent cases of non-indigenous people staging Bolivian indigeneity, but these apparently similar processes of displacement hold distinct meanings for Bolivians and Japanese. If for Bolivians it is all part of a nationalist discourse, for Japanese, it is about a longing and nostalgia for something perceived as lost in modern life. Processes of mediation move national and international identifications with staged indigeneity from a complex realm of antiestablishment statements in the 1970s to the realm of twenty-first-century multicultural pedagogies and indigeneity for commodified consumption. The shifting values of this music will be taken up in the next chapter. First, I turn to stories about how Bolivian music arrived in Japan, how staged indigeneity captured the attention of Europeans, Argentines, and then Japanese, and how conceptualizations of "the Andean" region were central to these processes.

What Paul Simon Did to and for Andean Music

For each performance, Hishimoto would give an extensive introduction to the show. For the audience of school children who were usually seated on a gymnasium floor, he would locate our point of origin as Bolivia, doing so via a discussion of the other countries on the South American continent, the Andes mountains, and the condor imagined to soar through their peaks. Our performances were visually presented with a painted scenic backdrop of the Illimani, the snowcapped Andean mountain closely associated with the city of La Paz. While the staged representation of Andean music had traveled to the opposite side of the globe, the pedagogical project of cultural difference required that place be reinscribed through the genre conventions of a particular geography and its fauna: the Andes mountains and the condor.[6] After Hishimoto's introduction, we would launch into "El condor pasa." We didn't play Simon and Garfunkel's arrangement that features only the opening ascending melody. We played a version that has two movements and ends with a fast danceable *huayno* (highland Peruvian dance genre). Our interpretation was entirely instrumental with no lyrics. Bolivian musicians rarely perform this piece at home, and when they do, they can be almost apologetic about it. One musician told me, "It's on the CD we launched, so we had to play it." He referred to a recording produced primarily for Japanese consumption, but that also had a limited release in Bolivia. Bolivian attitudes toward this single composition represent a morass of contradictions about Bolivian nationalism, indigenous Andean expressions, and the role of performed indigeneity in the globalization of Andean music.

In 1965, Simon and Garfunkel shared a Paris stage with an Andean folklore ensemble first known as Los Incas and later as Urubamba.[7] In fact the ensemble included several Argentine musicians, key among them being Uña Ramos, a quena player whose presence would resound in the Japanese context. Simon and Garfunkel became intrigued by the band's performance of "El condor pasa." The piece they played was only a small part of an entire musical theatrical production (*zarzuela*) that in 1913 was composed by the Peruvian Daniel Alomía Robles. The theatrical production carried a plot line about foreign exploitation of indigenous miners in Peru's central highlands. During its heyday in Lima, this extremely popular theatrical production boasted three thousand presentations over a five-year period.[8] Alomía Robles's composition was like other indigenista artistic expressions of the time, musical compositions that followed European patterns and aesthetics while drawing inspiration from indigenous music of the Andean countryside.[9] Indigenista expressions are much more varied and complex than this brief statement suggests. In admittedly oversimplified terms, one might say that indigenismo often involves mestizos representing an indigenous world, but without actual indians; these symbolic worlds as developed in art and music were key to early twentieth-century Latin American nationalist and regionalist projects.[10]

Fast-forward to Simon's meeting with the Andean ensemble in Paris.

Simon set his own lyrics to the opening melody ("I'd rather be a spar-row than a snail") and thus was born one of the most controversial tunes that fueled the Andean music boom.[11] Indignant about Simon's purported "theft" of the tune, Peruvians have clamored to reclaim this composition as national heritage. An entire website had been dedicated to reclaiming the composition under the name of Alomía Robles.[12] An irony here is that this composer's creation was supposedly inspired by melodies he heard while traveling in the Peruvian countryside, and these sources probably did not operate under the rubric of individual intellectual property that shapes claims to authorship. The realm of supposedly unauthored works ends up providing the raw materials for the symbolic work of national heritage.[13]

Unlike the Peruvians' concerns about theft of their national heritage, many Bolivian musicians instead feel trapped by the ongoing expectation that they perform this piece that many say "isn't even Bolivian." Although Bolivians are tired of the Peruvian tune, tired of Simon and Garfunkel's interpretation, and tired of having to repeat it endlessly for international audiences, probably no other piece did as much for the Andean music boom as this one. Simon's musical appropriation created an uncanny con-dition of possibility, providing the connection into a world music machine that would popularize in global metropoles an Andean sound before Peru-vian, Bolivian, and Ecuadorian musicians could do so themselves. The ethnomusicologist Dale Olsen, mentioning "hundreds of arrangements" of this tune for performance and recording projects as diverse as Muzak and the orchestral concert hall, suggests that the *melody*, not Simon's lyrics, helped carry this tune into global popularity.[14] Nevertheless, Simon's cul-tural capital, as a commercially successful US singer, also had much to do with this tune's eventual global reach and the subsequent Andean music boom in Europe and Japan. In reference to Simon's much later record-ing *Graceland*, Veit Erlmann interprets Simon's role as that of a "cultural intermediary"—a performer who on stage creates linkages and acts as a point of continuity between different musical practices.[15] With "El condor pasa," Simon was already playing this role. When his arrangement called forth the live presence of those who produced Andean sounds, musicians from Andean countries were brought into the boom.

As the end of a chain of borrowings, thefts, or reinterpretations—what might be called "schizophonic mimesis," to borrow a term from Steven Feld[16]—"El condor pasa" provided a major point of entry for Andean music. Peruvian highland peasants, who may or may not have identified as indigenous, played a short melody that was heard by an outsider. The tune was "captured" by Alomía Robles who rendered faceless the indigenous authorship as he used his indigenista sensibilities to put his personal name and nationality to a rearrangement of the tune. The tune was reworked through a US popular music machine and through well-known artists. Its performance finally became required implicitly of most musicians claiming to perform Andean music. Bolivian musicians often fulfill this requirement, but not without their own off-stage humorous and ironic commentary. When talking about this tune, they may refer to it through a phrase that completely transforms the title's literal meaning. Instead of calling it "El condor pasa" ("The condor flies by"), they often refer to it as "¿Qué te pasa, condor?" ("What's up with you, condor?").

A Gringo and a Milestone

At about the same time Simon and Garfunkel released their hit, the Swiss man Gilbert Favre (introduced in chapter 1) was making quite a sensation in Bolivia with his interpretation of the quena. If I single out "El Gringo" Favre in my discussion of how Andean music made it to the global market, I do so because Bolivian musicians often speak about him as they discuss the international boom (see figure 4). "El Gringo" Favre would eventually form part of Los Jairas, an ensemble founded in the mid-1960s that completely transformed the performance styles of Bolivian music. Its practical size—four members—facilitated international touring, and the attention brought to it by foreigners finally made Bolivians take serious notice of what could be played on those instruments that were considered previously as just "cosas de indios" (indian things). When Los Jairas appeared on the Bolivian music scene, they built on the ongoing process of folklorizing indigenous musical expressions, developing virtuosity on the iconic "Andean" instruments of quena, zampoña, and charango. They were one of the first nationally and internationally successful small Bolivian bands that performed what has been called the "Pan-Andean" style.[17]

The small size of Los Jairas was completely different from other ensembles that preceded it. For example, *estudiantinas* that were very popular through the first half of the twentieth century would feature fifteen to twenty-five players on guitars, mandolins, charangos, and sometimes violins and quenas. These ensembles often formed around trade guild organizations, and estudiantinas were a vital part of the social tapestry of urban artisans in La Paz. At the same time the panpipe troupe was another ensemble form that gained popularity among some sectors of the city—for example, among Aymara migrants who were establishing a precarious foothold in La Paz. Featuring twelve or more players, ensembles

4. Alfredo Domínguez, Gilbert ("El Gringo") Favre, and Ernesto Cavour around 1977. These musicians would participate in the ensemble Los Jairas. *Photograph used with kind permission of Ernesto Cavour.*

with names like Los Cebollitas (The Little Onions) and Los Choclos (The Ears of Corn) emerged from the organizations of *los canillitas* (a term that refers to those who sold newspapers and shined shoes). These ensembles reconstructed in the city a standard rural practice whereby musicians perform en masse on a single kind of wind instrument—a troupe style that later would become a main urban musical index of authentic indigenous performance.[18] Another principal ensemble of the early twentieth century was the *orquesta típica* (typical orchestra) often called simply *la típica* (the typical). Composed of piano, bass, drum set, and perhaps violin, la típica played for the urban, usually non-indigenous audiences and developed a repertoire of foreign genres like tangos, boleros, rumbas, and *cumbias*. While these orchestras were usually associated with a non-indigenous world, las típicas began to close shows with a "national set" of cuecas, *huayños*, and *taquiraris*. Even las típicas were beginning to play genres that would become known as Bolivian national folklore, but their renditions were aimed at non-indigenous Bolivian audiences.

The four-to-five person band of the 1960s, which came to represent Bolivian folklore in an international sphere, marked a major social and aesthetic break from the small ensemble that avoided indigenous instruments (i.e., la típica), and from the larger groups that did not travel well (the estudiantinas and indigenous instrument troupes).[19] Lynn Meisch's work with Otavalo musicians speaks to an eventual indigenous Ecuadorian presence on the global music stage,[20] but for the most part, Bolivian musicians who participated in and benefited from the boom were not indigenous but rather mestizos. The difference here may have to do with the ensemble forms that usually are associated with indigenous music in these two different contexts. The wind instrument troupe of twelve to twenty musicians that came to mark an indigenous Bolivian style at home does not travel well. However, the four- or five-person Pan-Andean band like Los Jairas had the wind instruments that indexed indigeneity (what the típica lacked), and its smaller structure and emphases on individual musical personalities meshed well with the organization of international tours. Today, Bolivians say Los Jairas marked "a milestone" in national music. The charango player of Los Jairas was Ernesto Cavour, a musician who would become a key Bolivian presence in Japan, but not until after his performing experiences in Europe and Argentina (see figure 4).

As I was heading to an interview with Ernesto Cavour, Rolando Encinas asked me, "Could you do me a favor? Ernesto has been asking for my quena." "Your quena?" I asked. "Yes, the one from years ago that shows how I was experimenting with the different sizes of the holes. He wants to put it in his museum, and I promised I would bring it to him." Encinas had told me several times about this experimental quena from years ago, on which he added wood filler, glue, tape, and so on, and cut the holes larger and smaller, experimenting with different sizes of the holes, striving to get an instrument with maximum range and quality tuning. His refashioned quena with an approximate three octave range has now become the standard that most professional players use. "Sure, I can take it." Carefully packing in my bag this relic of recent Bolivian music history, I headed up to Cavour's museum of musical instruments on the colonial street of Jaén in La Paz. Cavour dates the founding of his museum to 1962, but not until 1990 did he install his collection within the corner colonial House of the Green Cross, a building he was able to purchase after receiving a major payment for setting the musical score of a Japanese film. With the exception of minimal support received from the Dutch cooperation in Bolivia, the museum, according to Cavour, is a product of his own personal initiative (see figure 5).

I interviewed Cavour three times over three years. A man of seemingly infinite creative capacities, Cavour is a legend among his peers. He wears

5. Ernesto Cavour's Musical Instrument Museum in La Paz. *Photograph by the author.*

multiple titles: collector (of many things, including musical instruments, match boxes, and miniatures); inventor of multiple instruments that are featured in his museum and within his *Encyclopedic Dictionary of Musical Instruments from Bolivia*; published author (of several books, including miniature books of poetic sayings); and of course, composer and musician.[21] Having received many times the critical and even insulting gaze of classically trained conservatory musicians, Cavour proudly wears the label of "self-taught musician." One colleague who toured Europe with him commented on Cavour's endless on-the-road practicing, the sense that he never tired of working to perfect and expand the possible interpretations on his instrument.[22] Japanese fans commented on the robust and unique sound Cavour managed to get out of his small plucked stringed instrument. And they spoke admiringly about his own imaginative compositions that became hits in Japan. Other charango players commented on his invention of instruments, like the five-necked charango called *estrellita* (little star) or the *charango muyu muyu* (literally, "charango that turns around").[23] Cavour was also the first person to motivate Encinas to play the quena, and at my request, Encinas joined me during the third interview I had with Cavour. When we arrived at his museum on a cold, bright August morning, he introduced us to the two pet birds he kept in his patio: Juan Sebastian Bach and José "Jach'a" Flores (name of a Bolivian composer, 1941–98).

Cavour told me he came to music first through his experiences in Chela Urquidi's folklore ballet, which he entered in the early 1960s.[24] Cavour said he was "discovered" as a musician, as he switched back and forth between dancing and playing music. In 1965, he won a prize as a solo instrumentalist at the Festival of Latin American Music in Salta, Argentina. During these years, he played music at Radio Méndez in La Paz, on the Saturday show of Mickey Jiménez. It was there that Cavour met Favre, the quena player who would become known as "El Gringo," and who, along with Cavour, would form part of Los Jairas.

In the late 1960s, Los Jairas left Bolivia to work in Europe and reside in Switzerland. But after two years of performing in Europe, Cavour left the group. When he spoke about touring internationally, he talked about "escaping" back to Bolivia, of not really adjusting to the rhythm of life outside his country. When I interviewed him in the presence of Encinas, Cavour also mentioned the racism he experienced in Europe, turning to Encinas for confirmation of these unpleasant experiences that many touring Latin American musicians shared. Regardless of whether one is indigenous or mestizo, the Andean musician who tours transnationally experiences racism.

"Why were Los Jairas so popular in Bolivia?" I asked. Without skipping a beat, Cavour immediately responded, "Because the foreigners were interested in their music. So the Bolivians said, 'Well, it must be something good.'"[25] What was internationally valued finally came to be revered in Bolivian territory as well. Throughout the early twentieth century, Latin American musicians traveled to New York City, Mexico City, Havana, and Buenos Aires to record, thus cementing the transnational nature of many genres that eventually took on nationalist associations.[26] Because Bolivia's first recording studio was not established until the late 1940s, during the beginning of the twentieth century Bolivians often went to Argentina to record. The Bolivian-Argentine transnational connection, however, was not only about a lack of recording facilities at home. Long after Bolivia had its own studios, Bolivians were establishing themselves as folklore musicians by touring Argentina because there, beyond their own borders, they found audience acceptance of and desire for the indigenous sights and sounds that were only beginning to move into the nationalist stages at home. While Bolivians were performing in Argentina in the 1970s, they received some of their first invitations to tour Japan.

Rebellious Youth and National Folklore

Over a very long lunch in Shinjuku, Tokyo, I interviewed Luis Carlos Severich, one of the first Bolivian folklore boomers to tour Japan—preceded by Los Caballeros del Folklore (see chapter 1). Severich had married a Japanese woman he met on one of his tours, and they had settled permanently in Japan. During our tour in 2002, Bolivian musicians told me of Severich, but our hectic work schedule made it impossible for me to meet him until I returned to Japan on a separate trip. Other musicians expressed utter amazement at how well Severich had adapted to Japanese ways of being; he ate, spoke, gestured, and walked like a Japanese man. At the restaurant, he ordered our food in fluent Japanese and then proceeded to instruct me through the maze of plates that held different morsels and sauces. If several Bolivians have expressed to me their mixed feelings about Japanese food, it was clear that Severich savored every aspect of this foreign cuisine that he had made his own. Listening to him talk about Japanese food, I began to gather a greater appreciation for the more subtle tastes of this culinary tradition that differed greatly from the strong spices of Peru and Bolivia, the two ethnographic contexts in which I had worked previously. During lunch and in the long *sobre mesa* (post-meal discussion) he told me of his trajectory in Bolivian folklore music. It was a narrative that suggested a more rebellious, even antiestablishment, characteristic of folklore as performed by youth of that era. And it also brought to the forefront the place of Argentina in the development of Bolivian national folklore.

Severich told me a story of being born into a family of ten children, of attending primary and secondary school in Santa Cruz (Bolivia), of learning cabinetry, and of dreaming about music. As a student in the 1960s he said he was listening to the Bolivian groups Los Chaskas, and Los Payas, admiring the members of these groups who "manifested the Andes" and who were *young*. He compared the hairstyles, dress, and presentation of Los Chaskas with that of the Beatles, adding, "We [weren't] going to play the Beatles better than the Beatles. . . . But Bolivian music, we [were] going to interpret better than anybody." Young people in Bolivia admired the Beatles and looked to form their own homegrown version of their successes. Against his family's wishes, in 1970 Severich left Santa Cruz, heading for Lima, Peru, with his small band whose members played guitar, quena, and charango. Severich and his friends had heard of Andean folklore music accomplishments in Peru, and after their own respectable standings at Bolivian folklore festivals like Lauro in Cochabamba, they were anxious to try their luck internationally. They were told, "You're going to make money!" But on the way to Peru, they met a delegation from Argentina, and were persuaded to change their course of travels. Severich then described a trajectory of being "discovered" by Argentines, first in Salta, then in Cosquín, a small city in the province of Córdoba that since the early 1960s has hosted a "national folklore festival." After their Cosquín triumphs they were off to Buenos Aires where they settled into nightly gigs and recorded their first album—under the auspices of an Argentine harmonica player who, I was told, had attended music competitions in Germany. Severich and his band received their first invitation to tour Japan while they were working in Buenos Aires. The subsequent years were filled with numerous international tours and extensive work in Argentina.

Severich talked about why he left his band in 1982. While it was not the sole reason he gave, he alluded to working conditions in Argentina that were no longer what they used to be, and he twice mentioned that the politics of the Malvinas War (1982) interfered with folklore work in Argentina. Argentine history from 1976 to 1983 was marked by systematic state repression known as the Dirty War, a reference that was absent from Severich's discussion. Earlier in the conversation, as he described his band's total success in Buenos Aires, he referred to a time before subsequent economic crises and political repressions. "That's how Argentina was. It was a great country. The people, the economy. . . . The people could go out. There wasn't any problem around 1970, '71. Every night we could hardly get off the stage . . . because the public wanted us to keep playing." Argentina loomed large in this man's story about how he came to play *Bolivian* folklore. At the time of our conversation in Tokyo, during which Severich reminisced about his folklore boom years, he had been living outside Bolivia for more than half his life.

In addition to the French connections already mentioned, Japanese audiences were pulled into the world of "Andean" music through Argentine music performance circuits. From 1951 when Japan's commercial radios opened up, Japanese began listening to an assortment of new musical voices.[27] While Argentine tango had been heard in Japan since the 1930s, a music labeled "folklore" began to circulate on the B-side of tango records. When a famous tango orchestra came to Japan, "folklore" artists, also from Argentina, would fill out the staged presentation. Under these circumstances, Argentine "folklore" musicians got a foot in the door of the

Japanese performance circuit. By the 1960s, Argentine folk music artists like Atahualpa Yupanqui and Eduardo Falú began touring Japan.[28] Bolivians often received invitations to tour Japan after a stint of successful performing in Cosquín and Buenos Aires. Such was the case of Severich's Los Laicas, a mixed Bolivian and Argentine group. In Argentina, Ernesto Cavour of Los Jairas won a prize and also received his first invitations to tour Japan, although he would not accept them until a later date. Bolivian musicians also told me how the Japanese have recreated their own Cosquín in Kawamata, Japan, copying the form, dress, name, and repertoire of "original" folklore ensembles from Andean countries. Ercilia Moreno Cha wrote about the importance of Argentine folklore festivals in the development of the traditional Argentine repertoire,[29] but these festivals also were key sites where *Bolivian* folklore musicians sought validation. At the time, instruments of indigenous or rural association, like the quena, zampoña, and charango, were still viewed in very racist terms within Bolivia. These instruments had yet to be fully transformed into sonic indices of nationalism. The outsiders' view of this music finally brought these "culturally intimate" forms into a Bolivian nationalist project.[30]

Urban mestizo youth used indigenous instruments as a point of rebellion against their parents. According to the Bolivian sociologist Mauricio Sánchez Patzy, in the 1960s and 1970s, growing long hair, dressing like indians, and playing indigenous music was a way for youth to rebel against their parents' wishes. Young Bolivian musicians were inspired by global developments in pop and rock bands, as well as by local ethnic references. Thus young folklore musicians left Bolivia, not only to make a name for themselves, but also to challenge their parents, to do their local equivalent of joining a rock band, and to validate their performances on indigenous instruments.[31] While youthful rebellion and imitation of a Beatles form should not be ignored, nor should the radical nationalist edge of these key musical players. The musicians of the 1960s and 1970s might be seen as a second generation of indigenista nationalism, presenting more of a continuity than a rupture with folklorizing processes that began in the 1930s. From today's view, these folklorization processes are a central part of an establishment expression of Bolivian nationalism. In their heyday, however, these musical and artistic developments were still quite radical, and they came to the forefront when youth around the world were rocking the establishment, and when youth in Latin American countries were raising their voices in protest songs against brutal dictatorships and social inequalities, a movement that became known as Nueva Canción (New Song). For example, Chilean groups like Quilapayún and Inti Illimani that formed in the late 1960s took indigenous names (Araucanian and Quechua, respectively), purposely used "Andean" instruments, and wedded this aesthetic with the political revolutionary philosophy of Che Guevara and a Latin American political struggle.[32]

After the coup that overthrew Allende in Chile in 1973, these ensembles and other Chilean musicians of Nueva Canción performed in exile in Europe, providing the musical backdrop for solidarity movements outside the region.[33] Jan Fairley, in discussions of Violeta Parra's work on collecting folk songs that were then incorporated into Chilean Nueva Canción of the 1960s, suggests that Parra's work formed a bridge between rural and urban worlds.[34] In discussions of Chilean Nueva Canción, "rural," "peasant," and "Andean" become a conglomeration that is read through the lens of class exploitation. As Fernando Rios argues, the European audiences' fascination with Che Guevara and with his attempt to start a revolution in Bolivia, contributed to the use of the Andean indigenous world as a leftist emblem.[35] The Chilean representation of indigeneity as melded to radical leftist politics, and as appropriated by European solidarity movements, has to be considered in a different light next to the grounded politics of Bolivia. Relative to Chile, Bolivia has a much larger indigenous population, and a sizeable part of this population lives in urban contexts. These facts make for very different articulations of mestizo-indian race relations. The musical and cultural expressions of these years represented much more than a statement of generational resistance, and need to be unpacked in relation to class and ethnic relations of the specific national context.[36]

Genres of Indigeneity

In the pages that follow, I take a necessary detour to elaborate different genres of indigeneity at play in the Bolivian context—ones that seem, at first glance, to follow quite different paths. Many of the music performances described in this book involve mestizos staging representations of indigenous worlds, what might be glossed simply as "indigenismo." However, a second genre of "indigenous voice" is being heard within the contemporary Bolivian context.[37] More akin to Henri Favre's reference to "indianismo,"[38] this voice is connected to broad social movements, the election of an indigenous president in 2005, and the hope of radical social transformations through reference to indigenous cultural politics. I bring together these two apparently different genres of indigeneity for several reasons. First, an understanding of both genres is necessary to grasp how indigeneity works at the center of a Bolivian nationalist project. Second,

I argue that the past successes and present declines of Andean music are connected to shifts in the national political scene and the apparent present-day prominence of the second genre. Finally, I bring together these genres to question the seemingly stark division between the two.

While Bolivian mestizo youth were joining Andean bands, identifying with internationally famous rockers, and finding their indigenous nationalist roots, Aymaras were developing a political movement that drew on the memory of an eighteenth-century hero, and this movement crossed both rural and urban realms. In 1781, an Aymara man led an uprising that held the city of La Paz under seige for three months. His name was Tupac Katari, and his rebellion represented a protest against abuses of the colonial system. Tupac Katari's rebellion, along with others of the period, presented alternative emancipatory projects that in some cases proposed a return to indigenous rule.[39] Although Tupac Katari was publicly executed by troops sent from Buenos Aires—drawn and quartered—he has lived on in the collective memory of Bolivian Aymaras.

In the 1970s an indigenous political movement began to gather momentum, and its members took Katari's name. "Katarismo" was articulated on the one hand by university educated Aymara intellectuals. On the other hand, Katarismo was also associated with the peasant union organization founded in 1979 called the Confederación Unica de Trabajadores Campesinos de Bolivia (Sole Trade Union Confederation of Peasant Workers of Bolivia, CSUTCB). In their published political thesis of 1983 the CSUTCB renamed the heroes of independence—not San Martín, Bolívar, and Sucre, the creoles of nineteenth-century independence fame, but rather Tupac Katari along with a list of other rebel leaders of the eighteenth-century uprisings: Tupac Amaru, Bartolina Sisa, Micaela Bastidas, Tomás Katari, and others. They declared that the creole-sponsored formation of an independent republic had given them no benefits whatsoever. Their interpretation of Bolivian history emphasized two axes: exploitation as a class and exploitation as distinct ethnic or racial groups. Their political thesis was a challenge to what had been the national revolutionary project that included state-sponsored peasant unions, homogenizing assimilationist politics, and a nationalist ideology of mestizaje.[40] The CSUTCB also formed in contestation to the ongoing military-peasant pact that General René Barrientos implemented in the mid-1960s with the intention of co-opting and controlling the peasants.

While Aymara youth were setting the scene for the kind of indigenous politics that would emerge in the 1990s and into the twenty-first century, mestizo youth who joined Andean bands were also doing something radical in their time and within their social group; while they rebelled against their parents, they were also transforming mestizo attitudes about "indigenous things," even if attitudes about indians themselves were much more difficult to change. In response to Bolivian state repression of the period, some folklore groups leaned toward a protest style more akin to Nueva Canción. However, according to Sánchez Patzy, these "neo-folklorists" may have followed fashion rather than deep leftist convictions, with the possible exception of the singer and songwriter Benjo Cruz.[41] Benjo Cruz held to his ideals and died among the guerrillas of Teoponte—a column of sixty-seven young people who, during one hundred days in 1970, carried on Che Guevara's revolutionary ideals of "the armed struggle."[42] Bolivian musicians and ethnomusicologists describe a musical world where lines were drawn between those who, on the one hand, created and performed Nueva Canción—or who were at least politically inspired to alternative musical expressions—and, on the other hand, those who created and performed the supposedly apolitical *música folklórica*.[43] I suggest that this perspective narrows a view of "the political" and does not consider the influence these groups may have had on shifting mestizo attitudes about indigeneity, no matter how minor these shifts may appear from the present perspective. National folklore music, as embodied in Los Jairas and subsequently in Los Kjarkas (the long-lasting and commercially successful Cochabamba version of the Pan-Andean band that now has a Japanese charango player), may have appeared apolitical in relation to a conscious politics of the Left, but these ensembles were ultimately successful in articulating a national sentiment through indices of indigeneity.[44] The centrality of performed indigeneity on Bolivian stages was a radical shift in its time and place.

Intersecting genres of indigeneity are at work here: one shaped by international imaginaries about the Andean world, one shaped through nationalist folklorization processes since about the mid-twentieth century, and one shaped by increasing attention to the subjectivity and agency of indigenous peoples themselves. Using the terms "indigenismo" and "indianismo," Henri Favre makes the following distinction: if indigenismo is said to speak for indigenous subjects without including them, indianismo, emerging in the second half of the twentieth century, is said to critique the exclusionary cultural politics of the former, and to promise a project in which flesh and blood indigenous subjects reclaim their positions as agents of their own history.[45] According to Favre, contemporary processes of globalization and "tribalization" leave indigenismo in the dustbin of history as a new indian-ness emerges through indianismo.[46] Favre's discussion of indianismo might fit the Bolivian context of the late twentieth and early twenty-first centuries, as showcased by the election of an indigenous president and the subsequent attempts to implement pro-indigenous and decolonizing policies. However, given the global circulation and value of ideas about native peoples, and the corresponding actions of indigenous subjects, such a line between indigenismo and indianismo may not be drawn so easily. Positive ideas about indigenous peoples circulate through multiple realms of a global economy (the United Nations, NGOs, tourists, etc.), and make their way back to local indigenous groups.[47] Indigenous identities depend in part on the circulation of images and sounds of indigeneity, often as created, modified, and sustained by non-indigenous Others. In this sense, labels of indigeneity circulate as commodities that are sometimes taken up by or forced on those who may or may not self-identify as indigenous. For example, indigenous communities may modify their craft productions in order to meet the expectations of a global tourist market.[48] Or they may appear to "dress up" as indians when they interact in state and international arenas, recreating the very images crafted through national and global indigenista sensibilities.[49] Using the term "new indigenismo" to refer to the contemporary Bolivian context, Andrew Canessa points out that even Evo Morales's presidency seems to operate with very idealized notions of indigenous subjects; Canessa shows how these notions do not fit daily life within many communities that outsiders might label as indigenous, and how community members themselves actually reject the indigenous categorization.[50] While the Morales administration, according to Nancy Postero, has been reworking Andean utopias of the past to bolster radical transformations in the present, these politics based on cultural difference carry with them their own dangers of discrimination, particularly if a national agenda based on cultural difference begins to fail.[51] I do not want to deny the obvious differences between indigenous social movements and the folkloric representation of indigenous things. Nor do I want to discount the politics of indigenous groups simply because they may be dressing up as indigenous.[52] This second point would lead to the never-ending circular questioning about whether indigenous identities are constructed or essentialized, an inquiry that often means little to indigenous subjects themselves. In the world of indigenous representations, however, the boundaries between indigenismo and indianismo may indeed be more porous than often argued.

Global performances of Bolivian music carried multiple meanings—those of mestizo youth rebelling against their parents at home, those of mestizos exalting indigenous representations sans indians, and those of international audiences feeling themselves, through sound, in solidarity with popular struggles for justice that were occurring throughout Latin

America. During the 1970s, performed indigeneity moved in these multiple currents: through "El condor pasa," through nationalist folklorization, through transnational solidarity, and through a gathering momentum around an indigenous politics that would provide the rehearsals for the genre of indigenous voice that now holds sway in Bolivia. On its way to Japan, Bolivian music took circuitous routes. It was mediated through gringo associations, through Simon and Garfunkel's version of the allegedly Peruvian "El condor pasa," through a European Andean music boom, and through the rising popularity of Andean folklore in neighboring Argentina. In considering these trajectories of global cultural capitalism, and how the non-Western is mediated through the cultural and geographic metropoles before it gets to Japan,[53] the Bolivian-Japanese nexus seems to operate in a way that is, after all, not so far from the usual Western to non-Western encounter, at least in its historical trajectory. However, I do not want to leave the impression that everything is predetermined from that point on. Musicians challenge the traditional "Andean" framework in their choice of repertoire and in their own compositions. I will now follow stories about Andean music's arrival in Japan and its reception that drew heavily on the image of an imagined indigenous world, indexed by "El condor pasa" and by the sound of the quena instrument.

Quena Soul

I first "met" Takaatsu Kinoshita through the recorded sound of his guitar. He had put down the guitar tracks for Música de Maestros's first recordings in 1988. When Encinas decided to digitize and re-master these long plays in 1995, he asked me to put down four violin tracks, two firsts and two seconds. He had used the computer to produce a simulated violin sound on the original recording and now wanted to include "the real thing." At that time, the group had not yet shifted to the practice of simultaneous live recording, and studio work was often spread out over months and even years, as individual musicians would put in their hours in a one-on-two with Encinas and the technician or in a one-on-one with Encinas acting as both technician and director. We all look back on those days and shudder. It is difficult to muster the emotive feelings that should accompany an expressive musical performance when one plays alone, hour after hour, with a metronome beat or a single prerecorded guitar track fed through the headphones. But I remember Kinoshita's opening measures to "El olvido," a cueca by Simeón Roncal (1870–1953), a composer from Sucre. Kinoshita's touch was both light and majestic, a level of expression that is not easily attained. While our guitar and violin sounds were electronically mixed into this re-release,[54] we would not actually perform together until I began work on this project, and we played a small salon concert at the end of one of my trips to Japan.

Although I made arrangements to arrive early for our interview appointment in Tokyo, at fifteen minutes before the set time, Kinoshita was already waiting for me at the train station exit, cutting a slender figure and wearing his hair long, loose, and curly. After eating lunch at a nearby French restaurant, we walked to his small studio, perched on a top floor and accessed by narrow outdoor stairs. For three hours, he spoke in fluent Spanish about how he became involved in "folklore."

Kinoshita had been following Andean music since he was a young boy. In fact, several members of his family were involved in this ongoing hobby. At the age of nineteen, he bought a one-way ticket to Bolivia. Twelve years later he returned to Japan with his Bolivian wife and their son. He told me he might have remained indefinitely in Bolivia, but his sister's death made his more permanent presence at home a personal necessity. Of his boyhood attraction to this music, Kinoshita said: "At that time, '74, '75, Andean music came to Japan from Paris or Buenos Aires. [Uña] Ramos came from Paris. [Antonio] Pantoja came from Buenos Aires. . . . For the Japanese, Peru was closer because we had heard of the Inca empire. There had been exhibits of Andean culture or about the Machu Picchu ruins. We knew Argentina by the tango. But Bolivia, no. For those of us who liked Andean music, we thought Buenos Aires was the capital of Andean music. Or we thought everyone there played quena, that all the children played quena." Kinoshita depicted an imagining around the quena itself, the instrument played by both Pantoja, who was originally from Peru, and Uña Ramos, who was originally from Argentina. The quena was linked to an indigenous imaginary through the historically known reference of the Incas. Both Uña Ramos and Pantoja toured Japan, and Kinoshita remembered a course Pantoja taught in Tokyo. He recalled that in the 1970s it was very difficult to obtain a quena. But that situation would change. Pantoja and Uña Ramos began to sell quenas at their concerts. Suddenly Japan was flooded with Japanese fans who owned these instruments and who wanted to learn to play. By the late 1970s and early 1980s, a strong Japanese-Bolivian music connection had been established, particularly when Ernesto Cavour began touring Japan in 1981 and when a few Japanese youth began journeying to Bolivia for extended periods.

Kinoshita suggested that the popularity of Andean music in Japan has something to do with its accessibility. He pointed out that the wind instruments are relatively inexpensive and technically easy to play. Many Japanese learn to play the recorder in school, and this experience provides a starting point for learning Bolivian wind instruments. While Japanese may mention reluctantly that they have been studying the oboe for some time, they may be more open about their attempts to play Andean music. Kinoshita suggested that, unlike classical music or even jazz, less rigid hierarchies structure who is entitled to play Andean music in Japan. While the oboe player practices privately at home and hardly thinks of a symphony orchestra concert as a venue to purchase an instrument, Andean music fans are much more likely to engage in a public discussion about their own Andean bands, and a concert is often the place where fans buy their instruments. Kinoshita also suggested that many people find it possible to teach themselves to play Andean music, at least in a rudimentary phase. However, many Japanese fans eventually seek instruction, sometimes establishing disciple relations with a master musician.[55] If they can't travel to Bolivia to study with the masters, they might start in the Andean music classes offered in Tokyo by Ernesto Kawamoto and Shizue Shimada.

I first met Kawamoto and Shimada at an after-performance birthday celebration in a restaurant where Kawamoto treated the entire band, in addition to other fans and hobbyists whom I would get to know on my subsequent trip to Japan. In spite of our busy touring schedule, musicians still maintained contact with their Japanese friends, telling them when we would perform at a venue near them. This party had followed one of our few Tokyo theater performances and was actually the second postconcert social engagement of the evening. While on tour, there was little time for the weekly Friday or Saturday night social gathering around drink and music, or the postconcert music sessions that often mark the life of Bolivian musicians at home. On this night with Kawamoto and Shimada, food, sake, and music flowed easily, and the rhythm of the evening was only slowed by the nagging reality of the following day's early departure. Only when I returned to Japan, off tour, did I have the opportunity to hear Kawamoto's and Shimada's stories.

"I was born into Bolivian music when I heard Simon and Garfunkel's 'El condor pasa,'" Kawamoto told me at a café in Tokyo. "I also sang [Simon and Garfunkel's] other songs. But that one song! It was another kind of music! What instruments! It made me imagine something else. So I started to pursue the sound of the quena instrument." He started to learn quena as he watched another Japanese man within a folklore trio in which he himself was playing guitar. Before eventually offering his own classes, Kawamoto would teach quena classes as an assistant to this man. Through working for a magazine, *Revista latina*, Kawamoto began to learn Span-

6. Khantati performs at a locale in Tokyo. *Photograph by the author.*

ish as he followed tango and folklore performers in their concert tours of Japan. He was dividing his time by then between playing music and working his office job with the magazine. In 1982, when his boss forced him to choose between doing music and working at the magazine, he quit his job and went to Bolivia for three months. He described this trip as a transformative experience in which he met up with musicians in the legendary Peña Naira—a folklore nightclub in La Paz that was closely associated with the earlier performing days of Ernesto Cavour, El Gringo Favre, and Los Jairas. "Takaatsu [Kinoshita] was the first Japanese to enter the Peña Naira. I arrived after him, but during the same year. After that, many Japanese went to Bolivia. Takaatsu and I are part of that history." Kawamoto described hanging out at Peña Naira, getting to know the performing musicians, and even substituting for them when they didn't arrive for an evening's performance.

Kawamoto now has a name for himself among Bolivian musicians who have toured Japan, and among Japanese who are involved in Andean music. He is the director of an Andean music academy in Tokyo where he and Shimada teach classes, principally on quena and charango. Kawamoto also directs the Japanese-Bolivian music ensemble Khantati (see figure 6 in which Kawamoto is on guitar). He told me the name of his group means "the dawn" in Aymara, but he also pointed out its Spanish sonorous meaning: *Canta a ti* (He, she, or it sings to you). While its original founding brought together Severich and Kawamoto, Khantati's contemporary configuration includes only Japanese musicians, and their liner notes reference the group as "the first Andean, and specifically Bolivian, music group created in Japan."[56] Kawamoto, Shimada, and the other members of Khantati make short trips to Bolivia when they can, giving performances there and sometimes leading Japanese Andean music students to meet up with Ernesto Cavour in his instrument museum. For Kawamoto, the most important thing he teaches his students is the "soul" of the quena sound. "In Japan, many musicians play quena, but they play some other music. But this quena sound, that's what's important for me."

Playing "Andean music" in the 1960s, '70s, and early '80s involved radical antiestablishment aesthetics—radical for Bolivian youth who were transforming nationalist representations, radical for international audiences in solidarity with a myriad of Latin American struggles, and radical for Japanese youth wanting to break out of an extremely rigid and hierarchical society that was at the height of a process of modernization and economic success. By the 1990s, however, these various radicalisms had faded. No longer a radical statement, the Pan-Andean bands represented a mainstream expression of musical nationalism. Andean music abroad is no longer an aesthetic index of international solidarity movements, as Latin American dictatorships "returned to democracy," the Berlin Wall fell, the Soviet Union was dismantled, and neoliberalism ruled the day. Today, a different kind of indigeneity is central to the Bolivian context, one that owes much to the Katarista political organizing of the 1970s, a global attention to indigenous politics since the Columbus quincentennial in 1992, and the failure of Bolivia's neoliberal policies to change the dire living conditions in which so many Bolivians live. Folklorized indigeneity remains quite removed from the new realm of politicized indigeneity, in spite of the intersections I suggested earlier. I suspect these currently diverging paths of performed indigeneity may have something to do with Andean music's decline, a trend perceived by all musicians who make a living in this scene. Anxious to move beyond the confines of the Pan-Andean formula, Bolivian musicians still find themselves having to answer to international expectations. Those expectations in Japan often take the form of a pedagogical project about cultural difference, as many Bolivian musicians' concert schedules are filled with school performances—mostly for primary school students but occasionally for secondary level ones as well.

Bolivian Indigeneity Staged in Japan

For Música de Maestros, performing indigeneity for Japanese students started with "El condor pasa," but that was only the beginning. The group's director has always followed a proposal that was explicitly multiculturalist and nationalist. Costume changes in Japan, as described in chapter 1, were, on the one hand, about showmanship and spectacle. But on the other hand, they were also about Encinas's consistent desire to show world audiences that Bolivian music went far beyond the ubiquitous Pan-Andean bands whose fringed ponchos have become iconic in the international representation of this country's music. The ensemble's name, Música de Maestros, refers to the performance of master Bolivian composers, calling forth the parallel with European masters. But here, composers may figure as named individuals or as particular indigenous groups. Encinas takes pride in the fact that the repertoire is based on his extensive archival and field research in these multiple genres. After making more than fourteen recordings since the ensemble's founding in the 1980s, the group boasts a repertoire that includes mestizo-creole, highland indigenous, and lowland indigenous genres. As Bolivian politics have fractured around regional divides between the resource rich lowlands and the indigenous highlands (birthplace of President Evo Morales and the more radical social movements of the beginning of the twenty-first century), Encinas has begun to refer to the work of Música de Maestros as a "music for national integration." When the group's performances moved to Japan, the most significant changes involved the reduced size of the ensemble, the inclusion of indigenous costumes, and the performance of "El condor pasa." Even though the group's show was reshaped for the Japanese audience, often with the artistic advising of Hishimoto, it never completely abandoned a multicultural nationalist perspective.

During the first half of the show, we performed a segment that was introduced as "the Aymara fiesta" and that featured our playing of distinct instruments that are usually performed in the troupe style (*tarka, pinquillo,* and zampoña) (see figure 7). At one point two musicians would leave the stage and return in *khusillo* costumes (a jesting figure that appears within Aymara regions), playing the pinquillo instrument and literally acting out the part of the khusillo. While this dramatization of highland indigeneity gave many more details than one might encounter in a watered-down version of Andean folklore, it is difficult for a group of seven musicians to achieve the sonorous effect of a full troupe-style performance—an interpretation that requires a minimum of twelve musi-

7. Música de Maestros stages an Aymara fiesta for a performance in Japan.
Photograph from the author's collection.

cians. Throughout this research, I have only heard of one complete troupe
that made a brief tour of Japan. Because of the daily costs of maintaining
musicians on the road, companies rarely expand beyond the sponsorship
of five or six musicians. The troupe form that has become a key marker of
indigenous authenticity in La Paz becomes nearly impossible to replicate
in an international tour.

For the second half of the show, we performed in our mestizo-looking
costumes (see figure 8). During two moments of the performance, the
ensemble would leave the stage and Hishimoto would explain some of
the instruments that were unknown to the Japanese audiences, having
the individual musicians demonstrate their use, and asking the students
if they could guess certain materials that were used in their construction. In organizing our show, Hishimoto explicitly drew parallels between
a Japanese sonorous environment and a Bolivian one. During the dem-
onstration of the quena, Hishimoto would show the *shakuhachi*, a Japanese notched flute. Japanese and Bolivians consistently compared this
"traditional" Japanese instrument to the Andean notched flute. After featuring the quena and shakuhachi, Hishimoto and Encinas would interpret on quenas the song that runs through the credits of Hayao Miya-
zaki's popular Japanese animated film *Spirited Away*. The initial phrase

8. Música de Maestros performs in Japan wearing a "mestizo look."
Photograph from the author's collection.

of the tune often provoked a reaction of gleeful surprise, as the students heard a known tune on an instrument that was unknown yet somehow familiar. For middle and high school audiences, we all played another Japanese song, the Billboard hit of 1963 that was re-titled for English-speaking audiences as "Sukiyaki" (its original title was "Ue o muite aru-koo"—loosely translated as "Let's walk with our heads held high"). We began the second half of the show playing a *saya*, an African-Bolivian genre that features percussion and song. During this piece we moved into the audience, snaking through the aisles where the young audience members were seated, and giving them an up close view of performers and instruments.

Other parts of the show also were designed to connect unknown instruments to known sonorous environments. When Victor Hugo Gironda demonstrated the panpipes, he played a tune often heard in Japanese supermarkets as an advertising jingle for selling fish. Backstage, Gironda would refer to this part of the show as "going to sell fish," and his intervention was guaranteed to provoke laughter from the younger audiences. If from backstage we heard no response to the playing of this ditty on the panpipes, we knew we had a difficult audience to please.

We closed the show with a *tonada*, a genre considered typical of Quechua regions in Northern Potosí. With music composed by Hishimoto and lyrics set by Encinas, "Despiertan piedras" (Wake up rocks) was designed to bring the Japan-based show to a crescendoed close, and to rouse students who might have drifted during our performance.[57] The song's title also referred to what Bolivians identified as the most difficult audience to please: Japanese secondary school students. Bolivian musicians would call these audiences "rocks" because it was so difficult to get any reaction from these adolescent students. In contrast, the younger primary school audiences easily bubbled over with enthusism at our shows. Throughout our performances, Hishimoto was very conscious of the ensemble's use of a heavy drum beat that could potentially activate audience participation, and this final tune, in its straightforward rhythms (in 2/4–4/4 meter), was supposed to work the audience into a participatory frenzy, even an audience of "rocks." During one concert we gave for "rocks," we were almost too successful with this closing strategy. When we were part way through the piece, the students jumped on stage and began dancing with us, much to the consternation of the sound engineer who worried about the spaghetti of cords on the floor and the delicate microphones that were vital to our daily work.

The aesthetic approaches at work in meeting the expectations of Japanese audiences included making this Bolivian music seem less Other, foregrounding pieces with straightforward rhythmic patterns, and designing a program that aimed to produce audience identification and participation. The strange and exotic were made knowable by featuring Bolivian instruments that were "like traditional Japanese ones" and by referencing familiar sonorous landscapes of Japanese supermarkets, animated films, and popular songs. Bolivian cultural work for Japanese school audiences required citation to the Andeanist frame, which happened through the performance of "El condor pasa." This opening was followed, however, by a multicultural nationalist music project that was slightly reshaped to create performative intimacy between Bolivian musicians on stage and Japanese students in the audience.

The Condor Is So Over

According to the liner notes of his recording, Adrian Villanueva was "born of Aymara indian blood," plays the quena, makes instruments, and is the cofounder of the music group Kallawaya.[58] Because Kallawaya had toured Japan, I had interviewed several members of this ensemble (Villanueva, Edgar Villarroel, Fernando Jiménez, and Juan Carlos Cordero). With his

self-ascription as Aymara, Villanueva is one of the exceptions to the predominant presence of mestizos in the musical touring world. He taps into
those other genres of indigenous voice, designing and elaborating projects
that take on environmental issues. For example, he has a particular concern for the conservation of the trees and bamboos from which Bolivian
instruments are constructed. But he has another pet project that seems to
draw on both nationalist and more "universal" humanistic voices: he is
out to prove that Peruvians are wrong, and that "El condor pasa" is actually a Bolivian composition. In relation to this specific topic, I sought another interview with him and found him proudly busy with his work on
cultural politics for President Morales. Between his many other activities,
we spoke briefly while he was waiting for an appointment at Discolandia's
offices—a major recording company in Bolivia.

Villanueva claims that the music of "El condor pasa" was composed by
a music teacher, Modesto Narváez, who lived in Luribay, a town at the
foot of the Illimani mountain. According to Villanueva's account, the tune
carried the title "Kuntur p'usa" (Condor's breath) and originally featured
not quenas or zampoñas but mandolins. Framing a nationalist claim as
one of also defending what he specifically referenced as "intangible heritage of humanity," Villanueva has struggled to assemble evidence, much
of which he told me has been destroyed or never existed in the first place,
because of the late establishment of institutions where someone might
register such compositions. I am not weighing in on these different origin
stories, but rather calling attention to the symbolic work behind them.[59]
During the interview, Villanueva reasserted both a nationalist voice
(Bolivian) and a universal voice ("intangible heritage of humanity"). But
nationalism seemed more present in his thinking as he segued into telling me about what has become known as the charango controversy. In
2006, the Chilean president, Ricardo Lagos, gave U2's Bono a charango
as part of a ceremony to award him the Pablo Neruda arts medal.[60] The
assumption that the charango is a Chilean instrument was then coun-
tered by President Morales, who at the inaugural ceremonies for the new
Chilean president, Michelle Bachelet, gave Condoleeza Rice a charango.
Defending his gift, the former president of Chile invoked an indigenous
connection that extended across national borders, saying "there are also
Aymaras in Chile."[61] The charango controversy, like "El condor pasa," continues to operate in a complex interlocking symbolic world of indigeneities and nationalisms. The conversation with Villanueva moved seam-
lessly between different spheres that in other contexts might be assumed
to be competing or contradictory—indigenous worlds, national worlds,
and worlds that reference the whole of humanity.

Most Bolivian musicians I interviewed were ready to put "El condor pasa" to rest. Clarken Orosco, a charango player, instrument maker, and member of Grupo Aymara, remembered his band's reluctance to play this tune, even though Japanese audiences always requested it.[62] Members of Grupo Aymara responded to these requests with irony, saying, "Pero ya pasó el condor" (literally, "But the condor already went by," or more colloquially, "But the condor is so over" or "is so yesterday"). Only at the after-concert party would they oblige the Japanese, as the band and their accompanying Japanese fans would all play the tune. In closing this chapter, I reiterate the circuitous route through which Bolivian music made it to Japan. Mestizos in Bolivia first had to appreciate the value of their country's indigenous music, and this lesson was partially learned as foreigners from Europe and the United States began to esteem, appropriate, and reshape indigenous Andean sounds, and as Argentines gave significant space to "folklore" performances. The different appropriations of indigeneity—for a Bolivian mestizo nationalist project or for international solidarity and exoticism—almost always left out flesh and blood indigenous subjects and remained completely disconnected from indigenous social movements. Bolivian musicians have been asserting strategies to get beyond the exoticized sound and image associated with "El condor pasa." While they were not substituting indigenismo with the radical social politics of Bolivian indianismo, musicians realize the limits of the indigenista frame in which they feel trapped, and that ultimately shapes the value of their music in a volatile international market. In the next chapter, I turn to the issues of work and value as associated with the international performance of Bolivian music.

3 "The Chinese Food of Ethnic Music"

WORK AND VALUE IN MUSICAL OTHERNESS

After arriving in Japan, recovering from jet lag, and holding a first re-hearsal, we launched into an intense first week of work in which we were giving three performances a day in multiple locations, all in the still scorching summer temperatures. The temporal and physical demands of that first week quickly set a rhythm of activities that would remain with us for the duration of the tour. Music tours are not always the labor of love about which many musicians dream. Repetition dulls the artistic senses and reminds one that this kind of music making is indeed *work*. Our daily school performances varied little. Although Música de Maestros has a vast repertoire at home, cultural performances in Japan privileged a fixed program, carefully chosen to teach students about cultural differences as encountered through music of this South American country, and to fit within a time frame that was precisely measured to the minute. The occa-sional full concert program was aimed at a different audience of fans and enthusiasts, but during three months of touring we performed mostly for school children.

Knowing the exact time frame for each show, usually forty-five or fifty minutes, Hishimoto would advise us to add this tune here, take out that tune over there, move this way, dance that way. We also changed a few pieces, depending on whether we played for elementary or high school students. In these carefully structured performances we would give the audience a taste of Bolivia's musical diversity—a kind of cultural quickie in a school assembly before students returned to their studies and we packed up our musical magic and headed for another town.

Nearing the end of the tour, I begged Hishimoto to substitute just one piece, any piece within our now well-worn program. "How about some-thing different here, but in the same genre?" I asked. Hishimoto responded by sighing quietly, shaking his head, and telling me that the piece I sug-gested did not include a part for the *bombo*—the large goatskin-covered drum. The inclusion of this deeply resonating percussive instrument was considered crucial for animating young audiences at our performances. Disappointed with this response, but respectful of Hishimoto's decisions as to what was best for our work on the tour, I mustered up a smile and feigned enthusiasm for performance number seventy-one, playing music that, under different circumstances, is absolutely thrilling to me.

I was not alone in this struggle against the monotony of musical repetition, but many musicians who were well seasoned in the challenges of international tours seemed practiced in the acceptance of these conditions. The Japan tour is a temporary job and a relatively well-remunerated one at that. Musicians mentioned receiving individually between $1,000 and $2,500 per month, quoting these sums in dollars. For many musicians, the dangers of boredom on this tour were put in perspective against what is often referred to somewhat disparagingly as "playing on the street" (*tocando en la calle*). Once again let me call forth the image of that Andean band in the subway station or on the street corner of a cosmopolitan city. I attempted but failed to get interviews with Andean musicians who were performing in the streets of Tokyo. Those I contacted were understandably suspicious of a stranger asking them questions about their work, and I did not have the necessary time in Tokyo to secure their trust. While my fieldwork did not encompass interviews with those who were presently "playing on the street," musicians often measured their circumstances next to these experiences that most of them knew all too well from previous moments in their lives. For Bolivian musicians, "playing on the street" lurks as a possibility behind all other venues in which Andean music is staged. "Playing on the street" implies uncertainty in everything. Will the police be after them? Will they sell enough recordings to buy a proper meal? (A principal way that street bands make money is by selling their own independently produced recordings.) Where will they sleep at night? When will they make enough money to buy their airline ticket home? Bolivian musicians told me stories about tours that fell apart midway. Promises coaxed them into the international context: a certain number of concerts in theaters, a reasonable short-term living accommodation, the prestige of an international tour, and a respectable remunerative sum. After arriving at the international destination, the imagined pillars of organization crumbled, and/or the band splintered apart because of conflicts between members. Unexpectedly, they found themselves having to play on the street just to get a meal, just to tread water until either another musical gig materialized, or they could make their way home.

While Bolivian musicians' lives at home are usually financially risky, in their own country they can maneuver gigs more easily and draw on family support networks in times of crisis. At home, these musicians perform in municipal theaters and in late-night bar scenes. Música de Maestros has also performed in Bolivian schools as part of a cultural project. Occasionally a group may play in the streets, but they usually do so within the Sunday fairs organized through the mayor's office, performing on outdoor stages and with amplified sound. Some musicians talked about "playing on the street" as a first touring experience—something they did when they were younger and more willing to take risks, and something to which they had no great desire to return. The risk of musical boredom on a Japan tour paled in comparison to these other risks that knocked at the door of life's basic necessities.

While internationally touring Bolivian musicians know first hand what it means to play on the street, they also generally view this performance space as one that decreases the overall value of their music. Within conversations about the perceived fade-out of the Andean music boom, musicians ask: why would people go to the theater to hear music they can easily hear in the trajectory of their evening commute? When I returned to Japan, off tour, to conduct a series of interviews, I sought out a connection to another music world in which I dabble—Irish traditional music. When I lunched with another gaijin (foreigner), a friend of a friend who was connected to an Irish session scene in Tokyo, I explained to him my research project. After learning about the details of my work, he admitted he always thought of "that music" (Andean music) as "the Chinese food of ethnic music." The phrase stuck in my mind for so many reasons. For its mixing of taste and sound. For its problematic positioning of "Chinese." But also because it seemed to encompass an array of anxieties that Bolivian musicians themselves expressed about the value of their music and work. Chinese food is a cuisine found all over the world; even though it takes on different forms in local places, it is generally associated with something stereotypically recognizable as "Chinese." It is a tasty but sometimes less expensive dining option found in Los Angeles, New York, Lima, and La Paz. Bolivian musicians worry about their music losing its international value, losing its tastiness, as audiences grow weary of hearing the very tunes that the international performance context demanded of the musicians in the first place. With the problematic phrase "the Chinese food of ethnic music," I want to flag the ever-present possibility of playing Andean music "on the street," the exoticism often imposed on this music, and the ongoing concerns about the value of this music in different international settings.

Studies focusing on commodification and exotification of the Other often start from the premise of an economic distance between those represented and those watching the representations.[1] In the global scheme of things, one can certainly speak of an economic distance between Japan and Bolivia, and that distance constructs Japanese subjects who get to sojourn to Bolivia to learn music, and Bolivian subjects who travel to Japan under the limited parameters of contracted cultural work. Interpretations that read the world as a Disneyesque spectacle, however, attribute too little agency to the performers themselves and ignore the multiple motivations and complex outcomes of such work.[2] In this chapter, I want to balance out the usually distancing language of exoticized spectacles with the intimacy of daily cultural work and value. I examine what these touring contracts mean, unpacking musicians' economic, artistic, and cultural motivations in this work.

The mines of Potosí are perhaps best known as a site where indigenous laborers were exploited in order to extract silver, the value of which financed the Spanish colonial enterprise. Bolivian musicians in Japan might be seen as "laboring in the culture mines." Their work is located in the cultural economy of late capitalism, a context characterized by "the culturalization of economic life," and the privileging of cultural exchanges over economic and political ones.[3] A cultural economy builds profits through the commodification of difference,[4] and it also builds profits through the cultivation of multiple differentiated niche markets,[5] which may provide limited economic benefits for those who supposedly embody or perform that difference. The primacy of a cultural economy comes with the late or post-Fordist capitalist shift from a production-oriented economy to a consumption-oriented one.[6] This chapter explores the economic and cultural framings of Bolivian music in Japan, but without ignoring the deeply felt affective motivations—usually nationalist in tenor—that also put Bolivian musicians in motion.

When musicians engage in repetitive performance as contracted work they may feel dissatisfactions as artists, but these frustrations are not explained fully through a framework of alienated labor—a point Robert Faulkner made as he discussed Hollywood musicians' split between what they dreamed of doing in music, and the reality of everyday employment in this field.[7] Bolivian musicians too have complex motivations and frustrations related to their work as performers in Japan. The economic value of Bolivian music in Japan often is found in a cultural show or lesson in multiculturalism and less often in a creative artistic endeavor. Bolivian music entered a distinctly pedagogical venue in Japan that, through public schools, was also connected to the nation-state. While musicians make good money playing in Japanese schools, they still covet the theater venue as the preferred performance space, a place where one has a greater chance of being treated and expressing oneself "like an artist."

These transnational political economies involve physical work in culture, as well as the imaginative work of staging culture as difference and music as "art." In a postindustrial cultural economy, the cultural entrepreneur is replacing the artist,[8] and postindustrial capitalism profits "through the commodification of difference itself and the conscious production of that difference."[9] This chapter focuses on those realms of *production* that in a cultural world might be better encompassed through the concepts of *work* and *performance*. Working musicians explore multiple possibilities of revaluing their labor in Japan, even as they come up against the structured limitations of performing cultural otherness. While their contracts are always within the flexible labor regimes that characterize late capitalism, performers often struggle against the more inflexible representations of "Bolivian" and "Andean" culture.[10] A look at the work of musicians in the field of cultural representations begins to bridge what Peter Wade refers to as the divide between culture as a way of life and culture as a set of representations.[11] For all its requisite stereotypical representations, the musical performance of Bolivian culture in Japan makes a real economic difference for Bolivians who land these contracts, whether or not they play in theaters or schools, perform "art" or "culture," or manage to break out of the "El condor pasa" groove. These performances entail, on the one hand, processes that exotify and create distance between performers and what they represent. On the other hand, this performance work also creates positive feelings that structure a nationalist identification and an intimacy with what is staged.

Cultural Entrepreneurs

Not every Bolivian musician gets invited to tour Japan. René Noda of Los Caballeros del Folklore (introduced in chapter 1) described his invitation as "something like luck." A delegation of Japanese businessmen were visiting the National Bank of Bolivia. Looking for some local entertainment for their guests, the bank hosts hired Noda's group to perform. "We went. We sang them some songs. And they liked it. They asked if we would want to go to Japan. And I told them, 'Sure. Why not?' . . . This was something just said in the moment. But a few months went by and they began to confirm the details. . . . The Japanese, when they say one thing, they do it." When Noda remembered the invitation as "something just said in the moment," he referred to a practice I have found quite common in social circles of La Paz. In the enthusiasm of the moment, and in the presence of someone right in front of you who tells you of an idea, a dream project, or an upcoming party, you respond with due enthusiasm. You might even tell the person, "Of course I'll be at your party. How could I miss it?" All along, you know full well you can't possibly attend the event. Because it was just "something said in the moment," Noda recalled his utter surprise when he actually received touring contracts and an airline ticket to travel. Noda told me they were sponsored by a businessman who owned a hotel chain and golf courses. During three months, they performed all over Japan and stayed in these top-notch hotels. Each musician returned to Bolivia with about $3,000 in his or her pocket. At least that is what they remembered in their twenty-first-century telling of the tale. As they reflected back on these experiences, a good bit of nostalgia kicked in for the days of their youth. At the time of my interviews, the members of Los Caballeros did not play music regularly. For example, Edgar "Pato" Patiño had a television show, *Sábados de alegría* (Saturdays of happiness). Reynaldo "Tito" Peñarrieta combined music work with his job at the Ministry of Hacienda, where he has been employed for twenty-five years. Noda worked in the United States for the World Health Organization, but planned to return to Bolivia in his retirement.

While Los Caballeros toured in the mid-1970s — well into the phenomena of Los Jairas, "El condor pasa," and the European boom — Japanese audiences had been listening to many other Latin American genres. Hidejiro Mimura, a music entrepreneur who would become key in the Bolivian-Japanese connection, told me he was first attracted to Mexican music via Los Panchos, Los Diamantes, and Los Ases. He met his wife, Mariquita, through their similar musical tastes. As a disc jockey, she had a radio program that played music from all over the world, but she was particularly drawn to Latin American music, and more specifically to Mexican music. One day she gave up her job to sing in Mexico. She would subsequently form a duo with her husband, Mimura, and they would tour Latin America as Mariquita y Jiro. As they traveled, many local artists told Mimura they wanted to perform in Japan. To promote these kinds of activities, he founded Music Amigos or the Japanese Latin American Cultural Exchange Association. Since its founding in 1976, Music Amigos has produced performance tours of groups from Mexico, Argentina, Peru, Spain, Colombia, Venezuela, Paraguay, Cuba, Uruguay, Brazil, and Bolivia. Their website emphasized "cultural exchange," and some of the company's activities included commemorative anniversaries related to Japanese immigration to these countries.[12]

According to Mimura, the popularity of Bolivian music in Japan began with the Music Amigos–organized tours of Ernesto Cavour. "Before that, everyone wanted to go to Argentina. But after Ernesto Cavour, everything changed." Throughout the 1980s and 1990s, Music Amigos's annual performance list featured at least one Bolivian representation and, besides

Cavour, included Los Kjarkas, William Centellas (a charango player), Grupo Aymara, Luz del Ande, Kallawaya, and Alejandro Cámara (a charango player).

When I interviewed Mimura in 2003, he did not have his sights set on any future Bolivian music production, indicating what he suggested as a dearth of emerging musical talent in this country. In reaction to this sweeping comment, I felt my hackles lifting in defense of my Bolivian musician friends, many of whom are incredibly creative and talented. I kept my cool and asked what he looked for in a music group. "They must cause a sensational impact, like Ernesto Cavour. When groups come that don't have an impact, there are fewer [theater goers]. . . . It is very difficult to fill a theater." Through more discussion, the ability to "cause an impact" seemed connected with perceptions of talent, youth, skill, performers' personalities, and tasteful musical arrangements of the repertoire. The search for a performer who would cause an impact also appeared linked to the continuing hunger for exoticism and spectacle—the frame against which many Bolivians worked.

Although these productions are inspired by motives of cultural exchange—and Mimura's personal history speaks to a life of interest in this area—filling theaters is, after all, what interests someone in the business of producing music performances. Mimura talked about a present "boom" of the Paraguayan harp, as if this music were replacing Japanese audiences' interests in Bolivian and Andean music. But the producing company itself plays a key role in shaping the consuming audience for Latin American music. Music Amigos's recent performance schedules prominently featured Paraguayan harpists, some from Paraguay, and at least one young Japanese woman who performed in this tradition.

On one evening of the 2002 tour, Kinoshita (see chapter 2) invited us to attend a performance by this harpist. Kinoshita, living once again in Japan, was accompanying her on guitar. On stage the young harpist spoke in a high-pitched tone, wore a flowing frilly dress, and played (among other things) "El condor pasa." The fans lined up after the concert, asking for her autograph on the CD recordings they had recently purchased. She seemed to embody the sense of "cute" that has been associated with Japanese female pop singers, an expectation of soft, innocent, feminine display that according to Ian Condry takes its toll on the entire Japanese popular music industry.[13] Kinoshita, a relatively more mature musician, but still only in his early forties at the time of this performance, accompanied the headlining "cute" young harpist in this cross-cultural music performance. These stories, as well as others I have heard from Bolivians, point to an ageism in Japanese ethnic music performance. Companies want young energetic "fresh" faces in the performance of culture. The mature musician struggles to enter and remain on stages that, in the commercial sense, more easily accommodate youth who perform cultural difference.

While Music Amigos's touring contacts came through a combination of an entrepreneur's interests in a general category of "Latin American music" and Cavour's global notoriety through Los Jairas, for Música de Maestros, the Japan tour contact was at least ten years in the making and came through Hishimoto, after a chain of other Bolivia-Japan connections.

When Hishimoto met the director of Música de Maestros in the late 1980s, he already idolized Encinas's quena playing as he had heard it on recordings. At their first encounter, Hishimoto pointed at Encinas and said in his then limited Spanish, "teacher." He then pointed to himself and said "student." With these words, Hishimoto referenced a traditional learning structure (the *iemoto* system) through which Japanese learn an art from a particular master, and sometimes even take on the last name of their teacher. That was the beginning of an apprenticeship that became a partnership in the composing, arranging, and performing of Bolivian music, both within and outside Bolivia. While Hishimoto arrived in Bolivia with the intention of staying briefly, he ended up living seven years there, as he mastered playing Bolivian music, and specialized in the performance of panpipes and notched flutes. Hishimoto never told me why he left Bolivia, but when he returned to Japan with his wife and family, he did not yet have employment. His previous contacts with Kinoshita, who had preceded him in Bolivia, led to his employment as a guide and translator with a cultural performance company that contracted international groups to perform throughout Japan. Taypi K'ala was the first Bolivian band to tour Japan with this company. After a few years of working for this company, Hishimoto facilitated an invitation to Encinas and the latter opted to tour under the name of his group, Música de Maestros.

As opposed to Music Amigos's tours in which most concerts were in theaters, this cultural performance company contracted musicians to play primarily in schools. The company seemed to favor musicians from what might be called "Third World" contexts because these groups could be hired for a smaller fee. Part way into the tour during 2002, my Bolivian colleagues had to complete immigration paperwork to extend their stay in Japan by three days. En route to these bureaucratic dealings, I had a lengthy discussion with the company representative who accompanied the group and who spoke English very well. When I complimented her on her English and apologized for not speaking Japanese, she said she often had to use her English for the drafting of contracts for the different groups the company hired. From Latin America, she said they hired musicians from Mexico and Bolivia. She told me that Japanese like "happy music," and she quickly categorized under this term the music from these two countries. The company had tried to hire a Native American group, she told me, but they were unable to do so because the ensemble's fees were too high. Although I did not ask her directly about contracting groups from the United States, she seemed to volunteer her thoughts, responding to me as if I might wonder about my own country's representation in this company's work. They had considered bringing gospel singers, or even a country music band, but ultimately were deterred by what they thought these groups might charge. The geopolitical asymmetries of culture and power seemed to predetermine who would be hired as a performance spectacle for Japanese school children.[14] Operating out of a small office and rehearsal space in Tokyo, the company would sponsor simultaneously two or three groups; a Chinese theater group and a Korean dance troupe were on tour when I was in Japan in 2002.

The company representative also mentioned that groups from Asian countries were in high in demand. Since the cohosting of the World Cup in 2002, she suggested, Japanese had demonstrated a renewed interest in Korea. "There is a feeling we are becoming friends with Korea," she said. The head of the company was married to a Chinese woman who also worked in the company. Part of the interest in "Asia" may have been facilitated by this personal tie to another Asian country. But this trend may also be part of Japan's "return to Asia"—a renewed interest, since the 1990s, in the rising economic power of other Asian states.[15]

The company also sponsored performances abroad. For example, Hishimoto was contracted once to accompany a Japanese theater troupe on a tour of Mexico and Costa Rica. Hishimoto, who always underestimated his own abilities in the Spanish language, laughed shyly as he told me he had traveled as a Spanish translator on that tour. Hishimoto's, the tour manager's, and the sound engineer's contracts—like the Bolivian musicians' arrangement—consisted of short-term engagements that lasted as long as the tour, usually two or three months of work. Flexible labor contracts shaped the work of both Japanese and Bolivian members of this economy.

According to Hishimoto, each school in Japan is urged to sponsor one special performance each year, but it does not have to be a show by a foreign delegation. The company representative told me these foreign concerts were strongly recommended by the Ministry of Education. She referred to Japan's geography in her explanation, saying that because Japan is a country of islands, it is difficult for Japanese to get to know other cultures. From her perspective these foreign spectacles helped break a perceived cultural detachment of Japan. Her comment reflected a pervasive myth of Japanese isolation, one that even Bolivians repeated, and that flies in the face of a history of Japan's global connections.[16] According to the company representative, these cultural performances were perceived as a way for Japanese students to get to know the world. Even as the space-time compressions of labor and symbolic capital are surely at work here,[17] a myth of Japanese isolation seems to propel these cultural lessons in the first instance.

Our performances for school audiences should be located in relation to multicultural education in Japan. In a post–World War II context, the Japanese government followed UNESCO's argument that learning about others could be a preface to world peace.[18] Under the premise that Japan was a homogeneous society, projects of multicultural education looked first outside Japan for encounters with cultural otherness.[19] Even if multicultural education turned inward from the 1980s, beginning to recognize ethnic differences within Japan, practices in this area have focused on what Eika Tai calls the "three Fs approach" (food, fashion, and festivals), leading to a "boutique multiculturalism" that usually fails to get beyond culturally essentialist models.[20] Our musical presentations of difference did not stray much from these essentializing patterns. Encinas planned performances to demonstrate *Bolivia's* multiculturalism, but our shows were more often received as "Andean" at best, and more often as simply "Latin American" and exotic. The performances fit, however, in an overall attempt to know others through music—what Deborah Kapchan has called "the promise of sonic translation"; key here is the hope that music can translate affect across cultural and linguistic chasms.[21]

While Bolivian and Japanese nationalisms are, I argue, central to these transnational cultural performances, such shows are facilitated not by entities of nation-states, but by individual entrepreneurs who are willing to take the financial risk of sponsoring performers, and by individual Bolivian musicians who are quite eager not only to make money, but also to represent their country. As Louisa Schein has suggested through her work on transnational Miao, analyses need to work beyond the assumption that national identities are direct productions of state-based nationalism.[22] The nationalist sentiments of Bolivian music performers seldom benefit from state supports in the transnational arena.[23] I now take a closer look at the work conditions set by the company with which we toured.

Working for the Company

Música de Maestros in Japan took an entirely different shape from its home-based twenty-five- to thirty-person orchestra. Only five Bolivian musicians were invited, a number set by the Japanese company. The selection of these few musicians was a delicate matter, and one that stirred jealousy on the home front. Transnational flows of culture and capital have not brought an accompanying equality in the mobility of subjects.[24] While some people may insist on critiquing and dismissing these musicians as mestizos stealing indigenous music in representation of the nation, it is important to keep a more complex picture front and center. The musicians of this ensemble, indigenous or not, generally are not mobile subjects who have been emancipated by global flows. An occasional performer marries into a foreign context, taking up not just the art of performing in Japan, but also the art of living there. Bolivian musicians have remained in European contexts for more extended periods as well. But, in the case of touring Japan, Bolivian musicians' mobility has been limited to very specific, short-term contracts. Those who can participate in this temporary transnational cultural labor usually are underemployed at home and already existing within flexible labor conditions. If they are not in this tenuous position in Bolivia, a three-month tour and absence from any more stable employment is likely to move them into the realm of greater labor insecurity. Controversy emerged at home because just about anyone in the ensemble would be willing to drop everything in Bolivia to tour Japan. In selecting those who traveled, Encinas considered the musical demands of a small ensemble as well as the intense personal demands of sharing work, travel, and living space over a three-month period.

The company purchased the labor of the musicians for a set number of days, during which time they would schedule as many performances as possible. The company also arranged for the musicians' visas, paid their airfare and hotel, and distributed approximately $30 per diem to each touring musician for the purchase of food. Upon finalizing the tour, sometimes a mere thirty-six hours before departure, each member of the group received payment for their work.

Among Bolivian musicians a tour with this company is viewed as a no-frills job: a sure thing but with lots of hard work, mid-rate hotels, and uncomfortably long bus rides. After finishing the performances for the day, the group often had to travel by bus, three to eight hours, before arriving at the destination of the next day's performances and the night's accommodations. The moving bus sometimes became a space for rehearsing

9. Edwing Pantoja and Yuliano Encinas rehearse panpipes on the bus in Japan. *Photograph by the author.*

tunes that were not featured in our daily school performances, but that would form part of the repertoire for a theater concert (see figure 9). Musicians who had previously toured with this company would express their dissatisfaction in terms of whether or not they were being treated "like an artist," even using the term "exploitation" to describe these working conditions. Being treated "like an artist" translated to accommodations in five star hotels, comfortable travel arrangements that included bullet trains and air travel for long distances, and the ability to simply arrive at a performance, pick up an instrument, and play. In contrast, all members on this company tour—musicians, manager, and sound engineer—were involved in the grunt work of setting up and taking down a show, something that would happen one to three times a day.

Some musicians also expressed dissatisfaction with company rules and practices that stripped them of certain dignities as workers, and discriminated against them as Bolivians. One musician told me of his anger when a Japanese company employee took away his passport. In years of touring as a musician in Europe, this had never happened to him. "Without my passport, who am I? They gave me a photocopy, but what can I do with a photocopy?" Through an interpreter, he tried to reason with the company employees. They gave him their reason for holding the passports; they previously had problems with Peruvian musicians who had "escaped" and remained in Japan.

Several musicians reflected on the difficulties they faced on these tours as they had to accustom themselves to an early morning start of the work-day. Musicians' work in Bolivia is heavily weighted toward the evening and even the extreme early morning. Late mornings and early after-noons might be spent securing performing engagements, giving classes, and taking care of or acquiring musical instruments. With the exception of studio recording sessions—which may be scheduled at any time—Bolivian musicians usually rehearse and perform at night. Touring Japa-nese schools required a complete reversal of this pattern—a front-loading of the day.

Another musician, who had toured Japan after ten years of perform-ing in Europe and the United States—working those years as both musi-cian and tour manager—expressed his frustration when a Japanese com-pany would not communicate the daily schedule to the musicians: "[As tour manager in Europe] I always told everyone of the day's itinerary. Then you psychologically prepare for the day. . . . [The Japanese] had a schedule, but they never told us what it was. All of a sudden we would be leaving in the morning to go to three different performances. But you prepare yourself psychologically for the day. You rest more. . . . But they never told us this information in advance." By the time I toured Japan with Música de Maestros, more information of this kind flowed in our di-rection. Our guide posted the monthly itinerary with names of the places we would perform, how many performances we would give each day, and whether or not we would play in schools or theaters. When musi-cians weighed the troubles of these school performance touring condi-tions against the secure contract and remunerative gains, many still opted to accept the invitation, taking on the hardships of extended separation from family members—what all musicians spoke of as the most difficult aspect of these jobs.

Punctuality with a Smile

Hishimoto told me he once entered a school director's office and saw on his desk over one hundred brochures advertising different perform-ing groups. Many companies were competing for these contracts with schools. With this kind of competition, company workers, even those on short contracts like our guide, our manager, and our sound engineer, felt the pressure to meet high standards of work. Those standards included a meticulous attention to punctuality, a serious attitude about work, and a sincere attempt to meet perceived audience expectations in a performance of cultural difference.

Our manager would drive the bus into the school grounds about fifteen minutes before our scheduled arrival. But to make the first appointment of the day, we had usually traveled some five hours the previous day, making sure we were at a hotel within a twenty-minute drive of our first performance site. Each day the manager carefully studied maps, because his job was not about showing up on time to the same place of work every day, but rather about arriving punctually every day at two or three different and previously unknown places of work. Ideally, we would arrive two hours before show time, giving ourselves ample time to unload, set up, do a sound check, change our clothes, and perhaps even rehearse problem spots. Timing was crucial in the school context because students were scheduled to attend the special assembly of our show that had to fit within the already highly regimented school day. If we gave one performance during the day, being punctual seemed quite easy, but when we had three performances in a single day, at three different schools, being punctual became a real challenge indeed. In one case, we literally ran to set up a second show for which we had exactly twenty-five minutes from arrival to show time.

Until they proved themselves otherwise, Bolivian musicians were sometimes stereotyped as the late arrivers. One band was cited each morning thirty minutes before the actual departure time. To the dismay of band members, each morning the Japanese tour workers would arrive at the bus thirty minutes after the appointed hour. Again, the company workers justified their actions by saying they had problems with another group that would arrive an hour after the agreed time. Only after the Bolivians had proven their punctuality did the Japanese let them sleep thirty more minutes.

On previous tours with the company, Música de Maestros had already proven itself in the area of punctuality. At five minutes before departure, many of us would be seated on the bus, our luggage already loaded in the back. For those who didn't carry an alarm clock, other band members would give them a wake-up call or knock. If a band member sauntered on the bus even a minute after zero hour, she or he received flack, not from the Japanese manager, but from the rest of the band. Ultimate punctuality—sometimes taken by the group as a game, a test, or a challenge—was applied as well in other moments of the workday. After the last performance of the day, we were often taken to large shopping centers with supermarkets. Within an hour we were expected to purchase food and eat

10. Members of Música
de Maestros unload
the bus to perform at
a Japanese school.
*Photograph by the
author.*

lunch. Punctuality in returning to the bus was also emphasized because
we all knew that this stop would be followed by extensive cross-country
travel. A band member "got lost" one day in one of the shopping centers
and could not find the way back to the bus. For the remainder of the tour
this musician did very little wandering alone in shopping centers. Punctuality was internally enforced through the entire working day, which
lasted until we arrived at our hotel accommodations for the night.

The Bolivians emphasized the importance of teamwork to unload, set-
up, and strike the set (see figure 10). As the tour progressed, and we began
to get on each others' nerves, internal critiques inevitably surfaced about
members who didn't quite seem to be doing their share. If the situation became tense, we would have a discussion about it. After arriving at a school
and unloading, we usually had some time as the sound engineer prepared
his equipment. I used this time to play scales and exercises on the violin —
thankfully not putting fake braids in my hair! As we moved into the fall
months, and the mornings became cooler, many of the Bolivians began to

grab a game of basketball during this short interlude. Most of our school performances took place in gymnasiums that doubled as theaters for staged events. A basketball usually could be found in some corner of this venue. As the guitar player Yuliano Encinas told me, the physical activity warmed them up and helped them bring renewed energy and enthusiasm to what could easily become a monotonous performance routine. For the Bolivians, this kind of enthusiasm and energy, even if feigned, was a necessary element of good work on the tour. In fact, I was constantly being criticized by other members of the group because I apparently did not meet these standards of visible and demonstrable enthusiasm on stage. In the middle of the show another musician would remind me to smile. I thoroughly enjoy performing with these musicians—the fatigue of the tour aside—but while my stage presence in Bolivian performance contexts might be critiqued for my musical interpretations, in those contexts, lack of enthusiasm never entered the running commentary.

Exaggerated enthusiasm was a particular labor demand in the Japanese transnational context, where we were supposed to represent an Other for the audience. The demand for smiles and enthusiasm, according to Arlie Hochschild's work with flight attendants, characterizes labor in which feelings that might be expressed privately are managed as an alienable resource of service as performed in public and for remuneration.[25] In ritual entrance parades that run through the streets of Bolivian cities and towns, participants are also encouraged to show "more joy."[26] These taunts of encouragement, however, seem more like the response of a crowd that is both lending support to and demanding presence from performers. The direct connection between audience and performer makes the demand for "more joy" quite different from a similar demand as a reprimand made by fellow performers who are imagining how an audience might receive their show. The feelings on stage in Japan were not left as a resource to be invested in artistic expression;[27] rather they were mutually managed within the group because they mattered in terms of the overall impression the ensemble might leave, and the future contracts that accordingly might or might not be forthcoming.

The Bolivians' attention to pumping up energy and enthusiasm occasionally clashed with some of the Japanese expectations about work. For example, one school director became very angry when she saw the Bolivian musicians playing basketball. The Bolivians thought she was upset because they had not asked for permission to do so. According to Hishimoto, that was not the issue. Rather, the school director was miffed because her institution was paying them to work *as musicians* and to put on a show. She could not believe that these paid musicians were playing basketball on her yen, so to speak. On the other hand, the Bolivians defended their game of basketball as a way to bring energy to their performances. The musicians sought ways every day to laugh and joke on stage, and as the tour progressed I saw this as another strategy for keeping up enthusiasm. For example, in the second half of the show, we always introduced ourselves in Japanese—one of the few lines of Japanese we all had to learn. No one in the audience really knew our names, so we made a game out of giving ourselves alternative stage names. Our sound engineer, who was studying Spanish and who understood more and more about the daily on-stage jokes, would complain about our lack of a serious attitude. However, I would often catch him hiding a smile as he crouched behind the sound board and tried to keep a straight face.

Dancing was another specific demand of music performance in Japan, and one with which I struggled. Dancing itself was not the problem. But I am no Natalie MacMaster (the fiddler who plays and step dances at the same time). Following the Western penchant for splitting sensory experiences and the performance arts into their own semiautonomous realms,[28] I had learned to relish both dancing and playing music, but with each activity in its proper place and time. The trick was to dance *while* playing the violin. My classical music training had emphasized straight posture, a flowing wrist, and an otherwise unmoving body. To steady a bow across the strings, to apply an even pressure as the whole body is moving up and down, to flex the knees so as to move fluidly below the waist while steadying the torso—these are the challenges of playing the violin while dancing. Our performances in Japan were choreographed, with specific steps and moves, according to the genre at hand. All musicians were expected to move as we played. I was not the only one who had difficulty with dancing and playing, as this is a radical shift from staged music performances in Bolivia. Brass bands in Bolivia move through the streets as they accompany dance troupes in ritual entrance parades like Gran Poder in La Paz; and the troupe style performances of indigenous wind instruments also are particularly well suited to *playing and moving* through space.[29] But when Música de Maestros performed on stage in Bolivia, our movements were minimal unless we were playing the indigenous wind instruments. When I first began performing with this ensemble at the end of 1993, they were using microphones on pedestals, a technological detail that also constrained possible movements of a violinist on stage. As more members acquired microphones that could be attached to their instruments, the ensemble began to move more on stage. Yet our Bolivian performances were never choreographed like those in Japan.

Yuliano Encinas, completing his third tour of Japan when I interviewed him, reflected back on his first tour with Taypi K'ala. Yuliano spoke of a theater specialist that worked with the ensemble: "He completely changed what we were playing as a group in Bolivia. . . . We were a normal group without much movement. Maybe we would do one little thing like ask for hand-clapping. . . . But here they asked us to dance. They asked us to animate the show. We had to loosen up on stage." Yuliano easily adapted his performances to this new demand, but others, like myself, struggled with playing and dancing. Hishimoto, whose ears were always closely attuned to the sound we produced as well as the choreographed animation of the show, did suggest the violins engage in less movement in certain passages where we carried important melodic or harmonic lines.

When a couple of musicians left their instruments and took on the role of dancers, as occurred when we featured music from the Chaco region or when we played a cueca, the remaining musicians did not have to dance. The featured dancing couple would draw the audience's visual attention while the rest of us concentrated on the sound to which they danced. These choreographed performances were radically different from our concerts in La Paz's Municipal Theater, in which musicians generally did not dance and where we were accompanied at times by an entire dance company.

Working in the culture mines entails keen attention to playing a role on stage: the role of musicians who enthusiastically want to share the music from their country. The serious attitude toward work sat in contrast with the expectation of the ever-smiling representation of indigeneity. Tour members commented on the fact that this kind of energy, through one performance after another, is one of the most difficult aspects of this labor. As the basketball game incident demonstrated, Bolivian musicians' strategies for meeting the demands of these roles did not always receive the approval of Japanese hosts who sometimes held conflicting ideas about how one should approach working in music and cultural difference.

Playing for Adults

One musician summed up the difference between performing in schools and performing in theaters: in the former you play for children; in the latter you play for adults. I would add that our performances in schools were about cultural difference. In theaters, they were still about cultural difference, but with a leaning toward the art frame. The theater performances would attract fans, hobbyists, and friends who already knew not just about Bolivian music in general but also about details of the specific ensemble performing and the artistic trajectories of individual members. Several musicians mentioned their initial surprise when Japanese fans introduced themselves and cited their knowledge of other groups with which the musicians may have played. Enthusiasts seemed to carry a mental musical biography of each musician. Musicians' recordings had preceded the Bolivians in the transnational movement to Japanese soil. All of these factors created a situation in which more was at stake in the theater performance. Reputations had to be lived up to. If the band stood for "Bolivia" in a school performance, the theater called forth the ensemble's distinct identity within Bolivia. The group's repertoire had to strike a balance between old favorites and innovations. While the repetition of school performances took away some of that "tickle in the stomach . . . like what you feel when you are falling in love," as Luis Guillén (drummer of Luz del Ande) put it, some of that nervousness or excitement was welcomed back in the theater. After a theater performance, there was always the possibility of an after-hours scene, a celebration with beer, food, and sake, where fans, friends, and hobbyists would break out their own quenas, charangos, and zampoñas to join in informal playing.

Theater performances provided a glimpse into that other world of touring experiences about which musicians spoke with uniform enthusiasm—the space where musicians were given their due respect. If we were scheduled for a theater performance, usually the entire day was set aside for this activity. When we arrived at the venue, several theater workers met us to assist in unloading. When we performed at schools we often changed clothes in dusty corners, all while trying to keep our costumes as clean as possible. In contrast, at theaters we were shown to elaborate dressing rooms with mirrors, showers, and places to hang our clothes. With the appropriate space and time to do so, here we would break out the iron to remove the wrinkles that inevitably formed through the daily transport of our shirts and pants.

Sound checks for theater concerts usually involved a complete performance, a practice that, according to interviews with other musicians, is generalized in Japan. Once individual microphones had been checked and a general balance reached, we played in entire concert, start to finish. Even the stagehands, working elaborate lighting details, went through their paces. The sound check was in fact an entire dress rehearsal. We were usually thrilled with the theater sound. Our sound engineer, who was extremely thorough and detailed in his work, would occasionally complain about the low-quality sound equipment the company provided for our daily work. We each carried our own microphones, but the company provided everything else. The theater performance reminded everyone of the sonorous possibilities when performing with first-rate sound systems. Elsewhere, I have detailed a similar disregard for sound quality by those who organize folklore festivals in France.[30] Since that writing, Música de Maestros has made a habit of touring these French folklore festivals with their own microphones, cables, and console. When Bolivian music is sold as a pedagogical spectacle about cultural difference, sound quality takes a back seat only to be returned to prominence with the distinct status of the theater concert.

Even those who took contracts to perform in schools—often emphasizing the importance of developing a new audience for Bolivian music— also proudly counted the theater performances included in the itinerary. In assessing the tour in 2002, as opposed to his previous work for the same company, Yuliano Encinas remarked, "Look, this year we had more theater performances than in previous years." The street, the school, and the theater—as performance venues—represent a hierarchy of ascending values: music as a street corner curiosity or urban background noise, music as a lesson in cultural difference, and music as art. While the theater venue did not entail an instant transformation for folklore performances, these were the contexts in which musicians tried to challenge the expectations audiences often imposed on them.

Undressing Folklore in the Theater

"A fashion designer, to make a dress for a model, imagines the face without makeup, the body without anything, just as it is. Then over the body [the designer] puts on the clothes, the makeup. . . . But the designer never puts clothes on a body that is already clothed. I think it is necessary to undress folklore music." Kinoshita made these comments at the conclusion of our conversation in his Tokyo studio. He had been explaining his concern about Bolivian folklore music's lack of direction. Having lived so many years in Bolivia, he spoke with a sense of this music being *his*, but while also insisting on his Japanese-ness: "Although I put on a poncho, inside, I'm Japanese. . . . Living in Bolivia changed me a lot, but unfortunately, or luckily, I don't know, [before going to Bolivia] I had nineteen years of just being pure Japanese. I can't erase that. So in music, I think the same thing. To make Bolivian music we should not use only exoticisms." He uses the metaphor of undressing to point out his own sense of being Japanese, while also including himself as a creator of Bolivian music. The same idea of undressing is used to suggest that Bolivian musicians and Bolivian music are still there under the poncho, under what in the international performance context is the sartorial equivalent of "El condor pasa." These comments followed a discussion of his own attempt to redress folklore, so to speak, through his composition, *Suite ecológico ser* (Ecological being suite).

Suite ecológico ser, structured in seven movements labeled with titles like "Sun Theme," "Moon Theme," and "Ocean Theme," uses Andean instruments while also sitting easily with the categorizing adjective of "avant-garde." The liner notes, written in Spanish by Kinoshita himself, describe his own philosophical reflections on ecology, his experiences with music, and his very existence. He lays out what could be considered a universal theme—ecology as a way to "avoid planetary Holocaust." His proposal includes "preservation of the environment" as well as "the necessity of creating connections within ethnic-cultural diversity." The symbolic and activist world of indigeneity has often been associated with the natural world and ecology, a direct line often being drawn between those with "so much culture" and those "so close to nature." As previously mentioned, environmental stewardship is a powerful definitional frame of indigenous struggle.[31] On the other hand, indigenous peoples can read environmentalist politics as foreign and not necessarily in line with their own collective demands.[32] Representations of indigeneity also circulate in close proximity with ecological concerns, thus locking the imaginary indigenous native in an eternal embrace with the environmental good. In his *Suite*, Kinoshita brings together ethnic and ecological imaginaries and claims to call for a different way of understanding ecology. He writes that the musical pieces are written in "folklore language, *my* form of musical expression (emphasis added)." He then asks the question: "How can one explain all this in folklore language?" In other words, how can such a supposedly universal question be addressed through a music that evokes the particular. Answering his own question, he draws attention not to individual inspirations, but to the "collective identities" that might correspond to a more collective understanding of ecology.[33] Luz del Ande toured Japan with performances of this work in the late 1990s.

How did Kinoshita become director of this Bolivian group? According to Kinoshita, in the late 1980s he was approached in La Paz by Orlando Rojas, who offered him the name of his then defunct group. At the time, Kinoshita cut a prominent profile in the Paceño music world—performing and recording extensively, and playing in the famous Peña Naira with well-established musicians like Donato Espinoza on charango and Fernando Jiménez on zampoñas. Kinoshita accepted the offered name, Luz del Ande, forming a group whose membership shifted over the years. The group's directorship remained with Kinoshita, even after his permanent

11. Koji Hishimoto and Takaatsu Kinoshita pose with a poster for a salon concert in Tokyo. *Photograph by the author.*

return to Japan. Kinoshita is engaged with professional Andean and Latin American music performances in Japan, like those with the harpist (mentioned above), and also with other Bolivian-trained musicians like Hishimoto (see figure 11).

Luz del Ande had already toured Japan with their more traditional repertoire when Kinoshita proposed that the group return to tour with *Suite ecológico ser*. Each member of the ensemble spoke with great enthusiasm about this new project. Marcelo Peña (a quena player), remembered how Kinoshita pitched the project, "He said, 'I would like to create Bolivian music, but ours, of Luz del Ande. Like Piazzolla and his tango.'" Astor Piazzolla, an Argentine who considered himself a composer of classical symphonic music, went to France in the 1950s and studied with Nadia Boulanger who urged him to find his own roots through composing tangos.[34] Kinoshita was calling his ensemble to a project of artistic experimentation, but within Bolivian musical languages. Kinoshita, then residing in Japan, sent Luz del Ande members a recording of the composition as it was fashioned only on keyboard, and after listening to it, group members gave a green light to the project and the preparations began.

The *Suite* called for changes in both costume and choreography. If their Japanese performance of traditional repertoire called for Bolivian folklore costumes, usually some derivative use of the aguayo—colorful weavings characteristic of different areas in Bolivia—their costumes for the *Suite* were "completely different." They wore vests that had been made from the fabrics used to make cholitas' skirts in La Paz. Two ensemble members recalled this major shift from the typical indigenous woven cloth (sometimes hand woven and sometimes made simply to *look* hand woven) to the obviously machine-made cloth used in cholitas' skirts. Luis Guillén told me "they didn't use the aguayo. Nothing like that, but rather the urban." Wilson Molina, however, remembered that the new costumes were fashioned after a short jacket worn by men in Northern Potosí. Luz del Ande had toured previously with a small dance troupe that would perform the corresponding dances that accompanied each traditional genre. With the *Suite*, however, their dance troupe presented contemporary choreography, something more akin to modern dance.

How did Japanese audiences respond to the *Suite*? One band member gave it a completely positive spin saying it was well accepted "because it sound[ed] a little Japanese, as it was composed by Takaatsu, a Japanese." Everyone else admitted to the challenges of touring with the *Suite*, saying they lost some of their usual audience members who were expecting their folklore fix. Kinoshita was frank in his assessment: "The aficionados of folklore music here in Japan didn't accept it because . . . [they] like things they can guess already. They are people who like—." He paused and chuckled before making the following comment, recognizing that he was talking to an American, "—who like American movies . . . for the happy ending. That's why they watch calmly. They wait for this." While the *Suite* did not provide the expected ending for the usual folklore fan, Luz del Ande members told me the work attracted a new audience, one that might be more connected to the performance worlds of jazz and classical ballet.

The presentation in Japan of Kinoshita's *Suite* was one of the more daring attempts to break out of the folklore ghetto, to move these musical expressions not only into a theater, but also into a framework of high art. Other musicians also pushed the envelope here, taking advantage of the theater venue to present their own compositions that did not always fit folklore genre patterns. On theater stages, we performed a shortened arrangement of Encinas's *Supay*, a work in twenty-one movements that tells a musical tale of mythic and religious beings in pre- and postconquest moments.[35] The Quechua word "supay" often has been translated poorly as "devil." Regina Harrison, working with the translation of this word as "spirit," argues that such a being might be good (*allin supay*) or bad (*mana allin supay*).[36] The staged work *Supay* presents the idea of a forced incorporation of a Christian view of the devil, symbolized on stage when an angel forces Supay to wear a devil's mask. In Bolivia, this forty-five-minute work, orchestrated by Hishimoto, was performed as a modern ballet with the dance troupe Conadanz (short for Companía Nacional de Danza, National Dance Company). In Japanese theaters, we performed a shortened version of *Supay* without dancers and with Hishimoto's new arrangements for the smaller ensemble.[37] We also performed Hishimoto's "Memorias del Tiempo I y II" in Japan. These pieces would eventually form part of another longer work composed by both Hishimoto and Encinas, and recorded by the full Música de Maestros orchestra as *Surimana*.[38] While "Memorias del Tiempo II" followed a more traditional huayño genre, the first movement was described as "contemporary music elaborated with the harmonies of indigenous instruments."[39] Compositions like these provided performers with a welcome break from the daily monotony of the school performance repertoire. Bolivian musicians and Japanese who play Bolivian music are actively trying to get beyond the rigid expectations of folklore, but often they have to be in a theater context before they can make these moves. Their sponsoring entrepreneurs also have to be willing to take risks in terms of audiences' reactions.

As a less risky and seemingly quite economically successful way to "undress folklore" in the theater, some Bolivian musicians are mixing it up with jazz musicians in Japan. Donato Espinoza, well known in Bolivia as a highly skilled charango soloist and as a key figure in the group Savia Andina, began his Japanese connections through contacts with Japanese musicians who arrived in La Paz, went to the renowned Peña Naira, heard him play there, and began to study music with him. In the Peña Naira he also met and performed with both Kinoshita and Hishimoto and eventually met Takamasa Segi—a zampoña player who would transform this instrument's sound for a popular Japanese audience (see chapter 4). "Segi," as he is known artistically, would become one of Espinoza's main contacts in Japan.

When Espinoza travels to Japan, he says he presents "another type of music, not folklore." Often traveling alone from Bolivia, he meets up with Japanese jazz musicians who are "very well known in Japan." Sponsoring companies sometimes invite star musicians from several different Latin American countries, sending them written music to study before their departure, and then expecting the formation of ensembled sound once they arrive in Japan. On these tours, Espinoza told me, they play in huge theaters and jazz clubs, featuring a program of their own compositions and very few "covers." As Espinoza explained, these performances "have traces of Andean music, for example, in the sounds of the instruments. But the context is different. It's not exactly Bolivian."

While Espinoza's performance position seems the most open to creative possibilities, many musicians in the circuit I studied are negotiating a delicate balance between meeting audience expectations and refashioning the musical box called "Andean folklore music." Musicians fretted over these questions about cultural and artistic representation, but ultimately their economic earnings from this work in Japan transformed their lives at home.

Serious Shopping, Serious Patriotism

When I asked one Bolivian musician, who had toured Japan nine times, if these tours had gone well for him in the economic sense, he responded, "Absolutely! Eighty percent of my recording studio was acquired through this work." Through the 1980s, 1990s, and into the twenty-first century many musicians who tour Japan have dedicated their working lives to music—as performers, teachers, arrangers, instrument makers, independent museum curators, and sound engineers. Whether one travels as an invited artist to perform jazz-Andean fusion or as a school performer who gives musical lessons in cultural difference, whether one helps unload heavy speakers or hardly even lifts one's own instrument, and whether one has few or many opportunities to undress folklore in a theater performance, all musicians spoke of the economic gains made by touring Japan.

Before starting this project, money was not a topic of conversation I sought within my interactions with Bolivian musicians. I had certainly heard through participant observation about numerous conflicts over money problems, ones that sometimes split groups and made enemies out of the best of friends. Accusations of mismanaged concert earnings, rumors of small shadow ensembles that picked up extra gigs using the "look and feel" (repertoire and dress) of a larger established group, stories about a well-known singer's failure to pay an entire orchestra for their accompanying studio recording work—these are just a few of the sordid details about money that I have overheard, and that might be encountered in just about any other music context. Usually I say I do not make my living playing music, even though my colleague Barbara Yngvesson quite astutely pointed out to me that my music performance has been key to my professional work as an anthropologist. However, even as music may shape some details of my day job, I still have *a day job*. On the economic hardships of being a musician in or outside Bolivia, I am a mere observer.[40]

When I asked questions about the economic value of these tours, I received sincere reflections about personal financial plans, but they were often accompanied by assurances that this was not all about the money. Not that I ever thought it was. But I was originally drawn to this project as I noticed how work in Japan seemed to ease some of the economic challenges at home and facilitate continued creative work in a country where the majority of the population generally lives in dire economic circumstances. Marcelo Peña of Luz del Ande, who had managed to balance a regular job with his music performance activities, told me, "I'm not doing poorly. . . . But to be a musician [to live only from music] is really difficult. I have so much respect for my colleagues [who make a living in music]. You have to be a patriot to make music. You're not an artist anymore. You're a hero." This sense of sacrifice for the performance of *Bolivian* music—and the national adjective is not to be taken for granted here—was a commonplace throughout many of these discussions. That patriotic stance on Bolivian music was balanced with carefully researched shopping expeditions.

We spent few days in Tokyo, and the city often became a place for a "day off" if we were within close proximity and between school performances. Some people liked having the days off in Tokyo, taking full advantage of being in one place; of having already scouted out the nearest Internet cafes, markets, and used CDs stores; of having access to a kitchen to cook a home-style meal in the apartment where the company housed us; of being able to wash and dry clothes; and of pounding the pavement in search of the best deals on electronics. The younger musicians on the tour spent a good deal of their free time in Tokyo comparative shopping in order to make their big purchases in the limited time they would have between receiving payment at the end of the tour and boarding the flight to return home. Bolivian musicians often buy sound system and recording studio equipment, capital investments that significantly expand their limited employment options at home. They buy sound systems so they don't have to rent them every time they perform. They also "make them work" (*hacerlos trabajar*), renting them out for other activities. "I want to have a recording studio so I'm not paying someone else to record my music. But I can also use it for other work, like recording 'jingles' [advertisements]. Everyone needs to record something," one musician told me. Over several trips to Japan, musicians slowly put together equipment for complete recording studios. When in Tokyo, free time, jokingly called "dibujo libre" ("free drawing" or "free art"), was spent conducting consumer research about what systems to purchase, where they could be bought most inexpensively *a medio uso* (they literally say "at half use" rather than "used"), and how to transport them home within their limited luggage allowance.

Some musicians preferred to take their major earnings home to Bolivia. There they purchased a car that was "made to work" as a taxi. Others paid off the recording studio debts of their previous CD, hoping the studio owner would then agree to begin another project under an "I-owe-you" agreement. Japan tour earnings were also invested in living establishments. Musicians talked about family houses they had built or ones they were planning to rebuild. The unstable income of Bolivian musicians usually steers them away from seeking mortgages and loans for home construction or purchase. Even if they were not able to own their own home, Japan tour earnings allowed most musicians to move out of a situation of rent and into a peculiar real estate option in Bolivia called *anticrético*. When houses or apartments are offered in anticrético, the owner asks that the "tenants" put down a large fixed sum of money—say $10,000—upon moving in. The tenants then live "rent free" in the dwelling for at least a year and usually longer, with the understanding that the same large sum of money will be returned, without interest, when they move out. The owner is receiving a seemingly interest-free loan from the tenant; the tenant temporarily has access to a living space for which no rent is officially paid. Changing from a rented apartment to one occupied in anticrético moved musicians out of the precarious situation of monthly rent payments that were often extremely difficult to meet in the volatile world of music employment. Having toured Japan some four times, one musician expressed his sense of relief in this economic shift, however minor: "I was able to make some economic advancement in that now I can count on my anticrético. It's not a huge thing. But it has saved us from paying rent."

In addition to the lump sum received at the end of the tour, each ensemble member received daily travel allowances for the purchase of food. Musicians talked of depriving themselves of small luxuries while on the road, so as to take home even greater earnings. Daily shopping and saving strategies were applied vigorously as musicians got to know the best deals in food purchases, and even the time of day the supermarket would mark down their packaged and prepared fresh foods. Those who traveled on the higher-end tours were dropped off first at expensive restaurants where they could fritter away their travel allowances. But they quickly noticed the Japanese workers went elsewhere to eat—to smaller, less expensive establishments. It took little time for the Bolivian musicians to follow the

Japanese to these more modest culinary options. Like it or not, I also followed these economizing strategies to get me through this work in what is considered an expensive country, even for a US academic's pocketbook. With the combination of the tour company's choice of less expensive mid-rate hotels and my own lessons learned by following the Bolivians' shopping expertise, I actually spent less during three months in Japan than I spend in a comparable period at my home in western Massachusetts.

While some musicians complained about the tours that required heavier physical work, these contracts, in which one performed in schools, also tended to be of a longer duration, leading to overall greater earnings. Music Amigos, a company that tended to sponsor musicians in theaters, as mentioned above, might pay more per month and provide a higher on-the-road lifestyle, but they might contract the musicians for only a single month of seven theater concerts. As one musician put it, although he disliked the intense labor of performing in schools, he still preferred to tour for a longer period and take home more earnings. Edwing "Pato" Pantoja, the charango player and singer on our tour in 2002, who also works in another profession, framed the Japan tour as an opportunity to save: "There is a big difference that you have to note well. In Bolivia you can't save. In Bolivia you earn [money] to eat *each day*, to get through the month. . . . The difference with Europe, Japan, and the United States, I think, is that you can have a small savings, no matter how miniscule it may seem." Japan tours have provided musicians with this small opportunity to save and invest in areas that allow them to consider living on the musical edge in Bolivia.

Pantoja admitted that he viewed the Japan tour very much in terms of a job that he strived to do well and that he was very happy to have because of the financial rewards at its culmination. But the same musician, in the context of telling me of less lucrative tours he had completed in Europe, insisted he never measured his work by money, but rather by applause. Europe was often set up as the other touring experience, the one where musicians might even go into debt or lose money. From the previous chapter, we have seen the importance of the European scene for the popularizing of Andean music before it made it to Japan, but that scene has shifted since the late 1980s. Audiences are saturated. Since the end of the Cold War, Andean sounds are no longer so easily identified with movements of political solidarity. Bolivian musicians have noticed that a sound-image of a Native American, as shaped by New Age aesthetics, seems to be selling well in Europe, and some musicians have shifted their performances to meet these audience preferences.

Marcelo Peña—a quena player who grew up playing in the Peña Naira, and who would eventually tour Japan with Luz del Ande—told me a story that emphasized the deep emotional tie to performing Bolivian folklore music. He had been living in the United States where, to fulfill his mother's wishes, he completed a degree. A week after getting his diploma, Peña returned to Bolivia, leaving behind a decent job and a steady income. His family could not believe his decision. "It's that I'm a musician," he told me. "I'm a folklorist. I'm a quena player. . . . I made a good living [in the United States]. But I couldn't. . . . [The music] called me." Peña's story was about leaving one kind of work for the volatility of working in Bolivian music. Like others' stories, what emerged was a sense that "it's not all about the money."

Yuliano Encinas told me he made next to nothing on a recent trip to Germany: "We don't work with a company there. We work with a Bolivian who wants to put Bolivian music at a good level, in really good theaters. Because over there, Andean music is heard in the streets. The people are already bored [with that sound]. But we showed a different kind of work, and I felt great when all the people gave us a standing ovation. And it wasn't in the name of the group either . . . it was the group 'from Bolivia.' . . . And I was very happy about this. . . . I came home with about 100 dollars in my pocket from almost two months of work, of traveling without decent food, without sleeping well." Viewed next to these hardships in Europe—the uncertainties about accommodations, food, and even the final earnings—some musicians even referred to the Japanese contracts as "a vacation." As participants in folklore festivals in France, Bolivians enjoyed more security in terms of accommodations and food, but these activities, usually sponsored through local municipal governments, were not remunerated and they required that the musicians and dancers take on the debt of their own airfare to France. Because Bolivian state entities seldom figure in folklore sponsorship abroad, these activities are carried out by the group and the debts are individually assumed. As one musician put it, "we're representing Bolivia for free." Next to the risky single-band tour of Europe or the cheery folklore festivals of France where everyone wines and dines well, no one earns a cent, and everyone takes on at least $800 of personal debt, a Japan tour sits as an ideal music contract, whether one plays folklore in schools or art music in theaters.

We were in our final days of the tour when I interviewed most members of the group. You might say we were at points of maximum exhaustion, with each other and with the same repeated performances. In this context, my colleagues' upbeat attitudes about playing music as work gave me pause to reconsider my own weariness with musical repetition. It seemed like a trivial complaint coming from someone with the luxury of having a relatively secure job outside music. Of his own work in music, Yuliano Encinas told me, "It's work you enjoy. I think few people enjoy their work. Most people work because they have to. But many people here, myself included, enjoy what we are doing. In Bolivia, sure, you don't earn like you do here. There you might even leave music." His positive spin on working in the transnational culture mines placed in relative perspective the confines of performed exoticism and musical monotony, on the one hand, and, on the other, the small but significant gains made possible by such tours.

Laboring in the Culture Mines

Our director often reiterated that we were involved in a cultural labor (*un labor cultural*). For many touring members, this labor made financially possible other economic strategies at home. Making money in the Bolivian culture mines also permitted many of these musicians to engage in creative musical composition and performance in other contexts. Bolivians often talk about their country as "culturally rich." For example, those who work in culture spheres in La Paz were excited about their city being declared "Iberoamerican Capital of Cultures" for the year of 2009. Additionally, in contrast with their other intercultural connections with Europe or the United States, Bolivian musicians make positive comments about Japan being a country that is both modern and culturally rich. Performance of cultural diversity and exoticism, however, do not flow both ways here. Bolivians do not generally become involved in Japanese traditions. Economic distance between different national polities still provides the starting point for staging alterity.[41]

In structural arguments about having to perform the exotic Other, microeconomics and the economies of affect behind these performances are often left aside. A critique of exoticism may only see Bolivians who perform indigenous sounds without indians, or a Japanese fascination with indigeneity sans indians. Such an interpretation, however, misses the subtle point of Bolivian musicians' deeply felt patriotism—the intimate distance that founds nationalist projects. Such an interpretation also glosses over the racism experienced by most touring Bolivian musicians, whether they are mestizo or indigenous. Such an interpretation also overlooks the fact that individual musicians and entrepreneurs, not state entities, are pushing forward these transnational exchanges. While nation-state entities may encourage a process of getting to know cultural Others, in the end, private individuals and companies are underwriting this economy of difference. Individuals are risking their own money to bring these musicians to Japan; folklore musicians, Bolivian and Japanese in origin, assume the critical cultural and artistic work of representing a national frame, of breaking out of rigid audience expectations, and of presenting new musical proposals that aspire to maintain or raise the value of "folklore." The street always remains in the background as a possible but hopefully avoided performance venue. Bolivian musicians are keenly aware, however, of a decreasing international interest in their music. The flexibility of their work contracts sits in juxtaposition with the fixed expectations of performed cultural difference. Until when must they continue to perform "El condor pasa"?

A simple critique of exoticism also misses the significance of a Japanese musician who comes to see Andean or Bolivian music as his principal language of artistic expression. Japanese performers are now central to this economy of difference, and the intimate distance of their transnational nexus cannot be reduced to mere exoticism, imitation, or appropriation. In the next chapter, I take a closer look at the Japanese consumption and performance of Bolivian folklore music.

4 A Hobby, a Sojourn, and a Job

"Can I smoke here?" Takashi Sugiyama asked me somewhat nervously. Sugiyama had been living in Bolivia for thirteen years. I had not met him during my own ongoing interactions with La Paz's world of musicians, perhaps because Sugiyama located his primary interests in the troupe-style playing that characterizes genres associated with indigenous music from the countryside. While Música de Maestros stages some of these genres, the musical world in which I circulated had more mestizo associations, in genre as well as in personal identifications. Sugiyama prided himself on his connections to a performance scene of Bolivian indigenous music.[1] When I finally interviewed him, we met in Música de Maestros's rehearsal space on Sajama Street in San Pedro—an apartment in a relatively new building that overlooked a dusty, partially cobble-stoned street, located behind the central post office, behind the hole-in-the-wall ceviche restaurants, and across from a parking lot that, according to contemporary lore, used to be the site of an early twentieth-century bordello. "People who smoke here usually do so by the open window," I responded, giving Encinas's rule as I had heard it during numerous rehearsals. "Okay. I'll wait," he said politely.

When I asked Sugiyama to tell me how he became interested in Bolivian music, he recalled an early childhood interest in flutes—a concert flute at his grandmother's house in Japan, a recorder (*flauta dulce*) he learned to play in school, and even an ocarina that a friend showed him. When he was about twelve, a friend had him listen to a recording he called simply "folklore," meaning Andean folklore or music that featured quena, zampoña, and charango. It was a recording of Uña Ramos, the Argentine quena player who played with Urubamba, the ensemble of the Simon and Garfunkel and "El condor pasa" saga. Inspired by Ramos's playing, Sugiyama began his quena quest. But in the early 1970s, he said, there were no quena instruments, no quena method books, and no quena instructors. So he fashioned his own instrument from bamboo until, six months later, he was able to purchase an Argentine one at a store in Japan. Instrument construction would become one of his passions, as he described the experience of trying to make the perfect quena and of "almost sleeping with bamboo."

A few years later, he formed his first ensemble in Japan, calling it Kantuta, in reference to the Bolivian national flower. At the age of eighteen he had set his sights on traveling to Bolivia. Ernesto Cavour's performances in Japan during the 1980s may have been key in getting him to shift his attention from Argentina, or a more vague "folklore," to the specifically national category of "Bolivian" music. He attended Cavour's concerts in Japan, met the artist personally, and eventually would stay with Cavour for two months upon his initial arrival in La Paz. But getting to Bolivia took longer than Sugiyama had expected. He began to study architecture in Japan, but left this career to work in an odd assortment of jobs, saving his money to make the trip to Bolivia. At the age of twenty, when he had saved almost enough money, Sugiyama's father—his only surviving parent—died, leaving him in charge of his younger brother. With the postponement of his trip to Bolivia, Sugiyama spent his savings on a Harley Davidson, trading one dream for another, and began saving for the day when his sibling would be on more independent footing. He again took up many different jobs and said he hated most of them. As he reflected on these work experiences in Japan, from his current position in Bolivia he said, "That's why I want to work in something I enjoy doing—making instruments, playing music." He just kept telling himself, "One day I will go. One day I will go." At the age of twenty-nine, when he finally arrived at the airport in El Alto, he was overcome with emotion: "I was always imagining it . . . as I went down the highway into La Paz . . . I saw a cholita walking, carrying her aguayo. I almost cried, because before I had only seen this in photos."

He intended to stay three months, but at the time of our interview he had been living in Bolivia for thirteen years. "What could I learn in three months?" he added matter-of-factly. He began to travel in the highland areas, to Charazani and Italaque—ever in pursuit of the specific wind-instrument genres that in the city carry hefty symbolic associations with indigenous worlds. He recalled his first trip to the countryside, to Italaque where the research tables were turned on him. He had pulled out a notebook and was asking many questions about the panpipe troupe that was playing. Suddenly a man from the community approached him with another notebook and began to ask him questions. "It was in reverse," said Sugiyama with a laugh, "he asked me more things: Where are you from? Do you have family? What is your work? Married or single?" Sugiyama, while engaging in activities that occupy many anthropologists and ethnomusicologists, experienced the turn of the research gaze back on himself, and after this experience, he began to modify his approach.

When he lived in a community in Northern Potosí for a month, he felt frustrated because he could not find a charango "teacher," someone who would explain to him the different tunings, fingerings, and strumming styles. He therefore sought out a relation of exchange obligations with those who would sell him charangos. With each instrument purchase, he asked the previous owner for clarification of performance practice details. In other words, he would buy a charango from a seller if the latter would tell him something about how to play it. That is why, Sugiyama said, at one time, he had "more than ninety charangos."[2]

In Bolivia, Sugiyama eventually formed the ensemble Grupo Phaxsi Qhana. With a focus on indigenous music played in the troupe style, this group has three recordings in Bolivia and one with Japan Victor. Even before arriving in Bolivia, Sugiyama was drawn to what he called "the real native music," having heard a recording of Charazani's *k'antus* (a specific panpipe genre), and speculating about the lack of "authenticity" in any performance that included a guitar. While the troupe style is difficult to take on tour in Japan—because of the necessary minimum of twelve players—Sugiyama, in conjunction with two Japanese municipalities, managed to organize a twelve-day, two-concert tour that involved moving a troupe of eleven musicians. This is the only example I know of a Bolivian music *troupe* that has toured Japan. But this particular style has arrived in Japan by multiple means—recordings, videos, instruments— and remains an option for those who take up Andean music as a hobby, job, passion, or vocation. Touring Bolivian musicians have told me about seeing Japan's version of the Cosquín folklore festival, where numerous troupes of all Japanese musicians perform on different Bolivian indigenous wind instruments, imitating Bolivian ensembles as well as the folklore festival that has occurred annually in Argentina since 1961.[3] Japanese musicians are inventing their own instrument sizes, I was told, creating a panpipe that is even larger than the *toyo*, the largest in the Bolivian traditions.[4]

At the time of our interview in 2004, Sugiyama occasionally made trips back to Japan, but he had no plans for a permanent return. After all these years, does he still feel Japanese in Bolivia, I asked him. "Yes, but when I return to Japan, I don't feel Japanese. Neither Bolivian nor Japanese."

Japanese who are involved with Bolivian music represent a minuscule part of the Japanese population. The figures on niche music markets in Japan may take on mythical proportions when they become a point of national pride—for example, Argentines bragging about their tango having traveled *even* to Japan.[5] Such a musical niche may become a curiosity because of a perceived contradiction between an essentialized Japanese national character and the genre at hand—for example, Japanese play-ing and listening to jazz.[6] If the audiences for tango and jazz in Japan are often exaggerated in discussions, Andean music fans, aficionados, and professional musicians waste no time in telling one how small their audi-ence is in comparison—often setting themselves up in a hierarchy of other Latin American genres, where they perceive huge audiences for tango and salsa and tiny but dedicated ones for Andean music. I remind the reader that the economic importance of Japan tours for Bolivian musicians was one point that motivated this study, the other being the noticeable pres-ence of *Japanese in Bolivia* who were involved with the national folklore scene. The city of La Paz, with a population between two and three mil-lion (including population from the city of El Alto) is still considered *muy pueblo* or, literally, "very village." It is difficult to walk La Paz's streets without running into someone you know. The musicians within this scene all know each other, and they comment that since the arrival of Kinoshita in 1982, more and more Japanese youth have been finding their way into this scene.

While not all Japanese who become involved in Bolivian music live ex-tended periods in Bolivia, this path—almost like a pilgrimage—remains a common mode of learning.[7] Sugiyama has set the bar particularly high in relation to the number of years he has lived in Bolivia, as have Kino-shita and Hishimoto (see previous chapters). Other Japanese visitors with aspirations in these musical traditions measure their own stays in refer-ence to these well-known cases. Residencies of one or two years are quite common, more like the standard period anthropologists might spend in the field. Japanese musicians may state the time they have been in Bolivia and reveal the expected total length of their stay, badges of their commit-ment to learning this music through apprenticeship—to specific Bolivian musicians in a few cases and, more commonly, to Bolivian experiences in general. Those who cannot travel to Bolivia sustain the hope of a brief tourist visit, while maintaining their own music group in Japan as a week-end hobby or even as a source of income.

Sugiyama's emotion at seeing the *real* cholita—his fascination with a visual index of indigeneity—recalls a classic case of exoticizing: desiring, dressing, and performing like the Other, all while bolstering the identity of the self. Are Japanese Andean music enthusiasts who play Bolivian music "playing indian"? Examining the US case of whites playing Indians, Philip Deloria argued that white Americans have turned to Indians when-ever they have faced an identity crisis.[8] As hobbyists looked to American Indians for creative power, they did not want to become them, according to Deloria, but rather longed for "the utopian experience of being in between, of living a paradoxical moment in which absolute liberty coexisted with the absolute."⁹ My first draw to Andean music was admittedly close to the narrative about the utopias of playing indian. Like the Japanese I interviewed in this project, I was drawn originally to the exotic sounds of the Andean trio—charango, quena, and zampoña. But I never attempted to master any of these instruments, perhaps because during my initial anthropological work in Peru, and with migrants from Lucanas, Ayacucho, I encountered a "sufficiently indigenous" sound in the ensemble of violin and harp that characterizes music from that region; this was my window to an "authentic indigenous" musical world. My scare quotes here reflect a critical understanding of my own initial draw to Andean music and not a point about self-representation of the musicians with whom I worked in Peru. When I asked Japanese enthusiasts how they became involved in Bolivian music and why they liked Bolivian music, the Japanese often turned this question back on me, as if to say: "You are another foreigner playing Bolivian music. What's your story?" I sometimes responded with reference to my earlier Peruvian experiences, those in which I still felt what Diane Nelson has called "típica fever" (a passion for everything typical).¹⁰ By the time I entered the Bolivian music scene, however, I was still a gringa, but a more self-critical one. My disciplinary home of anthropology called for reflexivity and critique, charting for me a different path to knowing Bolivian music. While I, like the Japanese in this ethnography, came to Andean music through a fascination with indigeneity, my experience in Bolivian music began in a different way, through a disciplinary lens that in its contemporary configuration eschews essentializing.

If mestizo musicians might be seen as playing indian in the name of a Bolivian national project, the Japanese might be seen as playing indian as they long for a traditional utopia perceived to be lost within modern life. While Deloria recognizes the role of play in shaping identities, he also suggests that play is "a powerful metaphor for that which is frivolous and without significance."¹¹ In my work, I want to give more weight to play. The longing that motivates such play can be framed in terms of nostalgia—what bridges individual and collective memory.¹² Svetlana Boym elaborates two tendencies, "restorative nostalgia" and "reflective nostalgia," characterizing the first as engaging in a serious search for lost homes and the second as assuming a more ironic perspective while preferring to keep distance between the self and the subject of longing.¹³ When Japanese and Bolivians play indian, both reflective and restorative nostalgias are at work. Bolivian and Japanese ways of playing indian shape livelihoods and stir patriotism for Bolivians, and change life courses and even professions for some Japanese. While irony does not stand out in these performances, the subject that motivates longing and nostalgia is kept temporally at bay. The imagined ancestor who connects Japanese with Bolivian indians remains ensconced in a prehistoric moment, a theme to which I will return in the next chapter. The case of Japanese playing indian is further complicated because the articulation does not fit the usual colonizer-colonized model of the genre. But, as I will argue, neither does it stray much from the dual and supposedly opposing liberal subjectivities inherent within what Povinelli calls "settler modernity": the "autological subject" whose life is imagined through the lenses of freedom and choice, and the "genealogical subject" whose life is imagined as constrained by the baggage of kinship obligations.[14]

Povinelli's ethnography among Aboriginal Australians and US radical faeries lines up these two kinds of subjectivities. The radical faeries lean toward the position of autological subjectivity with a maximum sense of individual freedom. Think here of the liberal autonomous free-acting individual. The Aboriginal Australians are expected to carry the burdens of genealogical subjectivity, to show their responsibility to family and the collective group. The radical faeries turn to their local source of indigeneity—Native North American culture—to create alternative ritual worlds that they then fashion as their own.[15] When Japanese become Bolivian or Andean musicians, there is something of that search for a path not completely determined by the expectations of Japanese family and society, something like autological subjectivity raising its head in a society highly structured around the primacy of collective interest. But the Japanese attraction to Andean music is also wrapped up in other imagined collectivities, other genealogical subjectivities that they find lacking in their lives in Japan. The Japanese attraction to Andean and indigenous worlds expresses a critique of a subjectivity developed through "occupation modernity," if I may use this term in relation to Povinelli's work in contexts of "settler modernity." In following a path of Andean music, some Japanese are opting for an alternative to the US influences they find problematic within their sense of being Japanese. Their position is one consistent with Japan's mid-1990s turn away from the United States and toward greater focus on regional ties in Asia.[16] Taking up Bolivian music represented an alternative to consuming the globally circulating US popular culture, and opened exotic possibilities not necessarily granted in the pursuit of Japanese traditional music.

This chapter explores a wide range of Japanese serious play within Bolivian music—levels of involvement not easily subsumed under umbrellas of consumption, reception, or fandom. Consumption of Bolivian music in this transnational nexus looks like long-term travel to Bolivia, performance of this music, and even paid work in this field. The Japanese who become involved in Bolivian music are not passively consuming these sounds; they are in turn producing them at multiple levels of competency: poor, mediocre, and professional. Consuming Bolivian music here means playing it and being involved in the production of musical sound. Their participation in this realm reflects similarities with other studies of active fans: the hip-hop fan who not only consumes, but also produces through performance;[17] and the *enka* fans who must *do* enka by singing karaoke (enka is a "traditional" Japanese style of singing).[18] They are like fans who do not simply receive a mass-generated message but who have to work hard at play, as William Kelly suggests.[19] Japanese fandom, as Ian Condry argues, must be seen in terms that go beyond the frames of either the duped passive consumer or the dangerous crazy fanatic.[20] If fans usually emerge around mass mediated cultures, does Bolivian music fall into this category? One might question the *mass*-mediated character of such a small market, but recordings, radio, television, magazines, and the Internet all have a place in the multiple stories the Japanese told me. While this niche may not seem like a mass-mediated culture on a par with, say, comic books, it should be kept in mind that this music first entered Japan through the circulation of recordings and their on-air radio presence—a fact that almost every person mentioned in relation to their first experiences with this foreign music. But the label "fan" may seem rather incongruous with the professional levels at which Kinoshita, Hishimoto, and many others are contributing to Bolivian music. The consuming fans are now performing and composing this foreign music, and some of them are exceptionally good at it. In distinction with other examples of doing and performing fans, the Japanese pursuit of Bolivian music is strongly marked by long-term sojourning experiences, by multigenerational fandom, and by a significant presence of performing fans who go professional, albeit with mixed commercial success.

Rather than distinguishing who is and is not a fan, I assume the context reflects elements of fan cultures. I prefer to concentrate on the slippage between consumption, travel, performance, and the turn to professional work. I locate the complexities of Japanese fandom of Bolivian music in these spaces between a hobby and a sojourn, a hobby and a job, and a sojourn and a job. I contend that Andean music fans are almost always participants in producing the sounds with which they have become enamored. Here I remind the reader of Kinoshita's assessment of the democratic nature of Bolivian music (chapter 2). As he explained, the instruments are rather inexpensive to purchase and the melodies rather easy to play. Bolivian music fans are, more often than not, also performers of this music. So this musical world is not merely about passive reception. Nor is it about consumption within limited fields of production, where the act of consuming expends what is produced. Nor is it about a collection of artifacts. Instead, this musical world of participatory performance and hobby activities creates an ever-expanding web of social relations that counters the frame of isolated autonomous individuals.

It has been suggested that within anthropology *consumption* is coming to replace *kinship* as a key organizing concept of the discipline.[21] However, consumption as seen in this chapter needs to account for the production of one's own musical object and for the social relations (not necessarily about home and family) that emerge in this intercultural nexus. The case at hand points to *consumption as performance and production*, wherein issues of kinship persist, but are presented in terms of ancient, unnamed genetic ancestors—a theme I will explore in the next chapter. Japanese hobbyists, sojourners, and professional musicians consume Bolivian music by *making* it. A few professional-level Japanese musicians who are concerned about theater turnouts for Bolivian music in Japan have complained that the aficionados don't go to enough concerts, that they are too busy with their own rehearsals to show up for a theater performance! This hardly seems like the dutiful actions of adoring fans, unless they are viewed as fans not of specific artists, but of the genre category "Bolivian music."

Through their dedication to a category of music they hear first through recordings, they become admirers of Bolivian musicians and develop an expertise about different ensembles, their recording histories, and the individual artistic personalities within them. Sometimes Bolivian musicians were surprised by fans' detailed knowledge about their recording histories. Edgar Villarroel, a musician who toured with Música de Maestros, Kallawaya, and then as a salsa vocalist whose backup band was assembled in Japan, told me how amazed he was when a Japanese fan approached him and asked about an ensemble with which he had performed and recorded many years ago. Music fans consume much more than material objects, as Carolyn Stevens pointed out in her study of a Japanese rock band's fans; they are primary consumers of information about the band.[22] As I pursued one kind of information—stories through which to understand a Japanese-Bolivian connection around Andean music—the people I interviewed were after another not completely different kind of information about musicians, bands, and recordings. My own recording history in Bolivia—ten recordings with Música de Maestros at the time of this research—piqued Japanese fans' curiosity about me, opened doors to interviews, and facilitated some of my fieldwork contacts. They already knew me, perhaps through recordings whose liner notes had been carefully studied, or perhaps as Hishimoto told them about me under the reference of "a violinist who plays with Música de Maestros." While Japanese who play Bolivian music can indeed be considered as participants in a fan culture, rather than explore this realm as fandom, I find it more interesting to dwell on how these participants engage in a significant space of consumption, performance, and production, where much more than musical sound is produced and consumed. Consuming Bolivian music ultimately means playing it, manipulating it, making it one's own, and establishing different social relations in the educational and performance process.

Love at First Sound

Stories about first encounters with Andean music resounded with terms not unlike those used to describe falling in love. It was love at first sound. Upon hearing a recording through the radio or through a friend's record collection, the future fan described amazement, attraction, fascination, shock, and even spirituality. The love object was wrapped up in the sound, even if the visual packaging of these recordings and their associations with an imagined indigenous world did not lag far behind. Japanese consumers of Andean music focused first on particular instruments whose sound captured their imaginations, and the quena was principal among these. As Kinoshita insisted, "Folklore [Andean music] wasn't a fad; the quena instrument was the fad."

When I asked Japanese about what had drawn them to Bolivian music, most of them talked about a fascination with the sound of the quena. Of secondary importance was the genre actually performed on the instrument. For example, one hobbyist mentioned first becoming interested in the quena when he heard Mexican boleros played on it. A general field of Latin American genres—circulating through recordings, companies like Music Amigos, and the magazine for which Kawamoto and Shimada worked, *Revista latina* (see chapter 2)—provided the context in which the sound of folklore instruments entered circuits of consumption. As I detailed in chapter 2, Andean folklore entered Japan on the coattails of Argentine tango. Japanese fans and experts of folklore have continued to focus on specific instruments, usually taking up the quena, zampoña, or charango, and developing virtuosic voices through that choice. One professional charango player who performs in Japan with five different groups, interpreting Bolivian, Latin popular, and Japanese music, explained that he wanted "to express everything on the charango, not just Bolivian music."

While earlier fans had to dig up quenas in antique shops or fashion their own out of local bamboo, after the arrival in Japan of Uña Ramos and Antonio Pantoja in the 1970s, these instruments began to circulate more easily. Younger fans describe a similar process of falling for the sound of specific Andean folklore instruments, but this new generation now has more at its fingertips: brick and mortar music stores as well as online Japanese businesses that stock multiple Andean recordings and instruments, local teachers in Japan, method books in Japanese, online discussion groups about folklore recordings and activities, and, since the early 1980s, a tradition of Japanese sojourning to Bolivia.

For many hobbyists, a university "Latin American" or "folklore" club was the start of their performance participation in this world of an Other's music. While Japanese students studied forestry, landscaping, law, architecture, art, or sociology, they took up the performance of folklore through these extracurricular organizations. Even though it is notoriously difficult to enter Japanese universities, once one has gained entrance, the lack of academic rigor at these institutions is perhaps equally notorious. As Brian J. McVeigh wrote in his study about the crisis in Japan's higher education, the Japanese "describe their universities and colleges as 'playgrounds,' 'kindergartens for adults,' 'places for enjoyment,' 'resorts,' or 'moratorium' before regular employment."[23] In their personal stories, folklore hobbyists and professional musicians usually did not mention taking university courses about Latin America, but many of them noted an extracurricular Latin American or Andean music club. The professional musician who complained about hobbyists not attending live performances also leveled critiques at the university clubs that put more emphasis on social interaction than on improving musicianship. According to him, club members maintained only an ephemeral interest in Andean music, something he contended would end when they finished studying at the university. Nevertheless, a common tale of folklore involvement included a story of love at first sound and performance participation in such clubs.

The transition from listening to the love object to actually producing it was also marked by other educational experiences. Most of the Japanese I interviewed had some formal music training prior to their study of Bolivian music. Many hobbyists and professional musicians spoke of having learned to play the recorder in school and of then using the same eye, ear, and hand coordination for learning the quena. Since the Meiji era (1868–1912), Japanese have imported Western music to their military and educational contexts, taking these musical forms as one more applied technology that aimed to modernize Japan; as Atkins explained, "having observed the apparent effects of music on the 'national spirits' of Westerners, policymakers in Meiji Japan believed music (specifically music based on Western standards) was necessary for the success of a modern nation."[24] If Western classical music has been a part of this modernizing project into the twentieth century, Japanese folklore enthusiasts depicted Bolivian music as a space of refuge outside the rigid and demanding hierarchies of such a world.

On a Saturday afternoon, I interviewed a hobby group that rehearsed in a karaoke booth from 1:00 to 5:00 p.m. The group's name used to be Cuatro Cervezas (Four Beers), but shifted to Los Borrachos (The Drunkards) when the band began to expand beyond four members. I had met one of the participating musicians at a salon concert given by Hishimoto and Kinoshita (see figure 12), and through the musician's English language skills we made arrangements to meet at the hobby group's weekly rehearsal time. I was shown into the karaoke box, a completely enclosed room, lined with bright green walls, pink accents, and vinyl booth-type seats; the walls were covered with lots of mirrors. Everything was bright. Everything reflected light, even though there were no windows to the outside (see figure 13).

The group interview occurred in Japanese, as a daughter of one band member translated the conversation to English. One animated band member in her fifties, the only woman in the group, described her enchantment with folklore: "It's simple and short, not like classical music. You can enjoy it. . . . In classical [music] you have to just listen. In folklore you can join in and everyone can participate. And everyone can just bring a quena and play anywhere." One of her bandmates added, "Yeah, she likes to play anywhere, anytime." The suggestive comment sent a wave of laughter through the group. Her comments reflected the attraction of the non-exclusive musical practice and the pleasure of collective participation. When I asked her what it was like being the only woman in the group she answered, "They don't treat me like a woman," and then explained that music was something she could not do earlier in life. Now she does music along with other hobbies like playing the ocarina and making pottery. She is a devoted fan of Hishimoto, and her talk about him seemed similar to what adoring fans might say of male enka singers.[25] Los Borrachos perform at weddings, parties, and in charity work at places for the elderly and children. Their weekly rehearsals are about a long-term social and musical connection. They are weekend players—working Monday to Friday with Toshiba, with news agencies, in stainless steel manufacturing, in environmental consulting, and in housewifing. As one band member told

12. Koji Hishimoto and Takaatsu Kinoshita perform a salon concert in Tokyo.

13. Members of Los Borrachos pose during an afternoon weekend rehearsal in a karaoke box.

Both photographs by the author.

me: "The average age of our group is fifty to fifty-four. My dream is to be able to play when our average age is seventy. An old group, but good playing. . . . Something like a good wine. Yes?"

Next to the exclusions of classical music, hobbyists see the folklore world as free from the written page, inclusive of all levels of musicianship, spontaneous in its performance space, possibly flirtatious with an imagined bohemian world, and conducive to long-term friendships around the pleasure of informally performing music. Of course this music also has its hierarchies, and those Japanese who have become professional folklore musicians often have extensive previous training in classical music, even if they may downplay this background or disclaim any "real" expertise or talent in this more rigidly structured field.[26]

As folklore fans perform the very sounds that attracted them to this music, they form ensembles, giving themselves names like Los Vientos (The Winds), Kusi Kusi (Happy Happy—in Quechua), Raices (Roots), Cáscara de Durazno (Peach Peal), Los Sábados de Ch'aki (The Hangover Saturdays), Los Caprichos (The Whims), Ausencia (Absence), Ama Qhella (Don't be Lazy—of the famous Inca saying, "Ama sua, ama llulla, ama qhella," translated as "Don't steal, don't lie, don't be lazy"), Isla del Sol (Island of the Sun, an island in Lake Titicaca), Los Tomadores (The Drinkers), and Bolivia Deluxe. One group called themselves Boquechaguiza, putting together the initial parts of the words that named their instruments: *bo*mbo, *que*na, *cha*rango, *gui*tar, and *za*mpoña. While many professional Bolivian musicians may suffer a Saturday hangover, a hazard of the profession, Bolivians were always quite amused by the direct reference to drinking in many of the hobby groups' names. When a Japanese ensemble became more serious, they often underwent a name change, following Bolivian preferences for indigenous references, featuring Quechua and Aymara words. In general, getting serious meant getting indigenous. More serious groups include Khantati (The Dawn—in Aymara), Maya (number "one" in Aymara), Tinkuna (from the Quechua verb *tinkuy*—to meet or encounter), and Grupo Illamp'u (name of a snow-capped peak in the La Paz area). The transformation from "hobby" to "professional" ensemble might be subtle and in some cases difficult to pinpoint. Suffice it to say that the more ironic and humorous references to drinking do not appear in Japanese ensembles that have recordings. The studio brings a more solemn outlook, as well as a more focused attention on the imagined indigenous frame. For some hobbyists, it is enough to seek the weekend musical escape from the pressures and drudgeries of the office job. Others go deeper in their quest for understanding and interpreting someone else's music; they travel to the perceived sources of folklore.

Musical Sojourns

Travel to Bolivia is a principal way that Japanese fans and hobbyists edu-
cate themselves about Andean music. Some visit for a month. More often
they go for a year or two. And a few stay for many years. Most sojourners
I interviewed had traveled to Bolivia for the first time in their early twenties. If it were not for the loss in his family, Sugiyama too would have traveled in his early twenties. Many sojourners had started university studies.
A few had finished them and done nothing in relation to their degree.
Others traveled as volunteers with the Japan International Cooperation
Agency (JICA). Sojourners included young people who were not yet tied
to a career in Japan and others who had left their day jobs to play music
in a professional capacity.

  In Bolivia, I spoke with a twenty-six-year-old hobbyist I will call Hayao;
he was the only person I interviewed who specifically asked me to change
his name as I wrote about him. When he had finished an undergraduate
degree in anthropology at a Japanese university, he decided he wanted
to become a Bolivian musician. After working for one year as a security
guard at a construction site, he set off for Bolivia with his savings. He
ran out of money after his first year, and to remain in Bolivia he began
teaching Japanese-language classes. When we spoke, Hayao was in a second year of his planned three-year sojourn. He told me about his specific
objectives for each year: year one—learn to play one hundred Bolivian
songs; year two—get to know many Bolivian musicians; year three—
make a recording of his own compositions in Bolivia. He bragged to me
that his group had played in the Peña Naira. I thought to myself that this
place had been a touchstone of authenticity for Kinoshita, Kawamoto,
and Hishimoto, as each of them entered the Bolivian music scene, but
Hayao's age and trajectory did not correspond with the dates of its existence as the famous club. When I mentioned that the Peña Naira, in its old
sense, no longer existed, Hayao quickly brushed aside my comment and
said, "Yes, it's just a restaurant now, but we played a show there." Hayao,
still in the moment of his personal journey, took very seriously his plan
that he hoped would put him in a position to return to Japan and work as
a professional Bolivian musician. Hayao's narrative was the only one from
my interviews that seemed to shape the sojourning experience through an
itemized agenda that suggested a collector's outlook: learn one hundred
songs, meet so many musicians, complete one's own recording.

  Kinoshita, with the perspective of some twenty years' hindsight, spoke
with more self-reflexive irony about his sojourn and discovery in the
1980s. If he fell for the quena sound in Japan, he fell in love all over again

in Bolivia when he heard an indigenous troupe performance for the first time, and again when he danced in La Paz's carnival to the sound of a brass band. The brass band is a principal ensemble for major urban fiestas in Bolivia—celebratory contexts of indigenous and mestizo significance. He laughed at himself as he recalled how this experience led him to set the objective of spending the next years studying the different carnivals of all Bolivia's nine departments. While he seemed to suggest that this objective did not unfold exactly as planned, he did stay in Bolivia more than ten years, struggling at first with the groove of Bolivian music and life. He told me how he found the Bolivian musical groove only after he let go of his punctuality and went with the flow of *hora boliviana* (Bolivian time), which involves beginning activities well after the appointed time of arrival. Relinquishing his Japanese sense of time, Kinoshita was drawn into an extended foreign experience upon which he could now reflect self-critically and that could hardly be summarized as an inventory of songs learned or a listing of carnival participations in Bolivia's different departments. While the long sojourn in Bolivia ultimately shaped his career path in Japan as a composer and musician in Bolivian styles, in our interview, meeting within his own national context, he showed no signs of running on Bolivian time.

Other hobbyists and professional musicians have made multiple short trips to Bolivia over several years. Kawamoto and Shimada, who run the Andean music school in Tokyo, have guided students on annual visits to Bolivia. While in La Paz, they perform with their group Khantati, sometimes sharing the Municipal Theater's stage with Bolivian ensembles like Los Chaskas. Sojourning to Bolivia becomes a key aspect of consuming and then producing an Other's music. One musician told me that for the success of his own work in these traditions, he needed to breathe Bolivian air every once in a while. Another musician in Tokyo, Toyo Kusanagi, criticized those who were not taking seriously enough the sojourn experience, specifically those who were not going out to the countryside to conduct their own research. I interviewed Kusanagi over a traditional Japanese lunch in Misue, Tokyo, and his Bolivian wife from Llallagua, María Luisa, translated his words from Japanese to Spanish. Kusanagi told me: "Many play this music, but they play without heart. . . . To play this music, people used to go to the countryside, live in the same earth as the peasants. But not now . . . they don't go to the countryside." The sojourn, properly done, involves getting deeply into Bolivian musical life; it means delving into the countryside, the earth, the indigenous world, the fiesta systems, the workshops of instrument artisans, the urban bohemian musical scene, and love relationships that may or may not lead to marriage.

These sojourns—travel under very different circumstances than the

Bolivian musicians' tours of Japan—should be considered in relation to Japan's shifting socioeconomic contexts. In the late 1970s, at the start of the Japan-Bolivia folklore timeline, Japan was experiencing an incredible postwar boom with tremendous economic growth that peaked in the 1980s. High levels of production were guaranteed through business models that demanded of workers a life-long dedication to their company, and this loyalty was wrapped up in family and national commitments. The boom was accompanied by new approaches to leisure activities. During this period, the Japanese railway developed two different campaigns that encouraged Japanese to "Discover Japan" in the 1970s and to get to know "Exotic Japan" in 1984.[27] The Discover Japan campaign, according to Marilyn Ivy's research, motivated Japanese to get to know themselves through a tour into the premodern world that was already perceived as vanishing.[28] As Japanese were traveling within their country and getting to know the national self, in unprecedented numbers they were also beginning to travel internationally as tourists.[29] They were getting to know the premodern and exotic within and outside Japan.

Although the bubble burst in 1991, the recessionary context, according to Anne Allison, did not seem to limit consumer spending in department stores and leisure activities.[30] Studies of Japanese leisure tourism show continued travel after the economic downturn, although South American destinations do not even figure in their charts.[31] Nor do the sojourners of this case seem to fit the market-driven analysis about the Japanese travel life cycle.[32] The disconnect between these more commercially centered tourism studies and the cases of Japanese music sojourns to Bolivia reflects that the latter realm of performance, production, and consumption is not a particularly lucrative enterprise, and that other realms of symbolic capital are at stake in its articulation.

Allison describes a millennial or contemporary Japan in which materialist ideals of consumption rule the day, and individuals—rather than the household—have become the primary units of consumption; Japanese "spend more and more time alone, to be ever more focused on their own needs and desires rather than those of others, and to be socially detached from the kinds of relationships and commitments that are thought to have once grounded the culture (family, community, nation)."[33] In relation to the boom and bust pendulum, a tension surfaces between the genealogical and autological subjects, to borrow again from Povinelli's terminology.[34] National concerns were expressed about people becoming too individualist in their orientations and too far removed from an ethos of the collective good. In his study of *ikigai* ("what makes one's life worth living"), Gordon Mathews found that a postwar Japan, in the process of rebuilding the country, privileged a collective sense of this philosophical concept; one's reason for living was found in family and company. But with increased life expectancy and Japan's increasing affluence, ikigai took on new meaning as a project of self-realization.[35] If ikigai as self-realization opened up social space for activities like those of the hobbyists and sojourners in this chapter, its focus on the individual was telltale of other national anxieties, particularly in relation to youth culture. In a study of Japanese comic books and their fans, Sharon Kinsella outlines a national moral panic about youth; she details how intellectuals worried about youth who avoided company careers as they prioritized self, pleasure, recreation, and consumption.[36]

From the late 1980s and into the early 2000s, the term "freeter" emerged as a label for young Japanese who did not go directly from an educational context to full-time permanent employment. Combining the terms "freelance" and "*albeiter*" (German word referring to periodical or part-time side jobs) freeter has come to label those Japanese who have not been able to or who choose not to enter the model of Japanese employment that shaped the boom of the 1980s. In the media, freeters are often depicted as people who lack the will to work and who prefer to spend time in their leisure activities. Ian Condry wrote that about half of his interviewees in Japanese hip-hop clubs self-identified as freeters.[37] However, Akio Inui cautions against the media and policy misrepresentations of freeters, suggesting that for many who are classified as such, the problem is not a lack of will to work, but a lack of possibilities in gainful employment.[38] Japanese enthusiasts of Andean music who became professional Bolivian musicians, by the necessities of what it means to work as a musician, came to look a lot like freeters. They did not follow single career paths, did not join the family of "the company," and sought unique life experiences that might further shape their performance and aesthetic sensibilities. Yet, unlike Condry's findings among Japanese hip-hoppers, none of the Japanese I interviewed claimed the label "freeter."

I suggest that Japanese who sojourn to learn Bolivian music seek another alternative sociality, one that includes a focus on individual desires of knowing and performing an Other culture, but also one that develops other social ties that are not necessarily about family or material production for the nation. These cases cross multiple generations and therefore are far from a youth subculture framework. Becoming a hobbyist or sojourner in Bolivian music involves a project of self-realization. It is also about claiming social ties and an imagined genealogical subjectivity that Japanese feel themselves as having lost. As I will discuss in the next chapter, a more immediate genealogy of family, company, and nation has

14. Ernesto Cavour teaches a charango class in Japan around 1980.
Photograph used with kind permission of Ernesto Cavour.

been substituted with an imagined genealogy of unnamed indigenous ancestors.

Bolivian music's popularity in Japan preceded the emergence of the
freeter category, the former's heyday arriving with the popularity of
Ernesto Cavour's tours throughout the 1980s (see figure 14). The decade
was also marked by Kinoshita's pioneering sojourn to Bolivia. It was a
time when the founder of Music Amigos had no problems filling large theaters for multiple concerts of Bolivian music. While everyone talks about
a drop in theater performance draws in the 1990s, many young Japanese musicians are still finding their way to Bolivia. Within the bubble
of the 1980s, Japanese entrepreneurs were willing to take risks with concert tours of foreign musicians. These leisure activities, served up for listening consumption, were then refashioned into the practices of learning to play Bolivian music. Some Japanese may seek in Bolivian music
a work alternative to the salary-man model of corporate loyalty. Joseph
Tobin, in marking a shift in Japan away from a pattern of lifetime employment with a single company, suggests that in Japan, "What people
consume may be as important as what they produce in shaping a sense
of self."[39] Japanese hobbyists of Bolivian music who then become professional musicians are producing what they used to consume, and these
performance-consumption practices have come to define who they are. In

the post-bubble milieu, new Japanese consumers of Bolivian music may continue to seek alternatives to "brand name capitalism" and the atomistic social relations that Allison describes for present-day Japan.[40]

Japanese who undertake musical sojourns to Bolivia are also pursuing interests in indigenous worlds, but in these cases the commodification and consumption of indigeneity differ somewhat from those related to objects like textiles. While one can certainly point to the materiality of a packaged CD of Bolivian music, this form of "music" is more likely to be the starting point of the sojourn that takes the enthusiasts into a world of playing Bolivian music and draws them into different social interactions. Consumption here is completely entangled with different relationships that may or may not lead to professionalization, but that hardly look like individual consumption of stand-alone exotic indigenous commodities. Japanese enthusiasts, like Bolivian mestizo musicians, learn to perform indigenous music. While the mestizo musicians do so through a symbolic act of national incorporation, the Japanese do so in search of an alternative to other foreign cultural influences produced within occupation modernity. Their hobby and sojourn ethos is a turn away from inflexible and stifling structures of work, as well as a turn away from US-centric popular culture and policies.

Quitting Your Day Job

"This year I am celebrating twenty-five years of playing charango, a quarter of a century." With these proud words, Daiji Fukuda began our interview in Café Ciudad in La Paz. Fukuda sometimes joined Música de Maestros's performances, so I knew him from having shared stages that were crowded with microphones and cables. Off stage, I knew him as someone who was constantly joking and making people laugh. He had a reputation for moving easily in the bohemian life of La Paz. In his compositions and charango playing, he had picked up defining stylistic features of the country's master composers and charango players, so much so that colleagues often commented that his musical expression sounded "so Bolivian."

I came to know another side of Fukuda during the interview, a serious side with clear ideas about why, in his thirties, he would walk away from a more traditional career path in order to perfect his musical expressions on charango. Fukuda had studied classical guitar as a boy and first came to know the charango because his guitar teacher had one. But music was not his career. He studied political economy at the university and began a doctoral thesis on Latin American social movements. He first traveled to

Bolivia through an embassy job that had nothing to do with music. As he was drawn into the musical practices he had already studied at home, he wanted to perform in Bolivia. But his ambassador didn't want him to be involved in these activities, and Fukuda was left feeling "like a caged bird."

After finishing his mission and going back to Japan, he returned to Bolivia "exclusively to play and to record." "It was my dream, ever since I was a boy. I returned as a musician, not as a diplomat." Fukuda studied the contemporary Bolivian masters of the instrument, Ernesto Cavour and William Centellas. In Argentina, he also sought the expressions of masters like Jaime Torres. He studied the styles, fingerings, and techniques of each one. He also lived an extended period in Sucre, picking up the specific "chuquisaqueño" style of playing charango *punteado* (plucked melody as opposed to strummed chords).

At the time of our interview, Fukuda's stay in Bolivia was indefinite. However, he found it difficult to imagine supporting a family in Bolivia, mentioning both his limited income and lack of health insurance. If he were to marry, he would return to Japan, he told me.[41] For the moment, though, his objective was to learn as much as possible about Bolivian expressions on charango and to record his own compositions. Pointing to jazz as a musical tradition through which he could learn about creativity, he insisted his compositions were designed to innovate and enrich Bolivian charango music, but without becoming fusion—a point about which he was adamant. As of 2002, he had recorded with the singer and songwriter David Portillo, a CD titled *Para no caer al cielo* (So as not to fall into heaven). The recording features liner notes in Spanish and Japanese, and of the ten tracks, four showcase Fukuda's compositions, either alone or in conjunction with Portillo.[42]

Discussions anywhere about musicians giving up their day jobs are usually laced with comments about economic insecurity and sometimes unspoken speculations about whether or not someone is "good enough" to make it in music. In Japan, where great emphasis has been placed on life-long productive work with a single company, leaving one's day job, or even avoiding those jobs in the first instance, goes against the grain. Sojourners and professional musicians spoke of finding employment that would financially assist them in reaching a personal goal like living an extended period in Bolivia. Short-term employment in convenience stores and bread factories and doing outdoor painting and other odd jobs was a means to this end. Savings from work in Japan was stretched out over at least a year of living in Bolivia. While some Japanese sponsored their own Bolivian adventure, Fukuda insisted that some of the younger sojourners were supported by their parents in Japan, something I confirmed in one interview.

Practicing musicians back in Japan described a process of becoming overrun with musical activities that forced them to make a choice. Such was the case of Kawamoto, whose boss at the *Revista latina* forced him to choose between his job and his work in Bolivian music. "That's easy," he said from the position of hindsight. He chose music, quit his job, and made his first trip to Bolivia. Kusanagi, at the age of forty-two, is a professional charango player who has been working in this music for fifteen years, and who has about 150 students. But he was originally trained as an economist. When his musical activities began to spill over into his regular work schedule, he finally left his full-time job at a bank. Hitoshi Hashimoto, another hobbyist turned professional musician, left his job as a piano tuner with Yamaha and formed a group that cut its teeth playing on the streets of Japanese cities. Today he performs and records, teaches quena classes, and sells quenas that he himself makes. The lines between Japanese Bolivian music hobbyists, sojourners, and professionals are decidedly blurred. But to enter this realm through any of these doors means to seek forms of social interaction that are alternative to the expected norms and routines of daily life in Japan. The persistent theme of one's hobby coming into conflict with one's work underscores the implicit critique of a Japanese work ethic and its rigid structuring of time.[43]

Cultivating Expertise

While professional musicians are expected to have developed an expert knowledge about Bolivian music, hobbyists and small-business owners also cultivate the same expertise. Some hobbyists set up small businesses—an Andean-themed restaurant where appropriate performance groups are featured or a store where hobbyists can buy instruments and the latest recordings from Bolivia, Peru, Ecuador, and Argentina. As one entrepreneur told me, his online business depended heavily on information and contacts with artisans and musicians in Bolivia. Even if school performances demanded a staging of the stereotypically Andean, discerning hobbyists are no longer content with generic formulations of these genres. Rather they insist on following specific artists and ensembles whose independent recordings would not have international distribution if it were not for the individual initiative of entrepreneurs who may travel to Bolivia and Bolivian musicians who may carry these recordings to Japan. One shop owner makes annual visits to Bolivia where he says he avoids the tourist markets on Sagárnaga Street in La Paz and goes instead to artisans who "put their hearts" into making instruments specifically for him. The successes of these small businesses depend on the shop owners' web of contacts in Bolivia and on a continuing project of self-education about the Bolivian music scene. Such a project became obvious to me when, partway through an interview, one shop owner began to ask me numerous questions about my own work in Bolivian music. In this information-driven niche economy, he was just as interested in what I might have to say about Bolivian music, in what I had gleaned from participating in this world.

One online shop owner began his business simply as a website that posted information about Andean folklore activities and provided a chat space for those interested in the scene. Through this site, he formed an online group of twenty musicians who have participated in Japan's Cosquín Festival. Through Internet connections, members of this performing group met, planned prefestival rehearsals in culture halls of Tokyo and Osaka, and participated three times in this festival. Thus the disembodied online encounters became fully embodied performances by Andean music enthusiasts. The social spaces of hobbyists look like groups of friends, much like the hip-hop and rock band enthusiasts who also go against the stereotype of the alienated loner fan.[44] Only after setting up his site as a virtual space of connection did this hobbyist decide to establish an online business. He says most of his customers are in their thirties and forties, but he wishes he could reach those in their fifties and sixties—those who have more money to spend, who remember the Latin boom, and who would buy yesteryear recordings of tangos and boleros.

While the Bolivian music we performed in Japanese schools was often initially crafted to meet a simplified common denominator approach to Andean music, adult hobbyists and professional musicians develop detailed levels of expertise about Bolivian music. They come to recognize the differences between Bolivian music for export and for "domestic" consumption, admitting their own struggles with interpreting the latter strand. They mark the differences between the creole associations of genres featuring guitars, mandolins, and charangos, and the indigenous troupe style of performance on wind instruments. They spend extended periods in the countryside, learning indigenous performance styles, or in Sucre pursuing interviews and recordings with master charango players who are well known among Bolivian musicians, but barely known internationally. Their pantheon of musical heroes might therefore include names that appear rather obscure on the international level (e.g., the charango player Florencio Oros). Once they return to Japan, they may form specific groups for performance in different genres. Kaiya, a hobbyist and entrepreneur who makes and sells charangos, insisted he is not really a musician, that he simply follows already established customs. He told me that when he was attending the private Waseda University, he went

15. A Bolivian dance (cueca) workshop offered in Tokyo by Zenobia Mamani
in 2003. *Photograph by the author.*

to a performance of Don Mauro Nuñez that was sponsored by the university Latin American club. Mauro Nuñez, originally from Sucre, spent
many years in Argentina and returned to Bolivia with a folklorized performance on charango that emphasized an indigenous staged presentation.[45]
Kaiya had studied the recorder in school and law for his profession. But
Nuñez's performance inspired him, and he ended up making part hobby
and part business out of studying the intricacies of Bolivian music and
dance. At the time of our interview, he participated in three different ensembles that played respectively music from Sucre, indigenous troupe-
style music, and the charango style as performed in the countryside of
Northern Potosí. In our conversation, he mentioned struggling with running the construction company he inherited from his father, particularly
after the economic downturn in the 1990s. But what really made him
happy, he said, was working in wood, making charangos, and searching
for the ideal varnish to produce the perfect sound.

Hobbyists also cultivate their expertise through dance. Zenobia Mamani,
a Bolivian woman who had married a Japanese folklore musician, offered
workshops in Tokyo on how to dance the cueca (a Bolivian genre) (see
figure 15). Upon interviewing participants of one of these workshops, I
discovered most of them had their own hobby ensembles, and a principal motivation for taking the dance class was to better "feel" the groove

16. Members of Los Vientos rehearse in Tokyo. *Photograph by the author.*

of this more challenging genre that is played and felt through a simultaneous count of two and three.[46] One participant said that only when he began to dance did he really get to know Bolivian music. He wanted to learn to play and dance the cueca in all its regional variations—from Sucre, Cochabamba, Tarija, and El Chaco. A year after our interview I ran into him in Bolivia. He and his wife, both in their thirties, were spending a few months there, following their musical dreams. At the time, they had both left their jobs in Japan—he as a quality control inspector in a Toshiba cell phone factory and she as an insurance company secretary.

The Generational Question

The Miyamoto family was named in several interviews I conducted with Bolivian musicians; some Bolivians even referred to them as their "Japanese family." The Miyamotos have headed up a group called Los Vientos, an ensemble that has met weekly for the last twenty-eight years, also performing at friends' weddings and parties (see figure 16). Hishimoto had played with Los Vientos in the early years of his career, and it was through his connection that I found myself seated on tatami mats, listening to Los Vientos play and talk about their passion for this music. With the exception of their youngest member, a fifteen-year-old boy who was studying with Hishimoto, most of the members of this group were in their fifties and sixties, much like the age range of Los Borrachos as described earlier in this chapter. At first glance, Andean music hobby groups might appear to be populated by an older generation. But I suggest that the snapshot of hobbyists, sojourners, and professionals is multigenerational.

Christine Yano identifies a generation gap that emerged in the Japanese popular music scene in the 1970s, when a youth-oriented urban folk boom, featuring American singers like Bob Dylan and Joan Baez, did not appeal to older listeners; the invention and packaging of enka as a traditional Japanese ballad appealed to an older generation, and this genre sat next to these other more successful circulations of popular music in Japan.[47] The enka of the 1970s stood for the disappearing past and the soul of the Japanese, as opposed to the flood of foreign popular music.[48] But what about the youth who in the '70s chose Andean folk music? From the present moment, Andean folklore is uniquely linked to expressions of nostalgia for an unspecified ancient indigenous world, for old solidarity politics, and for a world imagined to exist before unfettered consumer capitalism. In these ways, even though Bolivian music is foreign and was popularized through a US singer's version of "El condor pasa," its meaning may resemble the symbolic readings of enka. If enka develops a nostalgia around an internal exotic of the past,[49] Andean music develops its nostalgia from an external exotic also located in a past. The world Andean music boom also was associated with global politics of solidarity in which youth identified with causes through listening to Andean music (see chapter 2). While solidarity politics did not seem to dominate the discussions I had with Japanese musicians, they were mentioned when interviewees of forty and fifty years of age reflected back on their initial attraction to this music, when they were in their twenties. Hobbyists expressed dislike for "modern" or "popular" music and claimed they had spiritual feelings when they heard the sound of the quena. A sixty-eight-year-old musicologist, Jiro Hamada, talked about a deep connection with these traditions: "We can appreciate their music as a fundamental culture, as a race, as humanity. This is why the message of Latin American folklore is so important to us. It's not just entertainment, but rather an expression of the soul, of the heart." In the next chapter, I will take up the racialized connection Hamada expressed here and that was almost uniformly present in my interviews. In spite of the commercial side of the Andean music boom, Bolivian music still indexed a kind of noncapitalist cultural alternative that hobbyists sought.

The market for Andean music in Japan has always been relatively small, and according to those who sponsor and book tours for Bolivian bands, general interest may be on a downswing. Nevertheless, my ethnography reveals cross-generational participation in this micro-niche musical world, and both younger and older participants talk of the pleasures of nostalgia they encounter in playing or listening to this music of Others. While more significant numbers of Japanese youth may prefer the developing hip-hop scene as an alternative youth space, a few young Japanese in their twenties and thirties are still sojourning to Bolivia, and this is the context in which Japanese presence is significant enough to be labeled by some Bolivian musicians as a "friendly invasion." The staidness of a hobby group in Japan is perhaps a bit incongruous with the still budding aspirations of twenty-something musicians, particularly when they now have a series of Japanese-Bolivian music success stories in Kinoshita, Hishimoto, Fukuda, and others. Like Hayao with his three-year plan for a Bolivian music education, the younger musician is more likely to be sojourning to Bolivia and dreaming of making it in this music. For at least one of those young musicians, that dream came true.

When I met Makoto Shishido, he was twenty-seven years old and had been living in Cochabamba for five years. His route to Bolivia was prefaced by a boyhood fascination with Los Kjarkas, a love affair that began when he heard them in concert in Japan: "I fell in love with Bolivian music and with the music of [Los] Kjarkas." His parents also played guitar, charango, and quena—making him a second generation follower of this music. Between the ages of six and eighteen, he also studied the cello, fulfilling the wishes of his parents that he learn "European music." During his teen years, he explored interests in rock, but at the age of nineteen he "returned to folklore" and the playing of charango. When I asked him to name his favorite groups, his musical heroes, he answered emphatically "Kjarkas, Kjarkas, Kjarkas . . . I have all of Kjarkas's recordings." When I mentioned specific charango artists, he insisted that his interests were located not in a solo style of playing but in the ability to perform within a group.

In his late teens, he made his first trip to Bolivia and during one month he studied with Fernando Torrico, a musician who used to play with Los Kjarkas. A year later he returned to Cochabamba and put himself forward in a long audition process to join Los Kjarkas as their new charango player. He told me that during an entire year, he auditioned at three different times, also competing with two other Bolivian charango players. When describing the results of this process he exclaimed excitedly, "I won. I had realized my dream." Shishido was settling well into life in Cochabamba: "It's uncomfortable in Japan. Lots of people, lots of noise."

He talked about how he dreamed of having a house and a recording studio in Cochabamba. Los Kjarkas is one of the most commercially successful internationally touring Bolivian ensembles. The weight of a young Japanese musician in such a group is indeed significant. Meanwhile, another young Japanese musician in his thirties was making a successful go of it as a headlining zampoña player in Japan.

World Zampoña

Takamasa Segi was a busy man. Scheduling an interview with him was no easy task. He invited me to a concert in Koshigaya (Saitama), a suburb of Tokyo where he performed as the lead artist "Segi." After fearing I had missed my train stop, but being reassured by helpful fellow passengers who communicated in a language I did not understand, I arrived early at the venue, as Segi had instructed, and was shown into the theater where the musicians were going through the usual full-concert "sound check." Top-notch Japanese jazz musicians accompanied him on piano, bass, and drum set. As I looked for Segi backstage, after the sound check and before the concert, it took some time to get beyond the entourage of black-suited bouncers who provided a major buffer between Segi and his fans. Apparently, this is what it means to be "treated like an artist" in Japan. With my lack of Japanese-language skills, it was impossible to explain my purpose for being there. I was seen as one more fan. When I finally reached Segi, I gave him a gift box of wrapped crackers—something I took to all my scheduled encounters in Japan—and asked if we might meet at another time for an interview. On his computer there, in his dressing room, he pulled up his agenda and suggested a meeting in Ebisu (Tokyo) where he would be playing at a shopping mall. He then invited me to enjoy the show.

He packed a large theater that seated about five hundred enthusiastic fans. He played a jazzed-up version of "El condor pasa," over which the audience went wild, and also a version of Los Kjarkas's "Llorando se fue," a tune that became popularized globally when the multinational ensemble Kaoma served it up as their own *lambada*—another tale of musical theft or appropriation.[50] Beyond these two pieces, the zampoña and quena instruments were almost the only Andean points of reference, as most of the repertoire consisted of Segi's own compositions and ones that relied heavily on the superb improvisational skills of his accompanying musicians. After the concert, the fans moved to the foyer where Segi's representatives marketed his CDs and "signature quena" (at the price of about $100, complete with a case made of aguayo fabric). Lining up with the other fans who had purchased a CD, I waited to obtain Segi's auto-graph, following a classic gesture in which fans honor Japanese artists. Christine Yano describes a set of formulaic practices through which fans of enka express intimacy with their favored artists.[51] The CD lineups for the harpist (chapter 3) and for Segi resemble these expressions of inti-macy. With Segi, I reconfirmed our appointment and then headed for the train station. It was a long ride back to Nakano.

Since he was ten years old, Segi was interested in music. With the guitar his father bought for him, he explored classical, rock, and jazz music, lis-tening to everything from Beethoven to Kiss. Within his father's record collection, he found an album with a cover that featured an image of in-digenous peoples who were playing bamboo panpipes. Upon listening to the recording, he was immediately intrigued by the sound. A few days later, he went to a concert of an Andean group he had seen advertised on television. Following this concert, Segi put aside the guitar and took up these foreign wind instruments, even though some of his high school friends chided him for leaving behind the popular rocker image that could accompany a guitarist, but that seemed to have nothing to do with someone who "just played bamboo." He told me he liked the zampoñas, the fact that you could play them softly or loudly, "sounding either like a light wind or an oncoming train."

Never having had a teacher, he learned from going to concerts of Ernesto Cavour, Savia Andina, and Los Kjarkas, and by listening to these ensembles' recordings. Although he formed what he called "just an ama-teur group" with his friends at home, he dreamed of playing with profes-sional Bolivian musicians. "I couldn't learn in Japan," he said. "Everyone just wanted 'El condor pasa' and 'Humahuaqueño' [another Andean music 'war horse' from Argentina]." In 1985, at the age of eighteen, Segi went to Bolivia for the first time, and since then he has returned several times. At twenty-one years of age, he found himself unemployed in Japan and de-cided to spend a year in Bolivia. A self-professed "fanatic" of all Savia An-dina repertoire, he decided to compose pieces in their style, while also de-veloping his own musical voice—what he calls "something like folklore, jazz, and rock." After Savia Andina's musicians heard a demo recording of Segi's compositions that the artist had sent, the ensemble asked him to come to Bolivia to record. At the time of our interview, he had made four recordings in Bolivia, including one titled *Una zampoña para el mundo* (A panpipe for the world).

Segi proudly told me his first CD in Japan had sold fifteen thousand

copies, when they usually expect these kinds of recordings to sell between three and five thousand maximum. What matters, he said, is "good
music." Crossing genres has not been a problem for him, and he even recorded a hit with a rock trio. He has adapted the zampoña instrument to
these different styles, using a chromatic and even what he called a "blue
note" zampoña. His Japanese-marketed albums—seven at the time of our
interview—carried titles like *Songs of the Wind*, *Nieve* ("snow," in Spanish), *Luna* ("moon," in Spanish), *Forest Rain*, *Silencio* ("silence," in Spanish), and *Tree of Life*. Although he is not fond of the moniker, Segi said
his music has been marketed under "what in the United States is called
'New Age,' and what in Japan they call 'Healing Music.'" As the titles of
his recordings suggest, Segi finds inspiration in what he calls "nature."
In his search for a natural world "that appear[s] unchanged throughout
the years," Segi told me he had traveled to Namibia, Sri Lanka, Borneo,
and the Amazon. For his thirty-seven years, he seemed quite the world
traveler.

Segi's story of discovery—through the indigenous image of a record
cover and the subsequent New Age marketing of his work—calls forth
the globally circulating image of indigenous peoples as eco-warriors. A
similar eco-indigenous connection propelled Kinoshita's *Suite ecológico
ser* (see chapter 3), although with very different aesthetics than those proposed by Segi. While mestizo musicians like those in Música de Maestros
draw out the indigenous connection in their expression of a nationalist
music, indigeneity here included reference to ecological secrets for which
indigenous peoples were imagined to hold the keys. If Bolivian musicians
referenced indigeneity as nationalism, a Japanese New Age reference to
indigeneity was about a global, somewhat generic, environmentalism—
a nod to the genre conventions of "indigenous voice," even if only at the
level of artistic representation.[52]

During our interview, I asked Segi if he was inspired by Bolivian music.
"No," he answered. His inspirations were located more within "world
music," he said, using the term in English in the middle of our interview
in the Spanish language. Steven Feld pointed out how the term "world
music" was set up next to just plain "music," as academics used the first
term in the 1960s "to celebrate and promote the study of musical diversity"; but the term also left entrenched the dual categorization of Western and non-Western musics.[53] In the provocatively titled article "World
Music Does Not Exist," Timothy Brennan claims that what goes by the
name "world music" is actually a very local or regional music that "has
no ambition to travel."[54] In contrast, Segi's "world music" reference was
very much about travel, a New Age expression of his encounters with

otherness, and ones that, because of his own position as Japanese, didn't fall easily into exoticism's West/non-West dichotomy. Segi's story sounds something like what Veit Erlmann calls the artist turned cultural entrepreneur: he is involved in "curatorial, promotional, and collaborative efforts across different cultural spheres."[55] Segi's New Age, eco-warrior, indigenous, and world music associations place his work within a genre category that sells well. Of the Japanese musicians making a living in "folklore" or Andean and Bolivian music, he was reaching a broader listening audience than any other musicians I interviewed. But he also drew a following that did not necessarily intersect with other hobbyists and enthusiasts of Bolivian music. The star image of "Segi" seemed to surpass rather than balance evenly with what concerned other participants in this musical niche: getting the details right about that Other culture, or simply getting to know people in that Other culture.

Concluding Thoughts on the Musical Love Object

In Jacques Attali's rather bleak picture of a political economy of music, the advent of recording possibilities was depicted as an endless cycle of musical repetition and stockpiling of music to which one has no time to listen. Within a Marxist frame and from a pre-iPod and pre-web 2.0 moment, he proposed a dialectic through which the contradictions of the "repeating" mode would be followed by a "composing" mode in which more people would have access to the musical modes of production, a democratization of the music-making process.[56] In spite of the critiques one might level at his work—its nonengagement with anything beyond Western music and its materialist reduction of the musical experience— something in the hobbyists' Saturday rehearsals seems consistent with a composing mode: the hobbyists' dedication to playing music for the sake of gathering as a social group, their nostalgia for something they cannot quite pinpoint, and their prioritizing of such rehearsals over seeing the latest hot professional Andean musicians in the theater. Hobbyists enter temporarily a world imagined as an alternative to the other foreign influences that flood Japan. In this alternative world, hobbyists perform the music they love, forging an emotional and physical bond to the sound of Bolivian music, and creating one level of intimacy that is then bolstered by the racialized imaginings I will discuss in the next chapter. The sojourning and performance cycle leads to no ordinary market circulation of cultural goods and artifacts that might be consumed within a tourist gaze.[57] In performing an Other's music for pleasure, the "goods" hardly

disappear in the process of consumption, and the thing-like logic of arti-
fact collection hardly fits these musical experiences that lead to a proliferation of different social connections. It is about pleasure and nostalgia
for an indigenous world, but it is also about the search for social ties imagined as vanishing within the modern structures of Japan's everyday life.

Hobbyists are not as concerned with the cultural authenticity of what
they play. In contrast, the quest for authenticities may strongly motivate
the sojourners who seek an unmediated encounter with cultural Others.
Those who talk about someone else's authenticity, or lack of it, often do
so from a relative position of power.[58] The Japanese who can choose to
sojourn to Bolivia for extended periods occupy a position of power in relation to the Bolivian musicians they encounter, much like my own position of researcher who comes and goes from this country on an almost
annual basis. If the sojourner turns professional, authenticity quests may
become retrospectively the subject of critical self-reflection, as the musician develops a different interpretive and creative voice. Nevertheless, I
want to insist on the blurred lines between the categories of hobbyists,
sojourners, and professional musicians, because in the stories I heard,
people are moving between these different ways of doing Bolivian music.
The common threads in these experiences include: the search for alternatives to a more commercial music scene they perceive as shaped through
a post–World War II context, the vague feelings of nostalgia that Bolivian
music evokes for them, and their fascination with Bolivian indigeneity.
When Japanese perform the Bolivian music they love, they produce much
more than musical sound. They produce nostalgia and racialized imaginaries that construe connections to an indigenous world, a topic to which
I turn in the next chapter.

5 Intimate Distance

In a noisy Tokyo restaurant, I chatted with Eduardo Prado during his brief lunch hour.[1] When we spoke, he was working an office job and playing "folklore" very much as a secondary project on the side. He was one of the few Bolivians I interviewed who made explicit claims to an indigenous Aymara identity. Prado praised the Aymaras' ability to adapt through the centuries to new and different living situations. As an example, he pointed to his own ability to get along in Japan while still maintaining his indigenous Bolivian identity. He explained that for Bolivians, anyone from Asia—Japanese, Chinese, Vietnamese, or Filipino—was simply called "*chinito*," and that Japanese similarly lumped together all people from the Andes. He said Japanese like Bolivian music because, "something calls their attention to native music. . . . Looking way back one might be able to see an ethnic connection between Asians and people who live in the Andes." Prado went on to frame Aymara and Japanese cultures as drawing strength from their ancient roots.

Throughout my interviews with both Japanese and Bolivians, I posed the question "Why do you think Japanese like Bolivian music?" or "Why do you think Japanese like playing Bolivian music?" In response to this question, a Japanese man in his forties told me the following in an interview in La Paz: "When I listened to Bolivian or Andean music on a folklore recording, I felt nostalgia. I imagined I had heard this before." I challenged him, asking with a purposefully stubborn rational edge, "How can you feel nostalgia for something you haven't experienced?" He responded, "Maybe it is history. Because there is a common connection between Japanese and the indigenous peoples of Central and South America." The Japanese enthusiast of Bolivian music explained his own nostalgia through an imagined prehistoric connection to indigenous peoples, and the Aymara Bolivian musician turned Japanese office worker similarly claimed to share ancient indigenous connections with the Japanese. In a transnational nexus of music performance, Japanese and Bolivians claimed a closeness with the Others of these encounters, but without identifying completely with them. If intimacy was mutually constructed through racialized narratives and imagined prehistoric indigenous ancestors, my interview questions about cross-cultural likes and dislikes also revealed mutual intimacy and distance between Japanese and Bolivians.

In this chapter, I explore more fully what I have called "intimate distance," the way both Japanese and Bolivians claimed closeness with and distance from the others with whom they engaged in a musical intersection of transnational music performance. From the Japanese perspective, a foreign music is brought into a system of desire whereby imagined genealogy, shared pentatonic scales, and similar musical instruments become metaphorical bridges that lean toward but never completely close the distance between Japanese musicians and their desired object of Bolivian music. Pentatonic music is built on a five-note scale, rather than the seven-note major and minor scales that generally form the basis for Western harmonic systems. Although also found in some Western classical music, the pentatonic scale often becomes a sonic sign of non-Western and premodern musical forms. Bolivian musicians also mentioned perceived similarities with Japanese in the areas of prehistoric genealogy and shared musical sonorities, while also pointing to their desired object: Japan's path of modernity, which they perceive as alternative to that of the United States. While I began with an exceptional example from a self-identified Aymara in Japan, most of the Bolivian musicians of this scene did not self-identify as indigenous. Thus the paradox: Japanese and mestizo Bolivian musicians invoked a racialized narrative of indigeneity as a point of connection, even though most of them do not self-identify as contemporary indigenous subjects. Their pride in dressing the part— Japanese and Bolivians dressing as indians on stage—contrasted with my own discomfort when asked to do the same; the colonial roots of my national history had followed a different cultural politics that assigned different taboos to "playing Indian."

With the term "system of desire," I refer to experiences that bring pleasure to a subject but that exist almost but not quite within one's grasp; the system is articulated through the subject's constant struggle to overcome the distance to that experience. Here I draw on the ideas of the philosopher Georg Simmel, who writes about how desire emerges when the subject experiences both closeness to and distance from the wanted object.[2] Music performance experiences, however, are not mere objects that one might obtain, possess, or hold close. The elusiveness of performance itself keeps this system of desire moving. For example, the Japanese genre of enka, according to Christine Yano, expresses a nostalgic longing for a perceived old traditional Japan, but nostalgia itself seems to demand simultaneously the maintenance and overcoming of distance.[3] As Japanese search for a closeness with Bolivians and their music, they construct racialized narratives that do that double work of familiarity and distance. When music performance is the "object" of desire, one's own body can become a performative site that both produces and attempts to satisfy desire; what is desired becomes associated with fandom, social relationships, and the performance experience.[4] In the case at hand, Japanese enthusiasts of Bolivian music sought intimacy through vaguely construed genealogies in indigenous worlds. Even so, distance remained in place as such imaginings were outside any contemporary positioning within the Japanese nation; blood may define who is Japanese within the modern context—who is allowed to return from Brazil or Peru because of Japanese ancestry—but the prehistoric blood connection is left to the realm of "nostalgination," if you will.

As discussed in other chapters, the Japanese-Bolivian encounter is not one of equals. The first reason Bolivian musicians seek connections with Japanese is, in most cases, not because of a desire to find closeness with Japanese but rather because of their pursuit of limited music employment possibilities in a global music economy. Once they are within these global encounters, Bolivians also used racialized discourses to narrativize familiarity and intimacy with the Japanese, even though they also marked a corresponding distance. This chapter explores the double work of desire as Japanese and Bolivians talk about both closeness with and distance from each other. Even if the Japanese and Bolivian narratives of intimate distance are doing different symbolic work, both cases highlight the centrality of racial imaginations not only in musical projects but in nationalist ones as well.

When one takes up musical practices that are framed through national, ethnic, or racial frames as *someone else's*, the results are celebrated by some as part of the wonders of global exchange and decried by others as cultural theft. The globalization of music tends to evoke these dueling narratives of creative appropriation and cultural theft.[5] When Japanese take up the music of others, the arguments focus on whether or not interpretations can ever get beyond the essentializing and ultimately insulting reading of Japanese as imitators. For example, some Japanese have taken jazz and hip-hop and made it their own.[6] But even the national modifier "Japanese" in front of "jazz"—what has now become an art genre with its own claims to universality—can become problematic for those who want to be known simply as "jazz musicians."[7] Insisting on the national modifier in front of "jazz," or for that matter in front of any other artistic line of work like "fashion designer," can ghettoize the musician, designer, or artist who wants to move beyond nationality and particularly beyond a national modifier that is heavily raced and exoticized in Westerners' eyes.[8] In contrast, only a few Japanese musicians I interviewed expressed designs on moving Bolivian folklore music into a realm of universal aesthetics. The category of Andean music or "folklore" is associated closely with the particular. But like Japanese musicians involved in jazz and hip-hop, Japanese folklore musicians used race thinking to position themselves close to someone else's music.

For Bolivians, the appropriation drama plays out at national and international levels. Mestizo musicians may play an indigenous Other's music as national music—something some people celebrate as patriotic pride, even while others discredit it as one more way to think positively about indigenous representations without the participation of flesh and blood indians. At the international level, as I have detailed in previous chapters, one can tell the story of Paul Simon's appropriation of "El condor pasa" or Kaoma's supposed theft of "Llorando se fue." The theft-appropriation scenario, I suggest, leaves out of these global encounters a serious consideration of desire, beyond a simplistic discussion of Westerners' desire for the exoticized non-Western Other.

While not dismissing the powerful effects of global capitalism and the economies of pleasure that do transform cultural life, often to the detriment of those "Others," I want to complicate perspectives on this system of desire that forms a central axis in music globalization processes. The Japanese desire to play Bolivian music is not so easily slotted in the Euro-American tale about the exotification of non-Western Others. Nor, as I will argue, is this desire completely outside Euro-American race thinking. This ethnographic case requires looking both within and beyond the standard postcolonial constructs of the West and the Rest,[9] pointing to the distinct ways that race thinking is implicated not only in colonial histories but also in national ones. To explain the intimate distance expressed between Bolivians and Japanese, I will need to unravel histories of nationalist thought and racial thinking. But first, I turn to several expressions of this intimacy.

Look Alike, Sound Alike, Rooted Alike

"When I listen to 'El condor pasa,'" said one Japanese man in his thirties during an interview in Tokyo, "I imagine the Andes . . . it feels like something very close, not that different. It's not foreign; it's very familiar."[10] In response to my questions about liking and playing Bolivian music, Japanese responded with a variety of answers. Spiritual kinship and reincarnation were cited within two interviews. One Bolivian musician told me the following: "It surprises me that being on the other side of the world, they like our music so much. . . . As many of them believe in reincarnation. . . . They tell me 'maybe in my previous life I was Bolivian.' . . . But it's also about feeling. It's something spiritual, like there is a connection of the heart." A Japanese enthusiast told me a story about how he was almost killed in a truck accident in Bolivia. "I was reborn as a Bolivian," he said, laughing lightly as he made this statement. Like Japanese who follow Argentine tango, Andean music enthusiasts reference "a spiritual kinship" between very different cultures.[11]

Even more common than spiritual kinship were the references to shared musical sounds, instrument types, and pentatonic scales—all tinged by an ongoing explicit or implicit reference to an Andean indigenous world. Japanese fans and musicians told me: "[In] Inca music, the melody is very similar to Japanese melodies." "The sounds and the scales of the music are very similar." "Native music is like ancient Japanese ritual music." "The native music they play by the Lake [Titicaca] is something like the music they play in Japanese rituals." "In Japan we also have a bamboo flute, the shakuhachi." Many of the same people who made these references to Bolivia's indigenous worlds were well versed in the intricacies of genres that highlight Spanish influence and mestizo developments within Bolivian music. However, in the moment of defining intimacy, more than five hundred years of Spanish influence seemed to disappear from their narratives.

Bolivians gave similar responses in relation to Japanese sounds and instruments. One Bolivian in La Paz referred to pentatonic scales and how Japanese use of them went against his own preconceptions about this country's position as modern: "They conserve pentatonic music, even though they are very modern." Bolivians also consistently referred to the shakuhachi as the Japanese equivalent of the quena, and this instrument's prominent place in our staged performances reflected these general associations as made by both Japanese and Bolivians.

In his study of Japanese diaspora in South America, Dale Olsen speculates that Japanese fascination with Andean music may have something to do with the shared pentatonic scales in Japanese children's songs and in Andean folk music. He follows this with a speculation about the "plaintive sounds" produced on the Japanese shakuhachi and the Andean quena.[12] While I would argue that there is nothing inherently "plaintive" about musical sounds, that emotion attributed to sound is fundamentally processed through sociocultural contexts, Olsen's ethnomusicological study is consistent with my interviewees' responses that reference the similar sonorities of these two instruments.

Japanese and Bolivians also pointed to other cultural practices they perceived as sharing with each other—imagined similarities between an indigenous language (Quechua) and Japanese, as well as similarities in sleeping practices. In comparative reference to Bolivian indigenous peasant practices of sleeping on the floor, a Bolivian mentioned that the Japanese "are very proud of sleeping on the floor." What is particularly interesting here is that the person speaking, and most other Bolivian musicians who tour Japan, generally sleep in beds at home and have very little fondness for sleeping on the floor anywhere, in Japan or Bolivia. On this point, Bolivians shared more with me, the gringa, than with their Japanese counterparts. Some Japanese also made this same comment about sleeping and sitting on the floor, claiming an imagined cultural closeness with Bolivia's indigenous peoples through a reference to daily bodily practices in which the body was kept close to the ground. The Japanese musician referred here to the low stools on which one might sit in an indigenous peasant home that likely had no chairs. Imagined peasant or indigenous bodily practices—squatting, sleeping on the floor, or sitting on low stools—became another point of construed intimacy through a perceived shared closeness to the ground.

A Bolivian musician who was living in Hamamatsu told me he became a Bolivian folklore musician only when he was living in Brazil. He subsequently married a Japanese Brazilian woman and moved with her to Japan where he now works for an employment agency and plays music on the side. In response to my question about why Japanese have an interest in Bolivian music, he told me, "There are many Japanese who look like Bolivians and Bolivians who look like Japanese. I think a long time ago, the Asians, I don't know, went to Bolivia, to South America and that's how the South American civilization was born." In interviews with both Bolivians and Japanese, cultural practices and forms slipped easily into racializations of culture: discussions of phenotype, blood, DNA, and supposed shared ancient ties to indigeneity. A Bolivian musician who claimed a Quechua background from Northern Potosí told me, "Maybe we have common roots with them. We are such ancient cultures. From back then there must be some connection to the contemporary South American [indian]." Another Bolivian I interviewed in La Paz told me, "I think we have many roots from Japan, especially the indians of Bolivia. . . . You must have seen the similarities with the indigenous people." He invokes what Mary Weismantel referred to as the "hollow claim to empiricism offered by race"; when Weismantel asked how one can tell that market women in Cuenca (Ecuador) are not white, she received the answer: "Just *look* at them."[13] Race's hollow empiricism was used in the present case to claim sameness rather than difference: "*You must have seen* how the Japanese look like indigenous people."

A Bolivian musician I interviewed in La Paz distinguished the Japanese desiring from that of other foreigners (like myself) and also regionalized the perceived racial connection: "I think we are connected in some way to the Asians. Especially [those of] the highland plain (*altiplano*). Long, long ago, centuries ago, there must have been a connection. . . . It's not the same with the European who likes the music for another reason. It's completely different. Nor with the American. It's totally different. With the Asian, there is an attachment." His reference to people of the highland plain signals people of indigenous Aymara or Quechua background. Another Bolivian I interviewed in Tokyo told me: "I think we are something alike. Maybe through the Bering Strait. We have something in common through our ancestors, they tell me. It might be true." Bolivians referred to descent and phenotype, even though within Bolivia indigeneity has not been defined through blood quantum, one drop ideas, nor necessarily by physical appearance.

A similar tale of ancestral connections emerged among the Japanese I interviewed, but not always with direct reference to phenotype. If race thinking in Japan has its ties to Western modernity—as I along with many others argue it does—it also has its own local articulations, one of which is its focus on "blood."[14] In my interviews with Japanese musicians, race was configured through references to Mongols, shared roots, and DNA: "I think they are of the same race; indians and Japanese are from Mongolians." "It must be a problem of DNA because Japanese and Andean pentatonic [scales] are the same." "Indigenous people come from the Mongol root. So maybe we feel something in common." One Japanese musician spoke of shared DNA between Japanese people "and the indians of South America." While the entire interview was in Spanish, he made the reference to "DNA" in the English language. The slippage between shared musical tastes and imaginings of shared genealogy was bolstered by pop-scientific references to genetics.

Diffusion stories via the Bering Strait, and now through genetic stories of connection, call forth powerful scientific discourses that in popular uptake often are positioned beyond critique. These scientific discourses then get reproduced in other representations of Japanese-South American connections. For example, Dale Olsen, in his discussions of the ways Peruvians and Japanese believe themselves to be genetically connected, cites a brochure from 1981 that was published by the Commemorative Museum of Japanese Immigration in Peru; the brochure states: "Peru and Japan have a common ancestry. In the distant Ice Age mongoloid ethnic groups from Asia crossed the Bering Strait, penetrated into the Americas, and became the first inhabitants of Peru and other South American countries. During the same Ice Age similar ethnic groups arrived to the archipelago of Japan. These people of common ancestry followed different evolutionary paths, accommodating themselves to the circumstances of their different environments and thus, created their own cultures."[15] My point here is not to debate diffusionist claims that feature the Bering Strait but to underscore the ways race thinking is reinscribed through popular and nationalist consumption of scientific narratives.

The Japanese and Bolivian narratives slide easily between references to similar musical instruments, cultural practices, pentatonic scales, and an imagined shared ancestry. In my interviews, "Mongol" emerges as a perceived genetic ancestor who is traced through reference to a racialized indigenous world. Nevertheless, this shared ancestor is devoid of historical specificity and quite detached from both the indigenous politics that characterize the contemporary Bolivian context and the narrative of cultural homogeneity that marks Japanese nationalist ideology.

The Japanese drew connections that seemed contradictory next to this country's dominant narrative of the Japanese as a unique homogeneous nation that resists the incorporation of foreigners. In their interview comments, the idiom of "Japanese blood," in relation to Bolivian indians, construed connections rather than exclusions, but only as funneled through a prehistoric moment. I would suggest that these ideas about race, as expressed by both Bolivians and Japanese, rather than representing a straight non-Western to non-Western intimacy, have been mediated by race thinking that was shaped through European colonial projects, scientific racism, and specific nationalist projects. Colonialism, nationalism, and scientific racism, however, have all played out in distinct ways. For example, Kosaku Yoshino, a scholar of Japan, has suggested that in contrast with Britain and the United States, racial discourse in Japan has been about positive in-group identification.[16] Similarly, Frank Dikötter emphasizes how racial discourse in East Asian contexts has provided a powerful narrative of inclusion for marginalized groups.[17] I want to emphasize that even if the race thinking noted here described a process of connection and inclusion—how Japanese felt connected to Bolivians and vice versa—it is nonetheless a form of racialization with all the real and potential practices of exclusion, discrimination, and marginalization that this thinking facilitates. Before turning to the specific colonial and national tales that shaped race thinking in Japan and Bolivia, something more must be said about the tenacity of race thinking and the slipperiness of race in relation to music.

Race Still Here and Everywhere

It is far too easy to point to these racialized narratives and say, "How strange! It must be something peculiar to Japanese or Bolivian thinking." Or "It sounds like something from the nineteenth century." "It's an old way of thinking," or "it's an Other way of thinking." But no one gets off the hook here; we are all caught in the webs of race thinking. Not only is such thinking ever-present in popular ideas about ethnicized musicians and the framing of their talent, but it is also taking on new life within popular adaptations of more recent scientific advancements. Recent genetic research projects have placed indigeneity front and center and have made claims to underscore human connectedness rather than differences. Racial categories continue to seep into these projects. While the controversial Human Genome Diversity Project was critiqued because of its lack of attention to real problems of living indigenous peoples who were merely scientifically interesting as "isolates of historic interest," the more recent Genographic Project, even as it attempted to distance its work from the previous Human Genome Diversity Project, still privileged indigenous DNA as a genetic marker.[18] As Kim TallBear shows, the Genographic Project seems to assume in a straightforward way that science will prove racism wrong and will show how we are all connected, even as persistent racialized hierarchies continue to shape our lives and institutions.[19] The Genographic Project's promotional video, however, relies on an image of indigeneity that is "culturally and phenotypically satisfying," featuring people who have been tested, found their ancient indigenous genes, and actually *look* like Indians.[20] Oh, the woes of those who do not fit race's empiricist bill! Another project, started in 2002 with private and public funding in Canada, China, Japan, Nigeria, the United Kingdom, and the United States aims to create an International Haplotype Map. As Jennifer Hamilton has argued, however, the categories of this so-called geographical ancestry map fall quite easily onto earlier racial taxonomies; geographic markers of African, European, and Asian, look much like categories of Negro, Caucasian, and Mongol.[21] Genetic research that fully assumes racial categories is sometimes justified in the name of medical science, but biologists suggest that race, rather than having any direct biological determination, consists of social processes that produce biological consequences that should be studied scientifically.[22] Race's social construction slips and slides dangerously in these debates.

Beyond these larger projects in the name of humankind, genetic science is now being marketed to individuals who want to know their "personalized genetic histories" (PGH). If supporters of the genome project believed this science would downplay human differences,[23] its applications seem to be doing quite the opposite. For example, using Karen Field's concept of "racecraft," Stephan Palmié draws parallels between Evans-Pritchard's study of witchcraft and the construction of Azande rationality, and the geneticization of race through personal genomic histories as sold to African American consumers. Genomic identity arbitration, according to Palmié, confirms rather than challenges the ideas of originary race making as based on "invisible essences" of relatedness and difference.[24] Genomic histories are being used to reinscribe race within a "natural" world.

I make this brief digression into contemporary genetic projects not because Bolivians or Japanese I interviewed told me about having their genetic histories charted, but because (1) when I have talked in the United States about these narratives of connection a few people mentioned having their own genetic histories plotted, as if to say, "But science did prove it for my case" (one person from Central America had volunteered within one of these genetic geography projects, wanting to solve some identity disputes within her immediate family), and (2) because the Japanese reference to "something in the DNA" flags how scientific discourse that was supposed to work against race, when taken up in the popular imagination, reinstates this thinking—even though it is being used to make a point about connection rather than difference. If scientific evidence points to shared genetic markers between Native Americans and people who live in Asia, Kim TallBear still asks "what does that mean?"[25] When Bolivians and Japanese claim musical affinities through reference to this narrative, they harness the symbolic power of science to a racialization of culture.

In reference to musical practices, racialization of culture is a commonplace in popular culture, and it surfaces frequently when a person is thought to be playing someone else's music.[26] Race thinking in the musical world, as in all other realms, is about both inclusion and exclusion. And each inclusion masks other kinds of exclusion. The racialization of culture I encountered in these narratives should not be dismissed as simply a Japanese or Bolivian thing, as something exotic and Other; this thinking is present in many cross-cultural musical encounters and ultimately shaped by discourses that emerged through a Eurocentric modernity. These racializations are part of what Radano and Bohlman call the "racial imagination":

> the shifting matrix of ideological constructions of difference associated with body type and color that have emerged as part of the discourse network of modernity. As a crucial aspect in the constitution of identities and groups, it

carries profound social meaning. As an ideology, however, the racial imagination remains forever on the loose, subject to reformation within the memories
and imaginations of the social as it blurs into other categories constituting difference. . . . As such, "race" defines not a fixity, but a signification saturated
with profound cultural meaning and whose discursive instability heightens
its affective power.[27]

The racial imagination works overtime in the musical world where the
site of performance, the body, is also where "race" and "nature" are read
as givens. Even as scholars have taken apart the naturalness of the body
in relation to sex, phenotypical variation, and race,[28] within popular discourse, these categories still hold sway as part of a "natural" world.

The racial imagination can authenticate a tourist performance, even
though in the case of indigeneity, race may be hiding behind the curtain
of cultural referents.[29] Such may be the equation in the standard Western
to non-Western tourist construct. The Japan-Bolivia music connection,
however, poses some variations. I have already argued that the producer-
consumer lines of the tourist enterprise seem inappropriate for interpreting this ethnographic case in which the Japanese themselves are performing Bolivian music. The case at hand is also unusual in that race is not
submerged but rather emphasized as a point of connection between those
who may not be equally marginalized in the economic sense but who feel
a common marginal position within a global racial geography.

Because the racial imagination emerges from discourses of modernity—a Eurocentric project—and is also distinctly read and refashioned
at the margins,[30] it needs unpacking in relation to Japanese and Bolivian
colonial and national trajectories. A study of race and colonial desire,
Robert Young suggests, calls for a focus on historical specificities that do
not always fall easily in the polarized model of black and white.[31] Therefore, I turn to the task of looking more closely at the emergence of race
concepts and their intersection with past colonial and present national
projects in Japan and Bolivia.

Someone might wonder why the points about shared bamboo flutes,
pentatonic scales, and sonorities take a back seat to the discussion of race.
I emphasize an analysis of racializiation for several reasons. First, similar racialized narratives emerge among Japanese fan cultures of hip-hop
and jazz, where no bamboo instruments are involved. Second, to focus on
bamboo flutes and pentatonic scales would be to fall into the more comfortable but uncritical examination of music apart from music-making
subjects. Such a project would replicate rather than challenge the problematic evasion of race by focusing on "the music" or "culture."[32] Third,
the racialized comments caught me by surprise and were present in al-

most every interview I conducted, thus demanding my attention as a critical ethnographer.[33] To interpret these narratives of indigenous intimacy,
I now turn to the intersecting and diverging histories of colonialism, scientific racism, and nationalism.

Race and Colonialisms

Bolivia and Japan each have their own separate colonial tales. In the case
of Latin America, one speaks of sixteenth-century Spanish colonization
followed by British economic imperialism in the nineteenth century and
US cultural imperialism in the twentieth century. Japan, on the other
hand, spearheaded its own imperial project throughout Asia between the
end of the nineteenth and the middle of the twentieth centuries, leading
up to its defeat in World War II and occupation by the United States. The
Japanese state framed its project through the ideology of the Greater East
Asia Co-Prosperity Sphere, promising "Asian unity and liberation from
Western colonial rule."[34] As such, Japanese imperialism was disguised
as the cure for Western colonialism. Here, a comparison of colonialisms
in Bolivia and Japan does not shed much light on a project that seeks to
compare and contrast racial thinking in these two countries. A classic
dilemma of postcolonial studies appears: how does one speak across such
different colonial experiences?[35] How is race configured through such
different histories? The project of modernity might provide one tenuous
thread.

Scholars have located the emergence of a race concept with modernity
and with the West's colonial encounters with Others.[36] Ann Stoler, for
example, makes no claim to locate racism's original moment, nor does
she argue that all racisms are the same. Instead her project focuses on
how racial thinking in colonialism sets up exclusionary taxonomies central to progressive projects.[37] But the colonialism she unpacks has its own
specificities that may not be compared so directly with the cases at hand.
For example, scholars of East Asia have also shown how racial thinking
has buttressed projects of inclusion.[38] Here, East Asian inclusionary racial
thinking is constructed as alternative to the exclusionary Eurocentric one
that places Asian subjects outside the realm of whiteness. While Stoler's
reworking of Foucault is useful in its broad approach to intimacy between colonizers and colonized, her arguments draw primarily from late
European colonialisms. An education of desire might look quite different
through the lens of sixteenth-century Spanish colonialism.[39] If we can't
talk specifically about the same concept of "race" in the sixteenth cen-

tury, what can we say about education of desire across difference in that much earlier European colonialism? Historians of Latin America are still tackling this question, but Peter Wade's anthropological analysis of race and ethnicity in this context insists that "the category 'indian' was an integral part of the colonial encounters within which the discourse of race emerged" and that it would be a mistake to see "indian" in only ethnic terms.[40]

Three centuries later, and under the influence of scientific racism, Japan's ideas on race were also shaped through their specific Asian imperial project. As Leo Ching has argued, Japan operated in seemingly contradictory ways, Othering its colonial subjects while also justifying its domination through a narrative of "yellow" interconnectedness.[41] In spite of the quite different and chronologically disparate colonial tales of Bolivia and Japan, both cases point to how colonial projects of expansion and exploitation produce racial identities and categories.[42] As I turn to the nineteenth and twentieth centuries, comparing and contrasting Japan's and Bolivia's experiences with scientific racism and national projects, it is worth repeating that nationalism can be seen as a continuation of, rather than break from, colonial experience. If Bolivian and Japanese colonial experiences are perhaps too different for any extensive postcolonial comparisons, their experiences with scientific racism and twentieth-century nation-building projects provide more fertile ground for comparing racial imaginations.

Race and the Indian in Bolivian Nationalism

Nationalism and race thinking haunted this project, and this double haunting is no mere coincidence. The race thinking in my interviews was about an inclusive narrative of transnational connection through an imagined prehistoric indigenous ancestor. However, the staging of indigenous Bolivian music as a national expression represents another form of race thinking and expression of intimate distance. Across several centuries, a ruling non-indigenous minority has grappled with how to include the indigenous majority in its governing structures. Such incorporation was slow, but the staging of indigenous music as Bolivian national music, as something near and dear to the nationalist frame, began in the first half of the twentieth century. While Bolivians have become proud of indigenous sounds as represented on stage, ongoing racism in institutional structures and everyday interactions has continued to mark a distance, whether those interactions occur when people pass in the street or if they occur in relation to organizing around specific demands.

What follows is a summarized sociocultural genealogy of "the indian in Bolivia"—the nationalist prism that features polemics of both imagined indians and indigenous subjects facing real resource dilemmas. Both configurations of indigeneity matter in an ethnographic understanding of how Bolivians and Japanese could express these narratives of intimate distance—the imagined indian because of its reiteration in these expressions of connectedness, and the materially grounded indigenous subjects because of their conspicuous absence in these conversations. The intimate distance formed within the Bolivian nationalist project has roots in Spanish colonialism, scientific racism, liberalism, and neoliberal multiculturalism.

If "indian" was a bureaucratic category of the Spanish colonial administration, independence did not bring an end to this rubric because the new states' coffers depended on the "indigenous contribution."[43] Though the Bolivian republic was formed in 1825, indians would not become enfranchised citizens until the mid-twentieth-century national revolution. However, in the late nineteenth and early twentieth centuries, scientific racism entered intellectual circles. As Nancy Leys Stepan has argued, Latin American intellectuals turned to European scientific influences as a way to modernize their countries, thus assuming a supposedly progressive stance by harnessing the promises of science as they also took on the fashionable European science of the moment: eugenics.[44] As Peter Wade suggests, Latin American elites, in some cases, had to adapt European ideas of eugenics and racial heredity to contexts where majorities were formed by mestizo, indian, and black populations; in some cases, racial determinism of European theories was substituted by campaigns about social hygiene and health.[45]

Under the influence of European ideas of scientific racism, Bolivian intellectuals debated the "problem of the indian," but they did so within specific social and historical configurations. Following the Federalist War of 1898–99, non-indians or creoles became particularly fearful of what they perceived as "race war." In this conflict, liberal elites who fought against a Chuquisaca-focused centralism entered alliances with Aymara communities. But in Mohoza, indians attacked their own creole allies because of local abuses by soldiers. The liberal General Pando then described the subsequent massacre in terms of a "race war," making this the official language that categorized the event. Historians, however, have shown how this conflict was really about indigenous self-government and ongoing conflicts over land, labor, and power in Aymara communities.[46] Key here is the collision of interpretations. While elites saw the cloud of race war, indians were organizing against the increasing usurpation of their lands, a problem that became more acute at the end of the nineteenth century. Parallel to the elites' fretting over the supposed threats of race war, indians were organizing through selected leaders (*caciques apoderados*) who would make legal land claims, sometimes going back as far as the colonial period to trace descent from indigenous leaders.[47]

Meanwhile intellectual elites framed the indian question in terms of the advantages and disadvantages of mestizaje for the Bolivian nation. In her study of several intellectuals writing between 1900 and 1910, Brooke Larson shows the development of an anti-mestizaje discourse, partially drawn from European ideas of race science, in which indians were not to disappear or become white but rather be kept separate and in their rural place.[48] The ideology of mestizaje, however, moved from being the root of Bolivia's problems to being the core of a nationalist project. The transformation of these ideologies began in education policies, involved discourses of hygienic practices, and was set next to momentous events like the Indigenous Congress of 1945 and the peasant uprisings of 1947.[49] In 1952, when mestizaje became articulated as the national project that would incorporate the indian, those known as "indians" became nominally "peasants," configured as a rural working class whose economic problems represented the principal contradiction to be addressed. While the state attempted to substitute the language of class for the language of race and ethnicity, racism did not disappear from the Bolivian map. The Agrarian Reform of 1953 may have been welcomed by some "peasants," but other indigenous groups read it as a direct threat to their ways of managing land, collective practices that reflected a specific ethnic identification, and that contradicted the prevailing politics of liberalism.[50] Next to but disconnected from these grounded indigenous politics about resource distribution and management, indigeneity entered nationalist symbolics. Staged and artistic representations of indigeneity became central to Bolivia's nationalist project at the same time as citizenship models, under the guise of liberal mestizaje, purported to erase indigenous differences.

Racism has flowed all too easily into the contemporary moment, in spite of, or some might say because of, other late twentieth-century reforms. In the 1990s, official mestizaje was replaced by official multiculturalism, but such politics have been viewed suspiciously by indigenous groups.[51] From the perspective of some indigenous peoples, neoliberal multiculturalism ends up looking not all that different from liberal mestizaje, as both seem to reinforce the power of non-indigenous elites. Bolivian "state-sponsored multiculturalism" led to a politics of recognition without a politics of redistribution.[52] Just as liberal mestizaje was viewed by many indigenous communities as a threat to their ethnic identity, neoliberal multiculturalism has been interpreted as one more attempt to celebrate indigenous difference without taking seriously indigenous people as political actors. Here, one might point to similarities with those who have argued that a politics of ethnicity that pretends to supplant race only ignores the persistence of racism.[53]

In the twenty-first century blatant racism has reared its head precisely as social movements and an elected indigenous president began to challenge the more institutionalized discrimination enshrined in state and constitutional structures. At the same time, according to the census of 2001, more people are identifying themselves as indigenous, leading some scholars to ask if the current moment has marked a nationalist shift away from mestizaje and toward indigeneity.[54] Felipe Quispe ("El Mallku")—an indigenous leader who vied for power in competition with Evo Morales— has made statements that hark back to Aymara firstness and recall the uprisings of the 1780s: "*Q'aras* (whites) who think with foreign heads must be Indianized"; Indians need to "unthink" mestizo ways;[55] and "If you quartered Tupaj Katari with four horses, you can quarter me with four tanks or four airplanes."[56] Quispe's political momentum, shaped around issues of land, water, and coca eradication policies, coalesced as a political party called the Movimiento Indígena Pachakuti (Indigenous Movement Pachakuti or MIP). In the face of Quispe's "radical indianismo," in 2000 Evo Morales began to emphasize his indigenous roots.[57]

Within the Morales presidency, the struggle over resource issues has been expressed through both regionalisms and racism. The special election of 2005 that brought Morales to the presidency was prefaced by the popular demands to renegotiate Bolivia's contracts that structure foreign extraction of its hydrocarbon resources, and to call a constituent assembly to rewrite Bolivia's constitution. These demands emerged through social movement politics of the Water War of 2000 and the October uprising of 2003 that ousted President Gonzalo Sánchez de Lozada. President Morales moved forward on these two popular agenda items, but not without opposition. The resource-rich eastern departments of the country formed a coalition called Media Luna (Half Moon; these departments form a half-moon on the eastern side of the Bolivian map) and have called for greater autonomy of their departments in relation to the control over these resources.[58] The power center of this movement is located in Santa Cruz, among wealthier non-indigenous business elites. Within this conflict of regionalism and resources, racist epithets were hurled at Bolivia's first indigenous president. Bolivians who opposed Morales blamed *him* for stirring up this racist hatred. Supporters point out that such racism has been there all along. Precisely as Morales's government challenged the structured racism of the Bolivian state, attempting to move forward with a Constituent Assembly and the renegotiation of resource contracts that would economically benefit the majority of Bolivians, racism and regionalism took center stage in Bolivian political discourse.

In summary, conceptualizations of difference in Bolivia have been shaped by the administrative colonial category of "indian," by the influences of nineteenth-century scientific racism as reframed in terms of education and hygiene, and by twentieth-century Latin Americanist nationalist frames that included mestizaje and multiculturalism as ongoing nationalist debates. In general, Latin American nationalisms are characterized by "recognized processes of 'race' mixture,"[59] and debates about racial and cultural mestizaje have been central to Bolivian national imaginings.[60] The management of racially inscribed indigeneity has been foundational to Bolivia's national projects, and such inscriptions have drawn on and modified European conceptualizations of race. One might wonder what the colonial period or even the early twentieth century has to do with race in Bolivia today, but these configurations continue to shape the contemporary political encounters about resources and the economic well-being of a country's majority. As already noted, these contemporary political themes ran a parallel course to the work of this ethnography; few Bolivian musicians or Japanese sojourners raised the contemporary political issues that very much highlighted the importance of indigenous politics. When Bolivian musicians identify with the Japanese through an imagined prehistoric indigenous ancestor, but do not necessarily identify with contemporary indigenous actors of Bolivia, this move of both intimacy and distance is made through the complicated historical hubris of race and indigeneity. An intimate distance places indigenous expressions, particularly musical ones, at the core of national pride; but shared national pride in indigenous expressions hardly budges the entrenched racial hierarchies that produce racist epithets for an indigenous president.

Race in the Japanese National Project

Japan's contemporary imaginings of a homogeneous national community stand in stark contrast with the Bolivian frame. Japan's supposed homogeneity is a *narrative* with its own historical trajectory as developed through Western influences related to Orientalism, scientific racism, social Darwinism, and the country's own experiences as an imperial power. Japanese enthusiasts of Andean music who believed they shared with Bolivians an ancient indigenous ancestor made no such connections to those who are presented as Japan's indigenous subjects—the Ainu. For the Japanese musicians I interviewed, the Ainu did not figure in the nationalist dynamic of intimate distance in the same way that Bolivia's indigenous people do within their corresponding national narrative. Below, I will say more about the case of the Ainu. In its history of race thinking, Japan shares with Bolivia certain historical influences, but these lead to quite different articulations of intimate distance, where the indigenous ancestor with whom one claims intimacy is usually safely beyond the nation's borders and outside specific histories.

When officials of the Meiji state embarked on a nation-building project, seeking to position Japan as a modern country, scientific inquiry was part of that modern garb as the state sent people to other countries and invited foreign scholars to Japan. Like the Bolivian and Latin American marriage of science and nation, this late nineteenth-century project brought scientific racism and eugenics into Japanese contemplations of nationhood. Through Japan's new international ties, they learned of Herbert Spencer,[61] and by the early twentieth century, around thirty translations of his work on social evolution circulated in Japan.[62] The anthropologist Jennifer Robertson has referred to this period of scholarship and nation building as "eugenic modernity"; science was used to build the nation and to constitute its national subjects.[63]

Debates for and against racial purity raged in Japan, not completely unlike the parallel debates in Bolivia about mestizaje. With concerns about the ties of race and power, one Meiji politician is said to have written Spencer, asking his advice about whether or not Japanese should be encouraged to intermarry with Europeans; Spencer is said to have advised against it.[64] While Bolivian mestizaje, by the mid-twentieth century, was given a positive spin within nation building, "racial purity" was increasingly emphasized in Japan during the 1930s.[65] Japanese anthropologists participated in scientific racism's rubric as they engaged in major projects that measured and compared skulls, facial features, and blood types.[66] In these ways, the forging of science and race was central to Japanese nation building.

As Japanese officials were drawn into the scientific discourses of the time—eugenics and social Darwinism—the country also embarked on imperial journeys that posed other challenges for a national project where racial purity and modernity supposedly went together. How would the Japanese position themselves in relation to other Asian nations and in relation to newly colonized subjects? First, Japan's historiographers had to find an identity for Japan other than that of being the West's backward Orient. As the historian Stefan Tanaka argues, Japanese historians adopted and transformed European Orientalism with their own unique twist: China became Japan's Orient, thus giving Japan a past and leaving China as a place stuck back there.[67] In its imperial projects, the Japanese state paradoxically brought diverse peoples under the emperor-system ideology in which the emperor posed as the metaphorical father of a family of national subjects.[68] Assimilation thus became the goal in relation to ethnic Others like the Okinawans and the Ainu.

The Ainu pose a case in point for a discussion of race, indigeneity, and the nation, and are significant to this project because these contemporary Japanese indigenous subjects, like those in Bolivia, remain key to nationalist imaginaries, but are surprisingly absent from the indigenous ancestor claims in these interviews. The Ainu of northern Japan are often narrativized as the geographically marginal internal Other, the aboriginal native against which Japanese-ness became articulated.[69] With the colonization of Hokkaido in 1869 and the incorporation of the Ainu into this imperial system, "Ainu studies" proliferated in which concepts like "survival of the fittest" were fully incorporated into assimilationist politics.[70] The Ainu supposedly lived by hunting, fishing, and gathering, and in this way they went against the grain of agrarian myths that located Japanese identity in relation to the agricultural production of rice.[71] But David Howell's work on the Ainu dispels the myth of their supposed isolation from trade and wage labor, and he points out the Catch-22 of state policies that only recognized those who had remained in Ainu communities.[72] The Hokkaido Former Aborigine Protection Act (in effect from 1899 to 1997) was supposed to provide agricultural land to the Ainu and encourage them to become agriculturalists, but it did not recognize the diverse activities in which they were already active.[73] Today, the Ainu still represent metaphorically Japan's internal exotic Other, but within the overarching ideology of Japanese homogeneity, a narrative that developed after World War II.[74]

Drawing on the metaphorical associations of "Japanese blood," the post–World War II Japanese state upheld an ideology of a homogeneous national community in which multiethnic categories were avoided and cultural differences were classified through the problematic Japanese-foreigner dichotomy.[75] In a provocatively titled book, *Multiethnic Japan*, John Lie debunks Japan's contemporary myth of homogeneity while also giving the myth's origins historical depth. At the beginning of the twentieth century, when Japan had embarked on its imperial project in Asia, its ideology was necessarily multiethnic; only after World War II, within Japan's quest for a postwar identity, and at the beginning of the country's economic prosperity did monoethnic nationalism emerge.[76] Next to Lie's re-reading of the homogeneity narrative, discussions of Japan's pre-war concern with racial purity point to the ambiguities of these different projects, as an imperial Japan and then a postwar Japan tried to squeeze into the camel hair suit of nationalism.[77]

A postwar nationalism thus drew on a myth of Japan as a nation that was isolated because of its geographic positioning on islands—another myth Lie dislodges by carefully looking at history.[78] With Japan construed as an isolated homogeneous island nation, race thinking took on a particular expression through *nihonjin ron* (discussions of the Japanese). The discourse of nihonjin ron establishes a "proprietary relationship between race and culture."[79] Kosaku Yoshino warns, however, against reading Japanese race thinking as genetic determinism; Japanese imagine themselves as possessing specific cultural elements that mark them as unique.[80] The discourse of nihonjin ron also assumes that the Japanese people form a homogeneous racial community that possesses an unchanging essence.[81]

Many scholars have pointed out the contradictions between official adherence to the narrative of homogeneity and the country's multicultural realities.[82] Foreign Japanese returnees and foreign workers in Japan are putting stress on the imagined seams of homogeneity.[83] Next to and in association with this strong national ideology, Japanese producers and consumers express strong desires to internationalize.[84] In finding a connection to an imagined Andean indigeneity, some Japanese enthusiasts of Bolivian music are finding an international connection that appears as an alternative to those with the United States, but one that is also safely located in the past, and that does not challenge the predominant national narrative.

The myth of Japanese racial homogeneity is not only believed by Japanese but also by others who comment about the Japanese. One Bolivian musician who toured Japan commented to me in his positive assessment of Japan, "the good thing I have noted is that they are all of one race. . . . It's not like in Bolivia where we are of different races, different regions, the *collas*, the *cambas*. . . . We are all at odds." His comment was made as regionalist tensions became more acutely felt around the issue of natural gas. These regionalist terms are heavily racialized in popular discourse. "Collas" from the highland areas are glossed as indigenous (mestizaje and mestizos aside). "Cambas" of the lowland areas, particularly Santa Cruz, from where the loudest cries for civic autonomy have emerged, are glossed as white and wealthy (lowland indigenous groups and highland indigenous migrants also aside). With his comments, the Bolivian cited here accepted as fact and even envied the idea of Japan as a homogeneous nation—as if this were a key to its relative successes.

While both Japan and Bolivia were influenced by Eurocentric projects of scientific racism, these countries' ideas on indigeneity, race, and nationalism have unfolded in distinct ways and under very different postcolonial rubrics. At the level of cultural expression, these configurations lead to distinctly motivated musical projects. The Bolivian nationalist project of intimate distance, as construed through the indian who symbolically makes the nation yet remains as a problem or embarrassment for the non-indian, is quite different from the Japanese sense of intimate distance that tends to look beyond the nation for difference. While Bolivians have stylized indigenous music into their national music, the Japanese have gained a reputation for getting deeply involved in many different musical traditions of Others—jazz, salsa, blue grass, tango, and so on.[85] Like other scholars, however, I want to steer away from the essentializing argument that the Japanese are by nature the great imitators. As Ian Condry writes in his book on hip-hop Japan, when we accept the idea that Japanese are good borrowers we essentialize a national character in order to explain transnational flows that are in fact much more complex, much more about both learning and transformation.[86] While E. Taylor Atkins recognizes as stereotypical the idea that the Japanese are great imitators, he also shows how this stereotype emerges within particular facts of the Japanese social context like the consensual value of conformity, the failure of the educational system to encourage critical thinking, and the primacy of the iemoto, or "school" system for musical learning.[87] However, in the cases of Japanese playing all these Other musical traditions, the imitation frame leaves out of the picture what these musical experiences mean to Japanese participants—the system of affect and desire, as well as the creative contributions they see themselves making.

When Bolivian and Japanese musicians of Andean folklore are asked about their mutual musical affinities, somehow the conversation shifts to discussions of a shared racial heritage. While these narratives that racialize culture have very different meanings within Japanese and Bolivian national historical trajectories, they still are imagined as points of connection and similarity. They talk about similar physical characteristics that supposedly indicate common ancestors who are located in a distant past, but who can never be named. Bolivian folklore performances in Japan foster this intimate distance between Japanese and Bolivian worlds, and the encounter hinges on musical intimacies and an imagined indigenous nexus in some unspecified moment of the past.

Relaxing to Pentatonic Scales

One Japanese Bolivian folklore musician who owns an Andean-themed restaurant in Tokyo said he liked Bolivian music because "it warms your blood and relaxes you." Bolivians were imagined as happy and their music as good for inducing relaxation. Japanese professional folklore musicians said things like: "Maybe we look to [Bolivians], well they are so happy. . . . Japanese are very nervous. We have a lot of stress." Or "Japanese who listen to Andean music say it reminds them of their childhood."[88] Another Japanese professional folklore musician referred to the common scales of Bolivian and Japanese music, stating matter-of-factly, "Japanese have a lot of stress. They relax by listening to pentatonic melodies." When Japanese pursue interests in Bolivian music, racialized cultural compatibilities are combined with exoticization and a search in the Other for what one perceives to have lost.[89] The intimate distance between Bolivians and Japanese also builds on essentializing and exoticizing ideas about the Other.

Exoticization also takes the form of admiring traditional clothes and of even donning those clothes for oneself. In describing his early days of infatuation with Andean music, one professional Japanese musician said he used to wear ponchos and abarcas (indigenous sandals made out of tire tread) around the city of La Paz. During the 1980s, this practice also was adopted among some mestizo musicians in La Paz who accompanied this daily sartorial style by letting their hair grow long. When I asked Japanese interviewees what they liked most about Bolivia and Bolivians, one fifty-seven-year-old entrepreneur and musician responded that he liked to see "indians selling ponchos in the street. They themselves wear their original clothes . . . they still maintain their culture. . . . Japan, under influences from the United States and England, has changed a lot. But in Bolivia, the people living in the countryside don't change their style." Of course all ethnographic evidence points to the contrary. So-called original clothes emerge out of over five hundred years of dynamic transcultural transformations, and Bolivian indians are far from fitting the bill of unchanging rural fixtures. The man's comment incarcerates the native, leaving indigenous people as romanticized, fixed, and unchanging.[90] Such imposed stasis also sidesteps the fact that many of the so-called natives continue to live in conditions of rural and urban poverty. It should be noted that Japanese volunteers do go to Bolivia to work in social projects. However, those who go to learn music tend to emphasize not social issues, but rather a slower-paced life they partly observe, partly imagine, and definitely admire in places like rural Bolivia.

The Japanese fascination with Bolivians is tied to both an imagined indigenous world and a nostalgia for a bucolic life where social contacts are perceived as easier to make and more meaningful, particularly when set in contrast with the fast-paced life the Japanese see themselves as forced to live in their own country. "In Bolivia it's easy to make friends. In Japan it's not like that." One Japanese enthusiast who was feeling the economic crisis in Japan told me, "I always ask myself why I like Bolivian music. I was born in Tokyo. I'm 100 percent urban. They have something I'm missing . . . something I'm always looking for. . . . I'm like a radio with a special ability to tune into Bolivian music." He went on to say, "Economically, the situation in Japan is bad. People don't have strength. Bolivians have strength. They always say they have no money, but they have strength." The "strength" of Bolivians was about a heightened sense of social connection. Said one Japanese musician who resides in Bolivia, "In Japan, it is a situation of winners and losers. Not in Bolivia. Family and friends there are very important. They have an open heart." He followed this comment by singing the praises of those who, in a Bolivian community in the countryside, extended their generous hospitality to him as a complete stranger. Throughout these comments, the Japanese I interviewed tended to associate the imagined indigenous subject with a rural context, even though indigeneity in Bolivia is about both rural and urban subjects.

From these comments emerges something like the individualist subject of modernity; at first glance this freestanding subject seems pitted against the other one that, according to Povinelli, modernity also produces—the genealogical subject who is construed as both constrained and strengthened by deep social ties.[91] Some Japanese are "free" to choose to sojourn to Bolivia for an extended period, but they admire the genealogical ties they see as providing Bolivians with another kind of intimacy beyond the intimate event of liberal love.[92] One Japanese enthusiast expressed the need to search for the lost culture of Japan: "When we lost [World War II], we started to throw away our culture. We need to find it again." He longed for those elements that Povinelli might refer to as constitutive of the genealogical subject,[93] and he seemed to critique a subjectivity formed in the postwar period. Bolivian indigenous culture provided a foreign connection, alternative to the US one that had heavily marked Japanese society. Such longing reaffirms rather than dislodges the powerful Manichean opposition between the two subjectivities that form the foundations of liberal modernity.[94]

In this case, however, the individualist subject is not simply opposing the genealogical one. Even if the Japanese may find themselves "free" to travel, their long journeys involve getting away, at least temporarily, from the other kinds of genealogical projects at home, those that draw on family metaphors to link tightly together work contexts, family obligations, and national sentiments. If Japanese flee one set of genealogical projects at home, they might be seen as choosing or adopting a different genealogy when they claim connections to a Bolivian indigenous ancestor.

As Japanese exoticized the "culture" of Bolivians, and more specifically of indigenous Bolivians, the indigenous social movements of the moment remained absent from the interviews. Not even the Japanese who had lived many years in Bolivia broached these topics during our conversations. Given the politics of the moment, the silence on this topic was remarkable. Indigeneity here, marked indexically by pentatonic melodies, was about imagined ritual, musical, and social worlds the Japanese saw themselves as having lost; but it was not about indigenous subjects marching in the streets, electing their first indigenous president, and drawing on non-liberal forms of governance for their organizing.[95]

Perfect Trash

"Please put this in bin E 29." Gironda handed a plastic bottle across the limited space of our tour bus so it could be placed in one of the few plastic bags that held refuse from our daily consumption on the road. His labeling reflected on-the-road banter about the specificity with which Japanese sorted their trash. These details seemed to stump all gaijin (foreigners) on the bus and sometimes got us in trouble when we were staying at the company's apartment in Tokyo; Hishimoto would go home to his family when we were in Tokyo, leaving us to fend for ourselves in deciphering the intricacies of Japanese trash sorting. On the road, Hishimoto would further separate the onboard trash bags' contents before placing the refuse in the appropriate bins at a rest stop. We had all taken up a mild jesting around this approach to perfect trash separation, inventing numerous lettered and numbered bins for a hyper-categorization of refuse. The joking reflected an admiration for the meticulous level of organization that nevertheless still left us bewildered. In other discussions, Bolivians would depict Japanese hyper-organization in both positive and negative lights, reflecting how stories of intimacy also have their negative edges. Systems of desire run on both attraction and repulsion.

When I asked Bolivians what they liked most about Japan and the Japanese, they responded with other exotifying narratives, and also with a replication of many myths about Japanese society. Bolivians used the following adjectives to describe positive attributes of the Japanese: organized, clean, polite, educated, meticulous, punctual, respectful, disciplined, and hard working. But these qualities were just as easily turned around and read through a negative lens. One Bolivian told me, "In Japan they work too much, as if there were no Sunday. They take those vitamins that give you strength. There is mass consumption of this." The positive aspect of the hardworking Japanese was depicted suddenly as a society-wide obsession that drives its members to addictive consumption of energy drinks. As an Andean folklore musician residing in Japan told me, "I don't want to be a clock. In Japan you can have a good job. The problem is you are going to be a slave. This would be something like the paradise of modern slavery." He also mentioned Japan's high suicide rates and said he didn't want his daughter "to marry someone who goes to work at 7:00 a.m. and comes home at 11:00 p.m." The hardworking Japanese subjects were framed as slaves of the modern system; they did not simply have jobs, but rather they were married to them. The attention given to meticulous work and the concern with perfection easily took a negative spin, as Bolivians described Japanese as "obsessed with perfection," "unable to improvise," and "lacking in inspiration."

Asking Japanese and Bolivians about likes and dislikes with respect to the other's culture opens the door to essentializing responses like those noted here. I should emphasize that most comments about their respective Others were overwhelmingly positive. However, these comments, as recorded in interviews, were also reflected in the day-to-day conversations and practices that emerged during the tour. Bolivians admired our sound engineer's drive to perfection as he took full responsibility for our amplified sound. "If only we had sound engineers like that in Bolivia!" I heard Bolivians comment on more than one occasion. But perfection as a goal also had its limits. Bolivians told stories of previous tours in which a manager made a Japanese tour member cry because a curtain was not raised exactly as scheduled, to the minute and second. On the tour in which I participated, we had a stage mishap at one point; but the postmortem comments by Bolivians included boasting about their own improvisational skills that had facilitated their navigation of these rough performance waters and comments about how the Japanese lacked these comparable skills: "If something goes wrong, [the Japanese] just don't know what to do." Though all of these comments are essentializing, these are the kinds of arguments that are made as musicians articulate an intimate distance with a Japanese Other.

Japanese admired Bolivians for being happy, but even such happiness turned sour at times. "Bolivians joke around too much," said one Japanese Bolivian folklore musician. "They make you stay up all night and drink," complained a Japanese musician I interviewed in La Paz. If the Japanese turn to Bolivian music for relaxation, they also mention that "Bolivians are always late" and "things are so slow in Bolivia." Time of arrival—punctual or late—was one of the key points of difference mentioned by Japanese and Bolivians, even as the Bolivians on tour in Japan proved in their daily work that they could indeed be just as punctual as the Japanese, and even as the Japanese seemed to long for a looser grip of the clock. Suddenly, a relaxing tempo of life was transformed into the tediousness of waiting for those who always arrive late. If Bolivians and Japanese used racialized narratives to mark intimacy around the performance of Bolivian folklore music, they also found many points of distance—looking through both positive and negative lenses to see themselves as very different from each other.

Stuck with Nationalism

While I began by suggesting that the Japanese-Bolivian intimacy breaks out of the usual Western to non-Western frameworks of exotification, I have also detailed how this nexus is shaped by global flows of Andean music and race thinking that are very much mediated through Western ideas. However, meaning is still articulated locally. A Japanese claim to genealogical intimacy with Bolivian indigeneity seems to project into a past; it looks like an expression of nostalgia for what Japanese perceive as having lost in modernity. The Bolivian claim to genealogical intimacy with the Japanese seems to project a future hope. Bolivian musicians placed great hope and promise in the idea that Japan was at once "modern" *and* connected to "ancient traditions," and they consistently held up Japan as exemplary in this regard—unlike, say, the United States. While Bolivians saw themselves aspiring to Japan's example of an alternative modernity in which modernization did not mean the erasure of ancient traditions,[96] Japanese seemed more uncertain of their own country's path. While the narrative of shared genealogy is doing different symbolic work for the Bolivians and Japanese, I would suggest that they are motivated by a common desire to distinguish self-other relations that fall outside the ongoing implicit location of many such positionings relative to the United States. Perhaps what deserves more attention is the Bolivian musicians' tendency to hold on to both the representation of an indigenous world, imagined to be rooted in the past, and the promise of a future as exemplified in their perceptions of Japanese modernity.

However, these narratives do not challenge or move outside Bolivia's or Japan's respective nationalisms—structures that seem forever tied to race thinking. Nationalisms are built on the myth of one people, one territory, one nation,[97] but of course all nations end up fudging this myth. They just do it in distinct ways. Japanese and Bolivian nationalisms have dealt differently with internal alterity. However, both countries faced the classic paradox of bringing multiethnicity under a single uniform nationalist framework, and race thinking, in varied forms, has been central to the construction of these projects. Bolivian nationalism depends on an intimately distant framing of indigenous peoples within the nation, whereas Japanese nationalism depends on intimately distant transnational connections. These nationalisms emerged from distinct colonial histories, but were both influenced by race thinking that emerged through European colonial endeavors to organize difference, and more specifically through the nineteenth-century interpretations of scientific racism.

Throughout this book, I have suggested that nationalism haunts the ethnographic work in this nexus of transnational music performance. These hauntings are not so much about the expected moments of national identification—the musical performance of a nationality—but rather the moments when the flag of nationalist ideology whips back in the wind and hits us in the face. If this chapter highlighted how race thinking is both foundational to nationalist projects of modernity, and reworked in transnational connections, my next chapter turns to nationalist hauntings that put in sharp relief the methodological issues I faced as a gringa conducting fieldwork between Bolivia and Japan.

6 Gringa in Japan

During three months of touring, we performed primarily in public schools and moved daily throughout the islands, going from the northernmost, Hokkaido, all the way to the southernmost, Okinawa. A small bus became our principal off-stage place of interaction—a moving capsule in which we were all rather captive and in each others' presence for three to six hours a day. Our instruments, costumes, and sound equipment fit in the large storage area of the back, while we fit into exactly nine passenger seats of the front—five Bolivian musicians, Hishimoto, a US musician (myself), a Japanese manager, and a Japanese sound engineer. At the beginning of the tour, conversations were boisterous and jovial, but as the daily monotony of repetitive performance work set in, we all sought our own escapes. Mine included a regimen of studying Japanese-language books and tapes for two hours, followed by a measured reading of a Murakami novel that I would try to make last until our next visit to Tokyo where I would shop again in the English-language section of the Shinjuku Kinokuniya Bookstore. The Bolivians did more music listening than reading. The Spanish-language section of Kinokuniya was very limited, and Bolivians had to pace their reading of the one or two books they brought with them from home. Japanese-to-Spanish language guides were difficult to find, making it less likely that Bolivians would attempt their own Japanese-language study on the bus. For a time, I was asked to create informal English-language study sessions, a plan that lasted the first few weeks, but then dwindled, in part due to my own limited abilities to improvise on-the-spot classes for language teaching. My captive students quickly lost interest. As one of them bluntly told me, "The problem is you don't have a method."

As we settled into our routines, or lack of them, this moving vehicle became a site of my fieldwork and the context of a particularly eye-opening conversation that made me reflect on the nature of doing fieldwork across areas—between Bolivia and Japan, between Latin America and East Asia. The phrase "gringa in Japan" is used to emphasize the methodological angle here, one that shook up my own ethnographic position with which I had become too comfortable. A gringa identity, like all identities, is relational; and as Diane Nelson has argued, it is constructed through movement; a US white woman must travel to Latin America before she becomes a "gringa."[1] The term may be inflicted as an insult as easily as it is rendered a term of endearment. Context is everything. I was sometimes called "the gringa who plays with Música de Maestros," although now some three different women might fit that description in relation to this ensemble. But at other moments, I have quaked in fear when identified through this term. On one of my trips in the Bolivian countryside, the bus on which I traveled had multiple flat tires. When the driver began to change the third tire, other passengers began to whisper to each other that the gringa had brought them this bad luck. When I am in the Bolivian context, "gringa" is an identity placed upon me by others. By taking that identity to Japan, I want to emphasize the ethnographic relations I brought to Japan—ones that were more about a knowledge of Bolivia, Latin America, and the Spanish language than about any equivalent knowledge of Japan.

While this unevenness of preparation can be seen as disadvantageous for my ethnographic interpretations, I instead propose that such variability is a prevalent yet untheorized aspect of multi-sited global ethnography, something that might be shoved under the rug because it reveals shortcomings next to time honored ethnographic traditions like learning the language of one's research context. Alternatively, such disparities of preparation might be dismissed as irrelevant because to pay it any attention at all would be to give too much credit to area studies formations that have come under attack.

In brief summary, "area studies" became central to the US academic context during the Cold War.[2] In 1958, the federal government began funding university area studies programs through the National Defense Education Act and Title VI grants. On one hand, area studies were championed as a metageography that avoided the dual East-West or Europe-Asia frameworks.[3] On the other hand, area studies were critiqued on several points. They did the informational work of US Cold War politics, leaving scholars in an ambivalent position in relation to the political implications of their research. Additionally, North America and Europe were left unmarked as areas. With this omission, Europe and the United States hovered above the empirical ground of proper geographic areas, but they were perceived as centers of disciplinary organization and theoretical production. Hypotheses that emerged from these unmarked centers were tested in the periphery. Theory was seen as coming from the geopolitical core, while those working on the geopolitical margins were thought to be forever stuck in messy empirical work. Scholars within some area studies became so parochial in their work that they had difficulty communicating with people who worked in the disciplines, let alone with those who worked in another area.[4] Some of these critiques became more clearly expressed as the Cold War ended and US academic institutions began searching for another metageography of a world in which "globalization" had become the operative term. In the late 1990s, the Ford Foundation funded projects on rethinking area studies, and many institutions shifted to academic rubrics of "international" or "global" studies.

I was trained as a Latin Americanist, and I am not so quick to shed this academic location under the current intellectual fashion. Therefore, I am acutely aware of what I must have missed in my understanding of the Japanese context. However, I suggest that many ethnographic insights emerge in this project precisely at the intersections of these unequal preparations—in what I call inter-area ethnography. Here are two proposed tenets of inter-area ethnography: First, the researcher recognizes rather than dismisses the unevenness in her own area expertise, and sees this as inevitable within multi-sited global ethnography. Here I am not dismissing area studies, but calling for the explicit and critical discussion of such training as a point of one's ethnographic location. Second, the ethnographic encounter, usually implicitly formulated in a dual self-other frame, becomes more clearly visible in triangular terms. Multiple others have always been present in ethnography, though perhaps not always accounted for as such. Inter-area ethnography foregrounds the multiplicity of Others and brings one's attention to the ways Others Other. I found it necessary to think in this ethnography through a triangular articulation between Bolivian musicians, Japanese enthusiasts of Andean music, and myself—a constellation of relations that turned out to be quite heavily weighted in nationalist sentiments and racialized undercurrents. Let me turn to the incident that precipitated my thinking on this methodological point, the first ethnographic puzzle that led to the interpretations of this book.

Alone on the Bus

On one of those rare days when we had no performances and simply had to arrive at the place of the next day's performance, we took time to stop at the Hiroshima Peace Memorial Park. The first part of the exhibit displayed details about Japan's pre–World War II imperialism. At one point, the Japanese sound engineer pointed to the part of the exhibit about the Nanjing massacre and said to me indignantly: "That is a lie."

When we were once again all captive on the bus, I asked him what he meant by that comment. He answered with a tale of being taught these things in school—being taught to hate his country through the stories of what Japan did as an imperial power. During his adolescence he wanted to leave Japan for the United States, a country he greatly admired at the time. He said that after he graduated from high school, he read other things and came to like his country, to like the fact that he was Japanese, and to like Japanese ways. He said he read things that retold Japanese history without what he saw as the exaggeration of his official schooling. Japan's curriculum, he insisted, was driven by the dictates of post–World War II US occupation. The Bolivian band members on the bus chimed in with what became an all-out anti-American sentiment that started with the heavy symbolic load of Hiroshima and then ran through a chain of associations based on elements of both Japanese and Bolivian nationalisms. The exchange left me unsettled, not only because of the denial of Japan's imperial past but also because I felt myself occupying an ethnographic space that was relatively new to me.

The sound engineer's interpretation of his own schooling intersected with ongoing textbook controversies. The Education Ministry was criticized in 1982 for euphemizing textbook descriptions of Japan's imperial past.[5] In 1991, Shintaro Ishihara, a member of the conservative Liberal Democratic Party, authored The Japan That Can Say No, a book that rejected Western liberal values, championed a distinct Asian model of capitalism that could challenge Western domination, and was read on the other side of the Pacific as "America bashing."[6] Many perspectives I heard from the sound engineer were similar to those in Ishihara's tome.[7] Besides calling for Japan to stand up to the United States and recognize the racism with which the latter has treated the former, Ishihara, along with others, questioned the official figures of the Chinese government in relation to the Nanjing massacre.[8] Our tour in 2002 also followed closely on the heels of the political furor over a textbook debate. In 2001, the Society for the Creation of a New History proposed a textbook that the Education Ministry approved for use in eighth grade social studies classes. Only three of the country's local textbook boards approved its possible classroom use, however, because this controversial edition toned down Japan's role in the war.[9] The sound engineer's comments might be read within the context of these shifting nationalist positionings, as Japan has searched for its footing in the crisis that followed the bursting of the economic bubble. I never saw Bolivians demonstrate awareness of these textbook controversies, even if they were quite aware of the Japanese economic downturn. How did the Bolivians come to identify with the Japanese sound engineer's position?

The Japanese sound engineer spoke better English than Spanish, so I had initiated the above-mentioned conversation in the English language. We quickly entered troubled waters, however, and I turned to Hishimoto for translation between Japanese and Spanish. Hishimoto did not speak English, so our language of exchange was always Spanish. When he began translating between the sound engineer's Japanese and my Spanish, the Bolivians began to follow the debate and express their own opinions on the topic.

The interlude on the bus contained multiple reflexivities: the Japanese reflected on interpretations of their national history; the Bolivians reflected on Japan's position in the world and in comparative view with their own national experiences; and I reflected on what my position might have to do with this moment of collective denial of Japan's imperial history. Rather than dismissing this denial, perhaps chalking it up to Bolivians' lack of education about the Japanese context, I chose to grapple with this moment as a conglomeration of concerns, all of which eventually became central to the interpretations in this ethnography. Anthropologists have been reflexive for some time now but, as Ilana Gershon argues, so are our informants; rather than distrusting these secondary explanations, as Franz Boas did, she insists on engaging with Others' reflexivity and doing so with an awareness of "how different contexts engender different kinds of reflexivity."[10]

The Bolivians immediately identified with the Japanese position of victim in relation to the United States. As our singer and charango player told me, "Remember that Japan did not just lose the war, they were also occupied by the victorious power. . . . Of course the US government is going to portray Japanese history in a light that is most complimentary to its own position. Of course they would present Japan as a ruthless imperial force." He based his argument on a shared empathy with the Japanese position of being under the thumb of the United States. For him it was completely logical that the United States had manufactured ways of knowing—just as they do for issues of coca production in Bolivia, for example. Contemporary Bolivian governments consistently have been squeezed between US pressures for eradication of coca plants and the small-scale Bolivian coca growers who have found a crop that provides an income, and who claim coca chewing as a millenarian tradition of the Andes. The United States has a history of wielding its influence in Bolivia by linking aid packages to Bolivian governments' willingness to accept US drug enforcement policies.[11]

While I side with the outcries against this form of US imperialism in a Latin American context, I was rather perplexed by the parallel lines that band members seemed to draw between this anti-imperialist stance and the stance that would deny Japanese responsibility in Nanjing. My undone-ness in hearing these remarks resembled Benedict Anderson's feeling of vertigo in 1963 when he heard Indonesia's president, a man who considered himself on the political left, extol the virtues of Adolf Hitler as a nationalist. While Anderson did not know how to name this feeling at the time, he later called it "the spectre of comparisons." With this phrase, Anderson evokes a kind of dizzying double vision on a subject that once was viewed from a single angle, a vision gained from new experiences that make it impossible to view the world again in any "just so" way.[12]

My position as a US citizen at the Hiroshima Peace Memorial elicited a Japanese and Bolivian comparison of nationalisms, as crafted through being on the receiving end of US policies. A view through the lens of Latin American studies might emphasize an anticolonial nationalism, specifically in response to US policies and presence. But an anticolonial stance in Bolivia that might produce solidarity or a politics of engagement had a different significance in Japan. In the inter-area moment I described, anticolonial nationalism—certainly a staple of Latin American studies rubrics—merged with the East-West dichotomy—a staple of Asian studies. Anthropology has long been a comparative enterprise, and it also has a long history of complicity with imperial projects. But graduate students of the 1980s and 1990s, intellectually raised within anthropology's critique,[13] still saw anthropology as the discipline most concerned with "a global society's dispossessed minorities."[14] Anthropology's comparative project has been somewhat up for grabs within the discipline,[15] but our informants have not stopped making their own comparisons. While I easily empathized with an anti-imperial Bolivian nationalism, I found myself quite alone on the bus when I expressed my disagreement with a comparative Japanese nationalism that used a similar narrative of victimhood in order to erase Japanese imperial history.

Any attempt I made to voice a more critical view of Japan's imperial past brought me, in the eyes of the Bolivians and Japanese, into line with a propaganda campaign of my own government in its role of occupying power. The timing of this music tour coincided with the Bush administration's initial bullying push to war in Iraq. The Bolivians and Japanese on the tour read these events as a continuation of US dictates of power, whether it was to establish peace after World War II, to eradicate coca in a War on Drugs, or to search and destroy imagined weapons of mass destruction. As I opposed the Japanese nationalist sentiments expressed on the bus, I was quickly pegged as a quintessential US patriotic citizen, even though at other moments I expressed my views against the war in Iraq, against Bush's cowboy approach to world politics, and against the imperial projects of the United States.

As a general category, gringas can stand symbolically for the imperialism of their country. They may be accused of child snatching, of fat sucking, or simply of being the bearer of bad luck flat tires.[16] In my previous ethnographic work, however, I had never faced such a forced association with the politics of my government. More often people went out of their way to distinguish between the US *government* and the people from that country. The oblique and triangular configuration of this inter-area research produced different fieldwork interactions, ones that explicitly profiled nationalist associations and more implicitly underscored globally racialized positions.

If I had been able to speak Japanese, the Bolivians never would have entered the conversation, and I probably would not have experienced the discomfort that led me to reflect on what it means to be gringa in Japan. Such serendipitous circumstances of fieldwork nourish anthropological reflections and call for another look at language in ethnographic and area studies projects. Our exchange that day involved more than a translation of languages. It involved a translation of nationalisms that called my attention to area studies frameworks and disciplinary expectations.

Transnational Ethnographic Orders

This story rallies nationalist ghosts, but it also plays with the spirits of ethnographic practice. In this project, I messed with some hallowed traditions of ethnographic work, although I am certainly not the first person to do so. Since Malinowski's early twentieth-century fieldwork, British and American anthropological traditions have been anchored in the concepts of long-term fieldwork, residence with "the natives," and study of the natives' language.[17] With a strong background in Latin American studies, fluency in Spanish, courses in the Quechua language, and previous fieldwork in Peru and Bolivia, I certainly brought the right credentials to be working with Bolivian musicians. In contrast, my training in the Japanese language was only slightly beyond point zero, minimal progress that reflected my limited study on the bus. With both Bolivians and Japanese, I used Spanish as my principal language of fieldwork. In some cases my lack of Japanese-language skills obviously hampered my communication with Japanese who participate in the Bolivian music scene. My involvement in the three-month music tour was followed by brief return trips to Japan and Bolivia to conduct interviews, mostly with individuals and occasionally with groups. In the interviewing process, I spoke with forty-seven Japanese, forty-six Bolivians, and one Argentine. While one interview was conducted in English, most others were completed directly in Spanish, and occasionally through a Spanish translator the Japanese interviewees appointed.

One might ask: what anthropologist does fieldwork without learning the language of "the natives"? Traditionally, ethnographers aim for an "active understanding" of a fieldsite language.[18] My "fieldsites" in this case were on the road in Japan with a Bolivian band, in the labors of transnational cultural performances, and in the system of desire between Bolivian musicians and Japanese Andean music enthusiasts. Through translations from Japanese to Spanish this disturbing conversation ensued, and in my order of ethnographic unpacking, it became one of the first stories I tried to understand. Ultimately, it referenced what would become key themes in this book: critiques of nationalisms, a decentering of the East-West axis of exoticism, and a transnational ingroup identification that drew on victimhood shaped within race thinking and nationalisms. While I do not want to discard the importance of language training for ethnographic work, it is worth considering the language limits anthropologists encounter in global and multi-sited work and balancing these with different ethnographic insights that emerge precisely because of these limits.

While attempting to maintain the depth that accompanies the ethnographic practice, anthropologists have grappled already with the necessities and implications of doing multi-sited research.[19] The multi-sited wave has brought entire revisions of what are considered as places or sites of fieldwork.[20] Even as this apparent shift in methodology grants an ethnographic view of translocal processes, ethnographers have come to rather frank admissions about a loss of depth in this process.[21] I have already suggested elsewhere that I suspect anthropologists have been "moving through places" more than is allowed through the Malinowskian imagining of fieldwork.[22] The difference today is that these movements have become central to the very telling of the ethnographic tale. As James Clifford has suggested, if dwelling has been the dominant metaphor for ethnographic work—that is dwelling of both ethnographic subjects and anthropologists—one might want to balance that focus with more attention to its metaphoric pair: traveling.[23] Within this ethnography, travel— of Andean music, Japanese sojourners, Bolivian musicians, and a gringa anthropologist—has been the dominant metaphor, eclipsing any concept of extended dwelling.

The conversation on the bus catapulted me out of an intellectual comfort zone as shaped through years of working in Latin American studies, years of thinking about those who were on the receiving end, rather than instigators, of imperial projects. Japan specialists might have been quite familiar with the issues of downplaying imperial histories. As the historian of Japan Carol Gluck suggested, with reference to Hiroshima and Nagasaki, the Japanese "turned atomic memory into imperial denial."[24] For me, however, the bus incident required an overhaul of my ethnographic location.

Akhil Gupta and James Ferguson, with their concept of "location-work," suggest that anthropological knowledge is less about geographic place and more about political location.[25] Through a critique of area studies, it might also be claimed that anthropological projects in geographic places are already about political locations. Donna Haraway insisted on the political location of all knowledge production as she also warned against the possible problems of "innocent 'identity' politics."[26] These issues might be framed in terms of how much we are able to identify with the subjects of our ethnographic research. While ethnographers may use identification as a strategy of fieldwork, Joshua Roth reminds us of the importance of knowing this strategy's limits.[27] In my fieldwork between Bolivia and Japan, I encountered these limits in no uncertain terms.

Building on Gupta and Ferguson's concept of location-work, Karen Kelsky develops the idea that ethnographers are constantly having to field different agendas; as she states: "I propose that what location-work is to anthropology, fielding, a verb, is to ethnography, especially ethnographies of desire, imagination, and mutual imbrication, when the field travels with the ethnographer and is mediated by his or her work, speech, presence, and praxis."[28] In my work, inter-area ethnography involved fielding agendas of three different nationalist histories that informed what it meant to perform on stage in indigenous dress. I fielded other agendas too, like the demands of performing music and the different racialized implications of being a foreigner in Japan. My unmentioned whiteness was a backdrop to the connections Japanese and Bolivians drew through imagined shared indigenous ancestors. Their narratives worked along an East-West axis and implicitly placed me, the gringa who plays Bolivian music, on the other side, with the West. Imagined indigeneity afforded the Bolivians and Japanese common access to a category of the non-West. The fielding of agendas in this inter-area ethnography has led to different insights, not in spite of, but because of the uneven-ness of my own area-related training. The Hiroshima-Nanjing ethnographic incident surprised me. When anthropologists face ethnographic surprises, Marilyn Strathern suggests that "we need to go precisely where we have already been, back to the immediate here and now of which we have created our present knowledge of the world."[29] For me, that meant going back to my own formations as a gringa and as a Latin Americanist.

Becoming Gringa

Gringas get excited about exotic things. They catch what Nelson termed "*típica* fever" and want to buy everything that looks indigenous.[30] Típica fever got to me as well when I took up Latin American studies as a second undergraduate major and, ironically, as a refuge from the more narrow Cold War framing of my first major, political science. Peruvian Shining Path guerrillas caught my attention; Quechua fulfilled my second language requirement after Spanish; and a year of my undergraduate work was completed in Peru. The irony here is that critiques of area studies have often depicted these knowledge production projects as uniformly representative of the US government's agenda. Area studies training, however, has produced mixed and even contradictory political agendas.[31]

My musical journey in Peru began with a desire to learn to play the violin in the Ayacuchano style. I sought to study with Máximo Damián, the violinist to whom José María Arguedas dedicated his novel *El zorro de arriba y el zorro de abajo* (*The Fox from Above and the Fox from Below*).[32] Arguedas, an anthropologist and a novelist, championed Quechua cultural expressions and lived between the white world that accepted him and the Quechua world in which he spent his childhood and in which he felt at home. During my violin lessons, where I found myself quite lost in one of my first attempts to learn music by ear, Damián would often remind me that he had played his violin at Arguedas's funeral. My quest for authentic Peruvian sounds was framed by lessons with Damián, his ties to the long-gone but much-revered Arguedas, and the fact that all this music came from Ayacucho, the supposed birthplace of Peru's Shining Path guerrillas. Eventually, the war itself would drive me away to work in Bolivia rather than Peru.

My initial entrance into Música de Maestros in Bolivia was facilitated not by my desire to pursue the authentic indigenous expression but by my classical music training. As I mentioned in a previous chapter, I was by then also more critically self-aware about any search for the authentic. Música de Maestros works with written scores and arrangements even though about half of the ensemble's musicians do not read music and have to be led through their parts until they have committed them to memory. Even if my ear and memory skills continued to lag far behind those of my Bolivian colleagues, my sight-reading skills—while nothing to brag about within the classical music world—were highly valued in Música de Maestros, and gained me relatively quick entrance to their performance stage. Playing with Música de Maestros is something like playing in a chamber orchestra. Unlike the hundred-plus piece orchestra where one violinist plays among forty, every violinist in Música de Maestros matters and can be heard. It is difficult to hide behind a microphone. Furthermore, although Encinas is the group's director and marks the start of pieces and specific passages, we often play without a conductor. The resulting sense of ensembled playing, if we are successful in achieving it, is one of the main reasons I enjoy playing with this group.

Throughout this book, I discussed how Japanese made connections with Bolivian music; I want to emphasize that I too have had my reasons for making these connections, ones that began with an attraction to the exotic, and ones that later drew on my classical music training. Before an annual trip to Bolivia, the classical technique is what I "woodshed" because that is what I need to perform with Música de Maestros. But both the exotic and the classical frames are flip sides of the same coin of a Eurocentric modernity, the same coin that makes possible the racialization of culture that surrounds both the division of labor between musicology and ethnomusicology and the ways Japanese and Bolivians come to terms with the indigeneity of the Andean music they stage.[33] Inter-area ethnography pointed to complex racialized schemes that took me into comparisons of nationalisms, colonial endeavors, and Eurocentric projects of scientific racism. These paths of inquiry developed as I became more aware of what it meant to be gringa in Japan.

Unlike the exoticized panorama that initially attracted me to Latin American studies, my knowledge of Japan came through critiques of this country's position within Asian studies—a construct that seems driven by an East-West problematic. Japan takes its place as an area through its historical positioning as an Asian imperial core and through Orientalism that marks it as Other in relation to an implicitly assumed construct of the West.[34] Anthropologists have addressed Japan studies' ambiguous, even awkward, position in academia. Anne Allison claims anthropological study of Japan, often too burdened by area specificities, has been positioned by its supposed lack of theoretical contributions to the discipline, as well as by an uneasy academic attitude toward this "superpower that is racially and culturally nonwest."[35] As Marilyn Ivy has suggested, Japan was the nonwhite nation that challenged Western colonizers by becoming colonialist, imperialist, and fascist.[36] I remember being completely baffled when I read about the postwar phenomenon of nihonjin ron, the discourses on what it means to be Japanese.[37] My amazement came from thinking about the number of Japanese intellectuals who seemed to be operating within and contributing to these discourses. I could not imagine Bolivian intellectuals involved in any kind of parallel essentializing project about what it means to be Bolivian, without hearing simultaneously several voices of self-critique and irony. To be sure, Bolivians wave their flags (both the official one and the indigenous one), and defend their devil dance against Peruvian claims, but intellectual production in Bolivia has not bought wholesale into an uncritical view of an essentialized Bolivian nationalism. However, William Kelly warns against a simplistic dismissal of nihonjin ron, and calls these ideologies of nationalist introspection the Occidentalist response to Orientalism.[38] Many of the contradictions I encountered in thinking about nationalisms in Japan emerge from the ambivalences produced by this country's framing as both Other and imperialist core. The Orientalism-Occidentalism question has not been a particularly relevant framework for Latin American studies,[39] but the East-West framework is central to understanding something like nihonjin ron in Japan.

Area studies are far from uniform; they develop their own cultures (the questions they ask, the issues that are important to them). These cultures of area studies become more clearly visible within the tasks of inter-area ethnography, when the ethnographer goes into a new area with the background of a different area.[40] This should sound familiar to anthropologists. After all, that is the anthropological project in reduced form: to know something about how other cultures work so as to reflect on how one's own culture works. My point is that anthropologists' intellectual cultures are often steeped in the *cultures* of area studies and an inter-area ethnography brings these cultures into high relief.

Of Chinitos, Gringas, and Gaijin in Japan

We were ready to leave the apartment and start the walk to the Mitaka train station. It was a day with no performances, and few of those came our way when we also happened to be in Tokyo. As a group, we had decided to give up our two days "off" in order to do a recording. Hishimoto had made the arrangements with the studio, and we would begin in the afternoon and work until fifteen minutes before the last train, somewhere between midnight and 1:00 a.m. If we missed that train, or its connections, we would have to shell out for taxis or wait four hours until train service resumed. Tokyo's public transportation system always amazed me, but its nightly closure seemed incongruous with the city's pace. The trains' break in service, however, hardly stopped nightlife. Those going out for a night of partying simply began their travels on the last train out and returned when the trains resumed.[41] In the recording studio they

17. Members of Música de Maestros meet at the train station with instruments and equipment en route to the recording studio in Tokyo. *Photograph by the author.*

worked long hours, but not that long; we would have to complete our work before the last train.

While the company bus usually transported us and all our instruments to the various performance spaces of the tour, we were on our own for the recording. Getting to the studio was a challenge. While we each carried our own instruments, the recording session also featured an array of Andean wind and percussion instruments, all of which also had to be transported to the studio (see figure 17). Our recording days thus began with a twenty-minute walk, carrying all our instruments to the Mitaka train station. Hishimoto, who lived two train stops away, arranged to meet us at Mitaka, preferring not to risk the possibility that we might get lost en route. As crowds of people moved in and out of the ticket gates, we kept our eyes peeled for a sighting of Hishimoto. When he was spotted but did not yet see us in the crowds, Encinas shouted to him "Chinito!" and waved. In a crowded Tokyo train station, Hishimoto was the only person who turned his head in response to the call of "chinito." With their nicknames, Bolivians do not distinguish between Chinese and Japanese, calling anyone of Japanese descent "chino." Some Japanese are annoyed by this confusion and will insist on their distinctness as Japanese. After all his years working in Bolivian music, Hishimoto has had ample experience with this nickname. If he was annoyed, he hid it well, threw his head back sideways, laughed, and came over to the gates to meet us. We followed him to the correct platform to begin the hour trip to the station closest to the studio.

Inter-area ethnography brings greater awareness to the triangulation of multiple others of any fieldwork context—how the Bolivians and I were gaijin, how the Japanese were all "chinito" to Bolivians, and how I continued to be gringa, even as I was seen distinctly by the Japanese. Depending on the context, "chinito" as said to a Japanese person can be just as insulting as "gringa"; "chinito" is a categorization used in many Latin American contexts to refer to anyone who "looks" Asian. Its use seemed out of place in the Tokyo train station, presenting something like the categorical dissonance of a "gringa in Japan." Gringas go to Latin America; that is the relational *place* that defines them as gringas. I was supposed to be gaijin (foreigner) in Japan, which of course I was. My ethnographic position was shaped by the national passport I carried, my Latin Americanist background, and the music I played. While Latin Americanists discuss an ambivalence about being called "gringa,"[42] and scholars of Japan want to cut through the "foreigner" (gaijin) framework,[43] my conditions of fieldwork necessitated embracing my foreigner status. During the tour, "participant observation" took on its usual oxymoronic tinge.[44] Even though my tour mates knew about my research project, on a daily basis my anthropological work appeared to take a back seat to the daily tasks of making music: arriving at the next performance space, setting up, practicing my violin, participating in a sound check, rehearsing, giving a full performance, striking the set, greeting members of the audience, and giving autographs. At the end of our performances, often after we had changed into our street clothes, every member of the group had a line of students asking for autographs (see figure 18). We were all flattered by these actions. This certainly never happens when I wear my anthropologist's hat! Students learn from an early age the proper roles of adoring fans. Primary school students would put tiny pieces of paper in front of me, saying "Sign, Kudasai" (Sign, please). Why did they grace me with such a request? After all, I was a gringa playing Bolivian music, and students noticed that I looked different from the Bolivian musicians on stage. When younger students drew the band, they usually represented me with a starkly different hair color (yellow) and exaggerated eyeglasses. (I was

18. Victor Hugo Gironda signs autographs after a school performance in Japan. *Photograph by the author.*

the only musician who wore glasses.) I was a foreigner to Japan, a foreigner to the nationalist music tradition I represented on stage, and a foreigner from the country that had dropped the A-bomb and occupied Japan after World War II. But it was precisely through my subject position as the gringa interacting with Bolivian musicians in Japan that a simple East-West dichotomy was decentered.

While Bolivians were also foreigners in Japan, I suggest my identity as imposed by others in this context was probably more aligned with "the West." Like it or not, my presence stood for what Japanese might oppose as they sought alternatives to a Western path. As Christine Yano writes, this opposition structures Japan's modernity: "One chooses to lodge in a Japanese inn or a Western hotel, to squat above a Japanese toilet at a train station or sit on a Western one, to eat rice or bread for breakfast. These choices are not neutral: these actions of the body are strategic assertions and practices of identity."[45] My choices followed that of a Western identity, but so did those of the Bolivians. Ah, the smell of toast! Each morning, between setting up the stage and completing the sound check, Bolivians would toast their morning bread backstage, using a toaster acquired secondhand in Japan. While Bolivians tended to opt for many elements listed above that were associated with a "Western" identity, the identity imposed on them differed from the one imposed on me.

Some Bolivians told me about experiencing racial discrimination in Japan—"no worse than in Bolivia," one person assured me. A shop owner might closely follow a person, afraid the Bolivian gaijin was out to steal rather than purchase merchandise. Bolivian gaijin experienced some of the same problems that have been analyzed by African American scholars who study Japan. Jacalyn Harden claims that Japan "occupies an ambiguous position in Western representations," and such ambiguities result from global hierarchies of race that Japanese experience as well as apply.[46] Through images of the black Other, according to John Russell, Japanese have played out the "insecurities and ambiguity of Japanese racial and cultural identity vis-à-vis an idealized West."[47] Bolivian gaijin presented a not-quite-Western reference. On the tour, Bolivians preferred eating toast, sleeping in beds, and using Western-style toilets, but in a shop Bolivians were more likely to be watched by anxious storeowners. The West and the Rest is, after all, also about the structuring of racism. On the other hand, I found that Bolivians and Japanese mutually imagined themselves as sharing ancient ties, and the cornerstone of that connection was found in imagined indigenous ancestors. Bolivians in Japan made for different gaijin than gringas in Japan, and racialized discourses structured those differences.

"Okinawans Are More Like Us"

As the temperatures began to drop, we all looked forward to our final week of work in Okinawa. Several musicians had already been there on previous tours, and they always mentioned how the Okinawans were "different from other Japanese," how they were "more relaxed," "more like us [Bolivians]." Of course, Norma Field shows how that difference can translate to a placement of Okinawans as Japan's second-class citizens who carry the burden of Japan's racist colonialism; in this spin Okinawans are read as the "lagging natives" who need to be "disciplined in the name of civilization."[48] Throughout the tour, I had taken to translating into Spanish the details from Lonely Planet's Japan guide.[49] Even if we did not have time to be tourists, members of the band often requested that I read and translate those juicy vignettes and historical notes that Lonely Planet includes for its readers who are fortunate enough to explore Japan this way. Upon arriving in Okinawa I began to translate some of the tragic details about the place. In Hiroshima, victimhood is writ large, but Okinawa's World War II stories are not so clear-cut. In the final battles of Okinawa, the deaths of civilians in caves are portrayed on the one hand as honorable deaths for the Japanese emperor; in a more critical view, these deaths are called "compulsory suicides," a term Norma Field uses "to suggest the dark inmixing of coercion and consent, of aggression and victimization"; Field describes how the ambivalences of Okinawans as colonized peoples, and of Okinawans who were forced to prove their full allegiance to Japan were horrifically played out in those tragic deaths.[50]

While the Lonely Planet guide does not give the nuances of Field's reading, some of these tragic details are included in the book's background information on Okinawa. As I was translating the guidebook, the charango player who was generally quite open to heated political and historical discussions, interrupted me and told me that he did not want to hear any more of my guidebook. Fair enough. We were all exhausted and looked forward to a single afternoon we would have on the beach. But this inter-area moment sat in juxtaposition with the one at the beginning of this chapter. The complexities of Okinawan history did not permit any easy Bolivian identification with both Okinawan and Japanese national projects. In spite of the contrast, both inter-area moments were located in historical readings of World War II and its aftermath—coincidentally also the historical juncture in which area studies emerged.

The post–Cold War reassessments of area studies tend to assume a uniformity in the knowledge-power equation between the United States and the rest of the world. Inter-area ethnography calls into question the homogeneity of these constructs, and raises different questions about how ethnography is ultimately shaped by assumptions within different area studies traditions. While my own formation as a Latin Americanist was influenced by a kind of empathy with Latin American anti-imperialist nationalisms, the fieldwork conducted between different areas productively unsettled this position.

My ethnographic position at the Hiroshima Peace Memorial put me in contradiction with the Japanese and Bolivian members of the tour. The point of disagreement emerged in my critique of a Japanese nationalism that combined victimhood with erasure of an imperial past. While Naoki Sakai, in reference to Japan and Korea, wanted to distinguish between an anti-imperialist nationalism and an imperialist one,[51] this ethnographic interlude demonstrates how the two seemingly different nationalisms can be patchworked dangerously into a single cloth. It is not a new idea to discuss how nationalism extends from, rather than opposes, colonial structures,[52] or that area studies traditions are haunted by colonialism,[53] but these ideas have important implications for ethnographers' subject positions. When the Japanese sound engineer questioned the reporting of the Nanjing massacre and the Bolivian musicians agreed with him, Bolivian and Japanese nationalisms came together: a right-wing Japanese nationalism that glossed over Japan's imperial past, and a sometimes left-wing Bolivian nationalism that responded to US interventionist policies that have tied coca eradication to aid packages. The specter of their comparisons led me to rethink my own ethnographic position in relation to area studies training and the demands of multi-sited global ethnography. Not really about immigrant communities—people moving from one place to another—nor solely about the popularity of a foreign music in Japan—commodities moving from one place to another—this has been a study of the intimacy involved in the movement of both persons and commodities, musicians and music performances between Bolivia and Japan. With my limited knowledge of the Japanese language and my relatively recent introduction to a study of Japan, there is no way to ignore what I lost in the depth of this study, and the particularly unbalanced way I entered the project. However, some ethnographic insights came in a flash, precisely at the interstices of these unbalanced preparations—in what I call inter-area ethnography.

7 Conclusion

Victor Hugo Gironda told me a poignant story about his own musical touring experiences in North America. He had received an invitation to Canada along with promises of performances, organizational structures, and a place to reside while he worked. Once he was in Canada, all those promises melted away, and he found himself unable to make an immediate return trip to Bolivia. In short, this was one of those international touring disasters that Bolivian musicians dread. As he was biding his time to return to Bolivia, he and his friends heard about activities of Canadian First Nations and attended some of its events. At one of them, they received an invitation to stay as long as necessary. Gironda told me about his tremendous gratitude to his indigenous hosts who saved him in a time of need. He also talked about a tie he felt to them, musing about the connections between them, in spite of the differences between situations of North American and South American indigenous peoples. Gironda is the musician pictured in figure 18, signing autographs for Japanese school children and wearing a Redskins T-shirt.[1]

At one level, this book has been about the intercultural nexus of Bolivian music in Japan as an ethnographic space through which to ground what often have been called sweepingly and ambiguously "transnational cultural flows." At another level, it is a critique of nationalism as an ideology, and an exploration of how indigeneity and race thinking work with nationalism in local and transnational places. At yet another level, it moves beyond mere references to exoticism, unpacking what it means to play "someone else's music." Through the critiques of nationalism and stories about playing someone else's music, I have aimed to maintain in the balance a serious consideration of the material and affective economies that might be dismissed too quickly in frameworks of exoticism, appropriation, and commodification.

Bolivian music took a round about route to Japan. First, it was transformed into "Andean" music, a process that moved through Argentina and European countries before reaching Japan. Bolivian music eventually captivated Japanese listeners and began to attract audiences with deep commitments not only to hearing this music but also to playing it, learning it from Bolivian masters, and traveling to Bolivia to experience its imagined original sources. The political economy of this nexus has involved the experiences of staging, for Japanese school children, "authentic" Andean music performances—representations that referenced an imagined indigenous world. The front door to an easily recognized Andean indigeneity has been "El condor pasa," the most immediate Japanese referent to the Andes that made a meandering journey through Simon and Garfunkel's trail of fame. The Bolivian musicians with whom I performed pushed back against these narrow expectations, balancing out a program that staged the multicultural specificities of their country, including indigenous music from the highlands and lowlands.

As many Bolivian musicians who tour Japan do not self-identify as indigenous, one might point the finger and say: they are playing someone else's music. According to these criteria, the Japanese, the Bolivians, and I were all playing someone else's music. The accusatory frame, even as it is associated with emotional responses to real historical injustices, can block off further discussion of how this borrowing, mimicry, appropriation, or theft works in nationalist ideologies, shared nostalgia for indigeneity, local economies of musicians in Bolivia, and transcultural systems of desire and affect.

The work of Bolivian musicians in Japan, in small but significant ways, has made possible other kinds of musical projects at home. From an economic perspective, those who might have quit playing music remained in this field because they were able to supplement insufficient earnings in Bolivia with their take-home pay from a tour of Japan. However, the picture is no more than relatively rosy. When I checked in with musicians in the summer of 2008, I was told that Japanese companies were decreasing Bolivians' pay, reducing their daily stipends, and scheduling just as many performances as in previous tours. Stories of work accidents and minimal health care responses to them revealed the limited coverage the sponsoring company carried for these musicians. Musicians now buy used computers upon their arrival in Japan in order to check their e-mail and chat through wireless connections available in most of their hotel accommodations. While these communication improvements eliminate the lengthy search for a nearby Internet café, the ongoing condition of being away from family members and loved ones continues to be a major hardship of work in the culture mines. On the road, Bolivian musicians also suffered subtle and not so subtle forms of discrimination, perhaps most commonly felt through the experience of the closely hovering shop owner.

Bolivian musicians remain concerned about the decreasing value of their music in the global arena, and they talk frankly about how these tours won't last forever. Even though most of them have played in the street at some time in their lives, they pointed to the proliferation of Andean street musicians as a principal reason their music was losing value in its global circulation. Many Bolivian musicians say the Andean music boom is over, and they are scrambling for new proposals as economic necessity forces some of them to consider what they themselves label as completely fake—dressing in the stereotypical image of a Native North American and giving a techno New Age spin to one's music. They call this, or any other kind of musical faking, "vendiendo la pomada" (selling the pomade), which translates to something like "selling snake oil."

When I wanted to know more about this new style, I was told to look up the Peruvian group Alborada. In a YouTube video of this group performing "Ananau," one sees singers and flute players standing on boulders in the middle of a river.[2] Members wear their hair long and loose, but with headbands and some with feathers. Their fringed costumes look something like those worn by scissors dancers of Peru's departments of Ayacucho, Huancavelica, and Apurimac. But other performers in this style don a stereotypical Native American buckskin suit with decorative details and fringes.[3] Alborada sings in Quechua to a music that features flutes and an electronic rhythmic background. Bolivians told me that groups like this one sell their recordings to street musicians who then promote the sale of the recordings in Europe through performances with playback. One person confessed that a Bolivian residing in Germany invited him to make a recording in this style; the producer asked him to alter his playing, to perform in a "flat" (plano) way, without the usual dynamics and inflections he would give a phrase. He in turn specifically asked that his name not be listed among the recording musicians. Another musician admitted he wanted to use his studio to make these kinds of recordings, but he wanted to leave it to others to perform this music on the street, to actually "sell the snake oil."

The disdain for these new styles, and the embarrassment about their own participation in their production, show the complicated positions of Bolivian Andean musicians as they face the shifting demands of a global market. Bolivians perform with pride their interpretation of Bolivian indigenous representations, but indigeneity here is not universally exchangeable. The national frame remains paramount. Bolivians feel silly altering their musical and sartorial aesthetics in order to look and sound like a Native North American and, perhaps even more problematically, like those from their rival neighboring country of Peru. To participate in this new music economy that meets an external shift in the desired exotic, some Bolivian musicians have preferred the anonymity the recording studio allows.

Work, pleasure, and national pride go hand in hand in the musical experiences represented in this book. "It's not just about the money," touring Bolivian musicians reminded me. They then spoke quite eloquently about the pleasures of representing their nation through music, even though their government had nothing to do with their sponsorship. The Bolivians' pleasure in performing nationalism sits next to the Japanese pleasure of falling in love with the sound of Bolivian bamboo instruments—something that seemed exotically Other, but also something that sounded somewhat familiar. When people play a music that is perceived as someone else's, they apply different strategies of authentication. Japanese and Bolivian Andean musicians imagine themselves to share blood, but these imaginaries have different meanings within the respective Japanese and Bolivian national projects. Japanese and Bolivians talked about feeling connected to each other, and in doing so they used narratives that racialized culture and placed them in an imagined genetic intimacy, even though this did not disrupt the national narratives operating within their respective countries: mestizaje and multiculturalism in Bolivia and homogeneity and isolation in Japan. Musicians from all over the world might claim what they do is "not about the money." While multiple motivations are at work here, I want to emphasize that global market forces and the flexible labor of Andean musicians partially shaped the articulation of an intimate distance and the ingroup identification between Japanese and Bolivians.

With the term "intimate distance," I have emphasized the apparent contradiction between feeling an emotional affective and even bodily connection with an Other—buttressed through narratives about sharing an indigenous ancestor—and yet feeling very different from each other and from living indigenous subjects. In the end, the Japanese I interviewed did not see themselves as Bolivian, nor did the Bolivians see themselves as Japanese. National identifications remained intact. Nor did the Japanese express connection to the Ainu, the indigenous peoples Japan colonized. And, with some notable exceptions I mentioned, many touring Bolivian musicians do not see themselves as indigenous. The indigenous connections are relegated to a prehistoric moment, and thus Bolivian folklore music remains rather disconnected from the breathtaking array of contemporary indigenous politics in Bolivia. I do not want to critique Bolivian musicians who have remained at the margins of these political processes, but rather my intention is to look seriously at the connections of race, indigeneity, and nationalism that leave so many people trapped in an endless dance to the expectations of others, while also considering the pride Bolivian musicians feel when they perform specific indigeneities as a part of their nationalism. For studies of immigration and the movement of labor, capital, and goods, Lynn Stephen has suggested the term "transborder" as more comprehensive than "transnational" because the former encompasses multiple kinds of borders being crossed within and beyond those of the nation-state; however, she also recognizes the continued effects of the *nationalist* frame.[4] Referencing an imagined genetic ancestor was a transborder move, but other elements of this Japanese-Bolivian encounter remained fully transnational.

A person who once worked closely with MAS, Evo Morales's party, once said to me, "Nobody really cares about music." This individual held strong political convictions about the potential change that a presidency of Evo Morales could bring. The comment was directed at a gringa musician who plays with a musical ensemble that sustains an unabashedly nationalist project, but a project that does not necessarily follow the more radical currents of the contemporary moment. While the MAS member's comment could be dismissed as superficial because it fails to acknowledge the symbolic world's importance for politics, it does beg the question: what is the place of music in what scholars are calling the latest of Bolivia's revolutionary openings? The historians Forrest Hylton and Sinclair Thomson locate this latest revolutionary horizon between 2000 and 2005, arguing that with the election of Evo Morales the revolutionary opening provisionally closed; even as MAS has acted in accordance with the demands for nationalization of gas (actually a renegotiation of existing contracts) and the calls for a constituent assembly, when MAS took the reins of the state and consolidated executive power within it, the social movements that brought MAS to power became fragmented.[5] As people ponder what happens to revolutionary openings when "the revolution" is elected to state power, one might ask how indigeneity plays out within the national frame when an indigenous man is president. While I do not intend to fully answer that question in the conclusion to this book, I will mention a relevant scene I viewed on YouTube, a video titled "Dancing with Evo Morales."[6] The opening scene of this video features a meeting of six thousand Bolivian band musicians who are attempting to enter the *Guinness Book of World Records* by the sheer numbers of band musicians present. As Evo Morales—also known in Bolivia as a trumpet player—presides over the event, what tune does the megaband begin to play? "El condor pasa," at the tempo of a dirge. Musical nationalism has not changed much and it continues to follow indigenismo's path: musical references that cite exoticized indigenista positions, rather than radical indianista ones, and claims to nationally exclusive patrimonies that "belong" to single nations. Nationalism does it again! Musicians *and* politicians who represent the nation continue to be trapped within this totalizing ideology that plays on indigenista and Andeanist symbolics shaped in part by global audiences.

While these expectations for staged indigeneity were enforced rigidly for Japanese school performances, Bolivian musicians as well as Japanese Andean music enthusiasts do not settle with merely giving audiences what they want. The latter develop expertise about different Bolivian genres, groups, and musicians. They live extended periods in Bolivia. Some of them even become major composers of Bolivian music. These are hardly the stories of mere imitators. Most of them *perform* Bolivian music, thus disrupting the usual ways one might think about consumption.

Like the Japanese I interviewed in this project, I too am a Bolivian music enthusiast who performs this music. But my strategies of intimacy varied from those of the Japanese, bringing my attention to the workings of race thinking in the pleasures of playing someone else's music. Beyond my previous training as a performer of Bolivian music, during this fieldwork other details about my subject position came to the fore and led me to propose that multi-sited ethnographers might pay more attention to the inter-area aspects of such work. I came to this ethnography with a strong background in Latin American studies, fluency in the Spanish language, and a long-term understanding of this region. I brought no equivalent expertise to my work in Japan, making me very much a gringa in Japan. The story on the bus that I describe in chapter 6 was one of the first ethnographic moments I tried to unpack; many themes within it became central to the book and my thinking about the methodological issues of this project. In the ethnographic order of things, this story and its insights came first. However, the book has several other narratives: one about Andean music going to Japan via recordings and then by performing musicians; one about Bolivians trying to make a living in music, even as their music seems to be losing value on the world market; one about Japanese going to Bolivia to get close to the sources of their Andean music pleasure; and one about Japanese and Bolivian musicians identifying with a common genetic ancestor. The issues that emerge in these narratives then bridge the gaps between theory and methodology—between the ideas of intimacy, race thinking, and nationalism, and the problematics of doing inter-area ethnography. Let me conclude by elaborating on the contributions this case study makes and the questions it poses for future consideration.

Race into Nationalism, Race into Transnationalism

The Japanese-Bolivian imagined racial link, even if it occurs through a prehistoric indigenous ancestor, is about an ingroup identification between two different nationalist peoples who find connections through a common experience of being under the political domination of the United States—even if such experiences are separated geographically and chronologically. Bolivians and Japanese deploy a racialized essentialism in the face of historical experiences of exploitation, marginalization, and racism as experienced in the world system.[7] In these narratives of racial connection, one unspoken point was that I was not *in* the ingroup, and the Hiroshima-Nanjing discussion drove home this point. Here was a possible non-Western to non-Western point of identification—with all the caveats about what "the West" might entail—an alternative to the Euro-American perspective on modernity. But a look at these countries' historical trajectories of nation building and race thinking shows how even these somewhat alternative connections are still very much part of Western modernity's frame.

Walter Benn Michaels, in an article about cultural identity politics in the United States, critiqued the way the "culture" concept reinstated rather than eradicated racial thinking; he titled his article "Race into Culture: A Critical Genealogy of Cultural Identity."[8] My own ethnography calls for further critical discussions on how race thinking has been integral to nationalist projects, not just as something to be addressed within an inclusive nationalism but rather something *foundational* to the nation itself. An examination of two quite different national contexts revealed scientific racism as a common historical thread in the weaving of a "modern nation"—a *race into nationalism*, if you will. This study adds another grain of sand to the questions about race thinking, nationalism, and music,[9] calling for further comparative research on race thinking's central place within nationalist ideologies. As I call for further analysis of nationalist forms and race thinking, I recognize the ambiguities of doing so. Critiquing nationalism is more comfortably done when one holds full citizenship in a "Goliath" country, even if that country's power is waning. "David" nationalism holds a different sense of urgency. "Musical integration," an expression now being used by Música de Maestros to talk about their work, must be evaluated within a context where national division, fragmentation, and disintegration hover daily as real possibilities with bloody consequences. Is there a national thinking outside of race thinking? The Japanese-Bolivian racialization of culture also provides an example of how race is rearticulated in a global context, persisting in transnational forms, at the intersection of national boundaries. National and transnational race thinking hardly contradict one another here but rather appear to work in tandem.

Triangulating the Postcolonial

> When we performed for students, some audience members learned better than others. At the close of our concerts, Hishimoto would ask the students to tell him the origin of the music they had just heard. The shouted incorrect answers included "Africa," "Mexico," "Brazil," and "Argentina." At hearing these responses, Encinas would shake his head that was dripping in sweat and say, "You can play your heart out in 40 degree [centigrade] heat and they still don't know you are from Bolivia." These incorrect answers never referenced the United States or any Asian country. Even for the inattentive listener, these performances were about non-US and non-Asian Others.

The intimate distance between Japanese and Bolivians was ultimately about fostering self-other connections that provided alternatives to the US-Japanese and US-Bolivian pairings. These avoided dyads more easily referenced histories of domination and occupation and more comfortably fit in postcolonial analyses. Ann Stoler, addressing the crisis of postcolonial theory, writes that we expect terms like "colonial legacy" to do too much explanatory work, and that the geographies of imperial centers and colonized peripheries (inside-outside, metropole-colony—other dual oppositional categories she mentions) simply don't match the worlds we study.[10] The only way to keep postcolonial studies out of the theoretical dustbin is to keep their forms plural and their histories particular, while also viewing the "post" not as a temporal referent but as a signal of critique. Just as postmodernity does not mean the end of modernity but rather a critical view of modernity's project, the "post" in postcolonial studies refers to critiques of colonial forms' multiple guises.

This book proposes a triangulation of postcolonial studies, a framework that forces analyses beyond the dual oppositional categories of colonizer and colonized, dominant and dominated, the West and the non-West. With the agenda of triangulating the postcolonial, I call attention to those relations that may appear skewed within a postcolonial frame that only sees the world through dual oppositional categories. Triangulating the postcolonial then leads to interpretations that refuse to fall for either-or propositions. Is playing "someone else's music" an example of cultural appropriation *or* cultural appreciation? I argue it is a bit of both, and neither interpretation, when taken alone, can sufficiently explain the social meaning behind these phenomena. Appropriation does not account for multiple subject positions of those playing this music, nor does it account for the material effects behind systems of affect and desire. Appreciation, on the other hand, can play a celebratory tune that too easily drowns out inequalities as structured in colonial and postcolonial histories.

The messiness of discussing a Japanese-Bolivian connection around the performance of Andean music required a look at each countries' respective colonial and national histories, pointing to postcolonial differences as well as the common theme of scientific racism's place in nationalist projects. Triangulation means delving into the contradictions a third term produces, while not abandoning the recognition of Western modernity's immense scope of influence. My own presence in this project, as a Latin Americanist anthropologist and as a US citizen who performs Bolivian music, implicitly and sometimes more explicitly evoked this third term. In our music performances, Bolivians, Japanese, and I were all playing indigenous music. "Playing Indian," however, meant something very different for me than for Bolivians and Japanese. In a US context, such practices can be seen as disrespectful of Native American cultures. Different dominant nation-states, each with their own colonial and postcolonial histories, shape diverse approaches to this performative practice. I have grappled with these very diverse examples of "playing indian," making sense of them through both local contexts as well as in terms of globally circulating ideas about indigenous peoples.

Triangulating the postcolonial also requires reexamining what has now become a commonplace in ethnography: multi-sited work.[11] Rarely addressed, however, are the articulations of area studies (e.g., Latin America) and culture areas (e.g., Andes) in relation to multi-sited and transnational work.[12] My intention here is not to argue for or against the reinvigoration of area-specific training. In an era of global ethnography, however, anthropologists can hardly claim a uniform expertise in the cultures of the world. Returning once again to Clifford Geertz's assessment that anthropologists don't study places but study *in* places,[13] I want to call attention this time to the second part of that idea, and to what happens in the formation of that plural form. I studied in many different places and my area studies training—thick in the case of Bolivia and comparatively thin in the case of Japan—set parameters through which particular ethnographic insights emerged, not by hiding that unevenness, but by recognizing it as central to my interpretations. Such are the conditions of multi-sited global ethnography, and anthropologists have much to gain by reflecting specifically on those unequal forms of preparation, rather than hiding them as an embarrassing anomaly within the ethnographic tradition. From this uneven terrain of preparation, the cultures of area studies became more obvious, and these insights helped unravel the knot of triangulated postcolonialisms. I adopted an inter-area ethnographic perspective to make sense of the Bolivian-Japanese point of intimate identification, without leaving behind the historically structured trajectories that, through indigeneity, made possible such imaginings.

What's Intimacy Got to Do with It?

Playing music with others is something like baring one's soul. But that statement has a particularly ethnocentric ring with its focus on the individual and interiorities. So let me say there is something *intimate* about playing music with others. It's not necessarily about kin, reproduction, or sex. But it is about desire as experienced through the body—through listening, tapping a foot, moving fingers in a rhythm, getting in a groove. Playing music with others calls forth Povinelli's idea of "carnality": "the socially built space between flesh and environment."[14] Bolivian musicians made indigenous music their own through nationalist ideologies. Japanese made it their own through a racialization of culture. When I discuss these projects in terms of intimacy, I join other analyses that are turning to a terminology of the intimate to discuss pleasure and a closeness with Others, while also accounting for the relations of power and inequality within these encounters.

These interactions across unequal social relations are nothing new. Nor are these interactions novel to the fieldwork situation. But a proliferation of "intimacy" within anthropological analyses of such contexts leads me to suggest that this term, as a disciplinary hook, is displacing or at least complementing and decentering other modes of making sense of social inequality (e.g., resistance and domination, world systems, the appropriated non-Western Other). I suggest that conceptualizations of intimacy make of desire a broader field of inquiry, even as they also potentially lead analyses into perpetuating dualistic oppositional frames—intimacy being balanced out by the public, the global, and the mass.[15]

If Daniel Miller suggested "consumption" has replaced "kinship" as an organizing concept of anthropology,[16] I suggest that "intimacy" may emerge as another keyword of the discipline. The case study of this book disrupts the usual ways one might think about consumption and follows others who have reworked consumption as performance.[17] In the world of Bolivian music in Japan, consumption is about performance and production of one's own musical experience. Japanese enthusiasts render their performances meaningful through strategies of intimacy. One such strategy is to claim ties to Bolivian indigenous ancestors. Thinking through intimacy provides ways into this complex realm of desire that is about a social connection as perceived through heightened sensations of musical experience. Such conceptualizations maintain parallel engagement with the global structuring of power, but without the more totalizing picture painted by world systems, the Manichean representations of domination and resistance, or the West and the Rest. Intimacy, as a concept, chaotically herds the unruly ambiguities of social relations that are infused with historical structures of power and the coexisting experiences of pleasure and affect. In thinking about desire in relation to playing someone else's music, intimacy also does the work previously encompassed by critical takes on authenticity, but without the ghost of "the real" that seems to haunt even critical perspectives on this topic.[18]

As a term that has opened different avenues of inquiry, "intimacy" is more than a secondhand thought. What might be intimacy's conceptual drawbacks? Perhaps it still holds the individual too central within its frame. Perhaps it sits too often within a duality, with the global or the mass-mediated acting as its pesky opposite. Like "love," "intimacy" is alluring but ultimately connected to an array of distinct issues that generate debate in the discipline. Within this book the term "intimate distance" points to how one can make an Other's music one's own, while not making that music's national origin one's own. Even though all the musicians described in this book have made Bolivian music their own, in the end, Bolivians remain Bolivian, Japanese remain Japanese, and I remain gringa.

Notes

1. Setting the Transnational Stage

1. Xavier Albó and Matías Preiswerk studied how both faith and power are revealed in this ritual's social organization in *Los señores del Gran Poder*. Also see Rossana Barragán and Cleverth Cárdenas, *Gran poder*; David Guss, "The Gran Poder and the Reconquest of La Paz"; and Jeff Himpele, "The Gran Poder Parade and the Local Movement of the Aymara Middle Class."

2. See Harris, "Ethnic Identity and Market Relations," 367.

3. See Lott, *Love and Theft*. Philip Deloria traces several key moments of American history through which whites construct an American identity by playing Indian (*Playing Indian*). Luke Lassiter tells his own complex story about his childhood participation in scouting and powwows and how he had to renegotiate the terms of his own fascination with Indians when, as an anthropologist, he studied the Kiowa (*The Power of Kiowa Song*). A note on terminology and capitalization: generally, I will use the lowercase form "indian" throughout this book because many scholars working in Latin America have given good reasons for doing so. For Latin America, the term is a contested cultural construct, refers to a colonial category, makes no reference to contemporary nationality, and points consistently to structured positions of marginality (Wade, *Race and Ethnicity in Latin America*, 121; Abercrombie, *Pathways of Memory and Power*, xviii; Canessa, *Natives Making Nation*, 24–25). For the North American context, the capital "I" is not so easily set aside, however. In the few cases where I reference scholarship about American Indians, I will use the term's capitalized form, following what is standard within that field. The term will also be capitalized when I reference other scholars who have maintained this form. These seemingly minor stylistic differences in scholarship point to contrasting conceptualizations of indigeneity, between North and South American contexts, that are yet to be unpacked fully, and that are beyond the scope of this book.

4. In his study of antebellum minstrelsy, Eric Lott moves away from a single monolithic interpretation of these performances as expressions of white domination; he reads minstrelsy through white working-class positions, arguing that these performers were motivated by "envy as well as repulsion, sympathetic identification as well as fear" (*Love and Theft*, 8).

5. Weismantel, *Cholas and Pishtacos*.

6. For a historian's discussion of the emergence of the mestizo-cholo in the city of La Paz, see the work of Rossana Barragán ("Entre polleras, lliqllas, y ñañacas").

7. I use musicians' real names in many passages of this book because these individuals wanted to be identified. They have artistic personas and some of them were even taken aback by my question of whether or not to identify them by name. However, in indicated passages I use pseudonyms to protect privacy and to follow more general analytical points. I have used pseudonyms here.

8. Nelson, *A Finger in the Wound*, 43.

9. Urry, *The Tourist Gaze*, 2.

10. Ibid., 2–11. For tourism studies that are recognizing the limits of the gaze frame, see Simone Abram and Jacqueline Waldren, *Tourists and Tourism*, 5–8; and Amanda Stronza, "Anthropology of Tourism," 272.

11. For example, Jane Desmond writes about the marketing and consumption of the Hawaiian hula girl (*Staging Tourism*). In her discussion of "eating the Other," bell hooks argues that the "commodification of difference promotes paradigms of consumption" (*Black Looks*, 31).

12. The authors writing in this vein are numerous. Davydd Greenwood, who in the 1970s wrote quite pessimistically about the commodification of culture in tourism, came to reassess his first readings of these transformational processes ("Culture by the Pound"). Daniel Miller has written extensively on the questions of material consumption and has come to see "consumption" as a disciplinary keyword that is replacing "kinship" ("Consumption and Commodities"). The global commodification of difference is the centerpiece of Jean and John Comarroff's *Ethnicity Inc.*

13. Pratt, "Globalización, desmodernización, y el retorno de los monstruos."

14. Rosaldo, *Culture and Truth*; Pratt, "Arts of the Contact Zone."

15. Ong, *Flexible Citizenship*, 32–35. Anne McClintock also develops a critique of postcolonial theory, claiming that it tends to be haunted by a nineteenth-century idea of linear progress, is too often presented in a singular form as "the postcolonial," and suggests an end to colonialism where colonial forms continue to structure daily life (*Imperial Leather*, 10–13). Juan Flores also points to the misnomer of "post" in postcolonial, a point that seems particularly relevant to his case of studying Puerto Ricans in Puerto Rico and in New York City (*From Bomba to Hip-Hop*).

16. Ong, *Flexible Citizenship*, 4. Also see Hall, "The West and the Rest."

17. Wade, "Working Culture," 462.

18. Andrew Canessa discusses the census of 2001 and Bolivia's "indigenous pluralism" that contrasts with the singular colonial and postcolonial construct that shapes many organizations working in indigenous issues ("Who Is Indigenous?").

19. Hale, "Between Che Guevara and the Pachamama."

20. Nelson, *A Finger in the Wound*, 128–69.

21. Gustafson, "The Paradoxes of Liberal Indigenism."

22. For a thorough discussion of Bolivia's relatively recent "revolutionary moment," see the work of Forrest Hylton and Sinclair Thomson (*Revolutionary Horizons*).

23. Elsewhere I have written about these urban folklorization processes that occurred between the 1930s and 1950s, see "Making Music Safe for the Nation," and "Embodied Matters." Bolivians "discovered" their own folklore when they were not at home; key figures who became significant folklore artists and promoters in Bolivia first worked and/or studied in Argentina.

24. See E. Taylor Atkins on jazz (*Blue Nippon*), Shuhei Hosokawa on salsa ("Salsa no tiene fronteras"), Toru Mitsui on blue grass ("The Reception of the Music of American Southern Whites in Japan"), Sean Williams on Irish music ("Irish Music and the Experience of Nostalgia in Japan"), Marta Savigliano on tango (*Tango and the Political Economy of Passion*), Ian Condry on hip-hop (*Hip-Hop Japan*), Marvin D. Sterling on reggae and dancehall culture ("The Symbolic Constitution of Japanese Dancehall"), and Yoko Kurokawa on hula ("Yearning for a Distant Music").

25. On Japanese immigration patterns to Latin America, see Daniel Masterson and Sayaka Funada-Classen, *The Japanese in Latin America*, 33, 45, 47, 80–179. In the 1950s, one of the largest colonies in the history of Japanese immigration to Latin America was formed: San Juan de Yapacaní; the Bolivian government granted them 87,198 acres of land and each household was granted 110 acres. Colonists were expected to work the land for at least two years, and they were expected to repay the cost of their passage to Bolivia (*The Japanese in Latin America*, 192).

26. Suzuki, "Becoming 'Japanese' in Bolivia" and "Viewing Nations, Narrating Hybridity."

27. Dale Olsen has studied the music in Japanese communities of Brazil, Peru, Argentina, Paraguay, and Bolivia (*The Chrysanthemum and the Song*).

28. Lesser, *A Discontented Diaspora*, 149.

29. On the privilege of the partial perspective, see Donna Haraway's *Simians, Cyborgs, and Women.*

30. The first category of foreign workers in Japan, according to Saskia Sassen, consists of "artists, religious personnel and journalists," not the "typical migrant worker" (*Globalization and Its Discontents*, 61).

31. Smith, *Hosts and Guests*, 11.

32. Graburn, "Tourism," 35.

33. Kelsky, *Women on the Verge*, 2.

34. As an aside, they use the term "North American" even as they mean "*estadounidense*" (US citizen), probably one of the most awkward words of the Spanish language, and one I rarely hear or use. Even in the English language we are limited in our nationalist nouns, and to the outcry of many people who live in Latin American countries, we have taken over the entire northern and southern hemispheres with our nationalist designation of "American."

35. For example, see Thomas Turino's *Nationalists, Cosmopolitans, and Popular Music in Zimbabwe.*

36. Abercrombie, "To Be Indian, to Be Bolivian," 119.

37. According to Luke Lassiter, the phrase "Indian at heart" is used to refer to hobbyists of the Native American world (*The Power of Kiowa Song*, 25).

38. Lassiter, *The Power of Kiowa Song.*

39. Pentatonic music is built on a five-tone scale within an octave range, and from a Western classical music perspective, it often becomes associated with a variety of non-Western musical expressions.

40. For Diana Fuss, identification is the detour through the Other that defines the self (*Identification Papers*). For Judith Butler the "inside" of any identity assumes the violence of an "exclusionary matrix" that produces "an abjected outside" to the subject (*Bodies That Matter*, 3). Within the context of Guatemala, Diane Nelson writes about "hostile markings" taken as identity as she attempts to capture the ambivalence within quincentennial indigenous identities that formed initially through relations of conquest and domination (*A Finger in the Wound*, 128–69).

41. Wolf, "Perilous Ideas," 7.

42. Michaels, "Race into Culture," 683–84.

43. Visweswaran, "Race and the Culture of Anthropology," 74. Also see de la Cadena, *Indigenous Mestizos*, 330.

44. Radano and Bohlman, *Music and the Racial Imagination*, 1.

45. Sanjek, "The Enduring Inequalities of Race"; Wade, *Race and Ethnicity in Latin America*; McClintock, *Imperial Leather*; Stoler, *Race and the Education of Desire.*

46. For a detailed discussion about the social construction of "talent" in the classical music world, see Henry Kingsbury's ethnography of a conservatory (*Music, Talent, and Performance*).

47. Radano and Bohlman, *Music and the Racial Imagination*, 8.

48. Ibid., 4.

49. Ibid., 9–10.

50. Chow, "Where Have All the Natives Gone?"; Clifford, *The Predicament of Culture*; Desmond, *Staging Tourism*; Errington, *The Death of Authentic Primitive Art and Other Tales of Progress*; Torgovnick, *Gone Primitive.*

51. Timothy Mitchell develops this argument in relation to an Egyptian delegation's presence at a Congress of Orientalists in 1889 ("The World as Exhibition," 218–22). Also see Edward Said's *Orientalism.*

52. Fernando Coronil makes this point through a citation to Noam Chomsky ("Beyond Occidentalism," 53–54). Also see Stuart Hall's "The West and the Rest."

53. Jansen, *The Making of Modern Japan*; Beasley, *Japan Encounters the Barbarian*; Gluck, "The 'End' of the Postwar."

54. Beasley, *Japan Encounters the Barbarian*, 216; Ching, "Yellow Skin, White Masks," 72.

55. Gluck, "The 'End' of the Postwar," 17.

56. Marvin Sterling emphasizes similar inequalities between Japanese who can travel to Jamaica and follow the dancehall scene, and the Jamaicans on the receiving end of these visits ("The Symbolic Constitution of Japanese Dancehall," 21).

57. Herzfeld, *Cultural Intimacy*, 3–4.

58. Wood, "The Yellow Negro," 329.

59. Robertson, *Takarazuka*, 90–97.

60. Berlant and Warner, "Sex in Public," 559.

61. Stoler, *Race and the Education of Desire*, 192.

62. Boym, "On Diasporic Intimacy," 499–501.

63. On stranger sociability, see Michael Warner's work ("Publics and Counterpublics," 56–57), and see Simmel on "the stranger" (*On Individuality and Social Forms*, 143–49).

64. Erik Ringmar discusses how intimacy between nationals sets up an exclusive "we" that does not cross into other nation-states ("Nationalism," 545). My work challenges the idea that national and transnational intimacies are mutually exclusive.

65. Povinelli, *The Empire of Love*, 2–4.

66. Ibid., 10.

67. Ibid., 14.

68. Wade, *Race and Ethnicity in Latin America*, 28; Harris, "Ethnic Identity and Market Relations," 353, 355.

69. Harris, "Ethnic Identity and Market Relations," 358.

70. For example, see Stern, "The Tragedy of Success."

71. Harris, "Ethnic Identity and Market Relations," 360.

72. Ibid., 361.

73. Platt, *Estado boliviano y ayllu andino*.

74. Barragán, "Identidades indias y mestizas," 21.

75. Brooke Larson's chapter focusing on turn-of-the-twentieth-century Bolivian writers (Bautista Saavedra, Manuel Rigoberto Paredes, Alcides Arguedas, and Franz Tamayo) details this anti-mestizaje tendency ("Redeemed Indians, Barbarized Cholos," 232). Also see Barragán, "Identidades indias y mestizas," 18.

76. Through her study of Bolivian education policies, Larson demonstrates the national ideological presence of mestizaje before the revolution of 1952 with which it is most commonly associated ("Capturing Indian Bodies, Hearths, and Minds," 50).

77. Albó, "From MNRistas to Kataristas to Katari," 381.

78. Other authors, working in multiple contexts about nationalism and ethnographies of the state, have highlighted this caveat. In her historical analysis of the Indigenous Congress of 1945, Laura Gotkowitz clearly demonstrates the eclecticism of Bolivian indigenistas ("'Under the Dominion of the Indian'"). For another critique of approaches that assume the top-down monolithic homogenizing state in Colombia, see Wade, *Music, Race, and Nation*, 4. For studies of nationalism, Michael Herzfeld warned against applying what he called "methodological individualism," an approach that treats the nation as if it were just a sum of individual wills (*Cultural Intimacy*, 9).

79. In another project, based on oral histories of dancers and musicians who worked in folklore between the 1930s and 1960s, I find that many folklore stars

of the period were sons and daughters or granddaughters and grandsons of ha-
cendados who, with the Agrarian Reform of 1953, lost their land holdings and
positions as overlords to indigenous workers (Bigenho, "Making Music Safe for
the Nation" and "Embodied Matters").

80. Roth, *Brokered Homeland*, 139.

81. Anna Tsing masterfully develops the concept of "global friction" to explore
how local articulations shape the tragedies as well as the promises of a globalized world (*Friction*).

82. Masterson and Funada-Classen, *The Japanese in Latin America*, 113. On a
Peruvian-Japanese experience in a US internment camp, see Higashide's *Adios
to Tears*.

83. Seeger, *Why Suyá Sing*; Turino, *Moving Away from Silence*; Turino, *Nationalists, Cosmopolitans, and Popular Music in Zimbabwe*; Wade, *Music, Race, and
Nation*.

84. Feld, "The Poetics and Politics of Pygmy Pop" and "A Sweet Lullaby for
World Music"; Erlmann, *Music, Modernity, and the Global Imagination*; Roberts,
"'World Music' and the Global Cultural Economy"; Goodwin and Gore, "World
Beat and the Cultural Imperialism Debate"; Meintjes, "Paul Simon's Graceland,
South Africa, and the Mediation of Musical Meaning"; De Carvalho, "La etno-
musicología en tiempos de canibalismo musical."

85. In her work on the intersection of Brazilian Indians with the Brazilian
state, Alcida Rita Ramos develops the concept of the "hyperreal Indian" as a
product of the bureaucratizations and noble savage ideologies as articulated by
nongovernmental organizations (*Indigenism*).

2. Performing Indigeneities

1. Listen to *Simon and Garfunkel's Greatest Hits*.

2. Albó, *Iguales aunque diferentes*.

3. See de la Cadena and Starn, *Indigenous Experience Today*, 4. Also see Butler,
Bodies That Matter. At the center of these discussions is the constructionist vs.
essentialist debate, distinctly experienced depending on one's position in relation to each term, and in relation to the indigenous identity in question. While
activists are often thought to deploy essentialist models of indigeneity, Joanne
Rappaport interpreted the complex networks of Colombian indigenous activism
as productive of frameworks that were not essentialist (*Intercultural Utopias*, 7).
James Clifford suggests the term "indigenous articulation" to get beyond the es-
sentialist/constructivist dichotomy ("Indigenous Articulations" and "Varieties
of Indigenous Experience").

4. Tsing, "Indigenous Voice," 38.

5. Ibid., 41.

6. Arturo Escobar argues that studies of mobility, deterritorialization, and the
production of cultural difference require a continued return to issues of place

("Culture Sits in Places," 147). While his study focuses on subaltern place-based practices, a global musical economy of cultural difference also depends on the imaginative recreation of place.

7. Meisch, *Andean Entrepreneurs*, 138.

8. See José Antonio Llórens Amico, who discusses other works by this composer and places this composition in contrast with the Inka operatic that was popular at that time in Lima (*Música popular en Lima*, 100–105). Deborah Poole uses the term "inca operatic" to refer more broadly to an eighteenth-century French fascination with and dramatization of an Inca world (*Vision, Race, and Modernity*).

9. Llórens Amico, *Música popular en Lima*, 102.

10. For some of these complexities in different contexts, see Favre, *El indigenismo*; de la Cadena, *Indigenous Mestizos*; Poole, *Vision, Race, and Modernity*; Muratorio, "Nación, identidad y etnicidad"; Mendoza, "Crear y sentir lo nuestro"; Salmón, *El espejo indígena*; Bigenho, "Embodied Matters."

11. For a history of the Andean-Paris connections that led to this boom, see Fernando Rios, "*La Flûte Indienne*."

12. Proyecto Condor Pasa, www.geocities.com/e_pomareda/alomia.html, accessed October 18, 2006; as of September 1, 2011, an archived version of the original GeoCities site is still available via ReoCities, www.reocities.com/e_pomareda/alomia.html.

13. In a chapter of my previous work as based on fieldwork conducted in the 1990s, I examined how indigenous music authorship played out in the recording and registration of audio cassettes from two indigenous Bolivian groups. In this work, I unpacked the colonizing logic of official registration processes that favored the naming of collectors, erased indigenous subjectivity, framed indigenous music as national patrimony created by "unidentified" authors, and ultimately unfolded with all the expected levels of bureaucratic inefficiency (*Sounding Indigenous*, 199–225). In her study of the global staging of Berber culture, Jane Goodman explored the ways indigenous peoples can also refashion copyright laws in new ways that challenge the supposedly oppositional categories of authorship and public domain (*Berber Culture on the World Stage*, 148).

14. Olsen, *The Chrysanthemum and the Song*, 69.

15. Erlmann, *Music, Modernity, and the Global Imagination*, 184.

16. Steven Feld uses the term "schizophonic mimesis" to refer to "a broad spectrum of interactive and extractive practices" that "produce a traffic in new creations and relationships through the use, circulation, and absorption of sound recordings." With his discussion of this term, I find particularly useful the move away from any simplistic discussion of cultural theft, but also the continued emphasis on the unequal relations of power that structure these exchanges and encounters ("The Poetics and Politics of Pygmy Pop," 263–64).

17. Céspedes, "New Currents in Música Folklórica in La Paz, Bolivia," 224. Listen to *Lo mejor de Los Jairas*.

18. Bigenho, "Embodied Matters"; Bigenho, *Sounding Indigenous*, 109–13.

19. My perspective on this break has developed through interviews and through informal discussions with Rolando Encinas (personal communication, 2005–6).

20. Meisch, *Andean Entrepreneurs*, 117–53.

21. See Cavour's *Diccionario enciclopédico de los instrumentos musicales de Bolivia*. Cavour locates his interest in miniatures through the January Alasitas fair in which it is a Paceña tradition to purchase in miniature those items that one wishes to acquire during the coming year. He told me his collection of miniatures is held in another museum he calls "The Smallest Museum of Bolivia."

22. Listen to *Ernesto Cavour: "De Colección."*

23. See Cavour, *Diccionario enciclopédico de los instrumentos musicales de Bolivia*.

24. Urquidi's folklore ballet was one of the first of its kind in Bolivia, and it was born in the 1950s as part of a music and dance revue called Fantasía Boliviana (Bigenho, "Embodied Matters").

25. This comment brings to the foreground Michael Herzfeld's work on "cultural intimacy" in nationalism (*Cultural Intimacy*); as Andrew Shryock reiterates, with reference to Herzfeld, this concept of intimacy internalizes and makes necessary an outside observer ("Other Conscious/Self Aware," 10).

26. See Wade, *Music, Race, and Nation*, 74.

27. Yano, *Tears of Longing*, 40.

28. Insights on the tango-folklore connection in Japan emerged from an interview with Jiro Hamada and Takaatsu Kinoshita (2003).

29. Moreno Cha, "Alternativas del proceso de cambio de un repertorio tradicional argentino," 96.

30. On the concept of "cultural intimacy" and nationalism, see Herzfeld, *Cultural Intimacy*.

31. Sánchez Patzy, "La música popular en Bolivia desde mediados del siglo XX y la identidad social," 282.

32. Fairley, "La nueva canción latinoamericana"; Rios, "*La Flûte Indienne*."

33. Fairley, "La nueva canción latinoamericana," 112, 108.

34. Ibid., 110.

35. Rios, "*La Flûte Indienne*," 163.

36. With his work in British punk music, Dick Hebdige draws attention to looking beyond the interpretation that reads youth subcultures as mere expressions of generational resistance (*Subculture*).

37. See Tsing, "Indigenous Voice."

38. Favre, *El indigenismo*.

39. Sinclair Thomson's re-examination of this period provides fascinating historical details on the diverse emancipation projects of this time and locates the Andean projects' obscurity next to the well-known cases from the Age of Revolution (*We Alone Will Rule*).

40. Rivera Cusicanqui, *Oprimidos pero no vencidos*.

41. Sánchez Patzy, "La música popular en Bolivia desde mediados del siglo XX y la identidad social," 283.

42. Rodríguez Ostria, *Sin tiempo para las palabras*.

43. Sánchez Patzy, "La música popular en Bolivia desde mediados del siglo XX y la identidad social," 284; Monroy Chazarreta, "De la protesta a la proyección," 98–102. In another Latin American case, Peter Wade details how in Colombia a modernized costeño music—the racialized "black" music that became nationally popular—"began to appeal to middle-class youth who identified with left-wing radicalism" (*Music, Race, and Nation*, 147).

44. Sánchez Patzy, "La música popular en Bolivia desde mediados del siglo XX y la identidad social," 280; Céspedes, "New Currents in Música Folklórica in La Paz, Bolivia" and "'Huayño,' 'Saya' and 'Chuntunqui.'"

45. Favre, *El indigenismo*, 11.

46. Ibid., 149–50.

47. Clifford, "Indigenous Articulations," 472.

48. Zorn, "From Political Prison to Tourist Village."

49. See Turner, "The Social Dynamics of Video Media in an Indigenous Society"; Ramos, *Indigenism*.

50. Canessa, "'Todos somos indígenas.'"

51. Postero, "Andean Utopias in Evo Morales's Bolivia."

52. Laura Graham cautions against a purely instrumentalist interpretation of indigenous peoples' use of such representations ("Image and Instrumentality in a Xavante Politics of Existential Recognition").

53. Marta Savigliano found the same metropolitan detours in tango's travels from Argentina to Japan (*Tango and the Political Economy of Passion*).

54. Música de Maestros recording, *Volumen I y II*.

55. Japanese musicians of different traditions establish real and fictive kin relations with their master teachers, following their respective *iemoto* or school. According to Atkins, within a school, "disciples are not free to interpret a style" (*Blue Nippon*, 34). The focus on a school and a master's lineage is not all that different from the studio lineages within a classical music conservatory in the Euro-American tradition (see Kingsbury, *Music, Talent, and Performance*). Citing one's master teachers as an artistic genealogy is a central part of the classical music tradition. For example, see Arnold Steinhardt, *Violin Dreams*.

56. From liner notes of Khantati's recording, *Charla del Viento*.

57. Listen to *Septeto Mayor de Música de Maestros*.

58. Listen to Kallawaya, *Shaman*.

59. For example, see Peter Wade's analysis of the "origin myths" of different Colombian music genres (*Music, Race, and Nation*, 53–66).

60. Associated Press, "Bono Receives Chile's Neruda Prize," Billboard.com, February 27, 2006.

61. La Nación, "Lagos sobre charango a Bono: 'En Chile también hay aymaras,'" Lanacion.cl, March 3, 2006.

62. Listen to Grupo Aymara, *Live in Japan*.

3. Work and Value in Musical Otherness

1. Stanley, *Being Ourselves for You*, 182.

2. On Disney and the world as spectacle, see Stanley, *Being Ourselves for You*, 17.

3. Ching, "Globalizing the Regional, Regionalizing the Global," 285.

4. Ibid., 288.

5. Jameson, *Postmodernism or the Cultural Logic of Late Capitalism*; García Canclini, "Cultural Reconversion."

6. Comaroff and Comaroff, "Millennial Capitalism"; Ellmeier, "Cultural Entrepreneurialism," 5.

7. Faulkner, *Hollywood Studio Musicians*, 10, 178–79.

8. Ellmeier, "Cultural Entrepreneurialism," 10.

9. Ching, "Globalizing the Regional, Regionalizing the Global," 288.

10. Post-Fordist capitalism is characterized by widespread tendencies toward labor flexibility and flexible specialization (Amin, "Post-Fordism," 4). Hand in hand with this form of capitalism comes a trend of "formalizing difference" (Geschiere and Nyamnjoh, "Capitalism and Autochthony").

11. Wade, "Working Culture," 449.

12. Information was drawn from the website of Music Amigos, or the Japanese Latin American Cultural Exchange Association on March 15, 2007 (www.music-amigos.co.jp). The website no longer exists.

13. As a way to understand why relatively few women become involved in Japanese hip-hop, Condry sets up a discussion of "cutismo" next to the "machismo" that characterizes Japanese hip hop (*Hip-Hop Japan*, 165–66).

14. Here, like Nick Stanley's argument, the performance of alterity is conditioned first by economic distance (*Being Ourselves for You*, 182).

15. Iwabuchi, "Nostalgia for a (Different) Asian Modernity," 547.

16. Lie, *Multiethnic Japan*, 131. Carol Gluck, in her discussion of various Japanese "postwar" frameworks, mentions that the "closed-off country" was one of the important metaphors of the early 1990s ("The 'End' of the Postwar," 21).

17. Harvey, *The Condition of Postmodernity*.

18. Fujikane, "Approaches to Global Education in the United States, the United Kingdom and Japan," 135.

19. Ibid., 137.

20. Tai, "Multicultural Education in Japan"; Murphy-Shigematsu, "Challenges for Multicultural Education in Japan."

21. Kapchan, "The Promise of Sonic Translation," 468.

22. Schein, "Importing Miao Brethren to Hmong America," 185.

23. In a contrast to this point, Jeffrey Lesser's work on Japanese Brazilians documents examples of government involvement in cultural exchange; in 1968 the Brazilian government sponsored a carnival parade of samba schools that performed in the streets of Kobe (*A Discontented Diaspora*, 14).

24. Ong, *Flexible Citizenship*, 11.

25. Hochschild, *The Managed Heart*, 7, 19, 55.

26. For example, see the ethnography of Lazar, *El Alto, Rebel City*.

27. Hochschild, *The Managed Heart*, 55.

28. Barbara Kirshenblatt-Gimblett discusses the partitioning of sensory experiences and their associations with specific art forms, a disciplining of the arts through parsed experiences (*Destination Culture*, 57). Diana Taylor suggests that the field of "performance studies" challenges the disciplinary compartmentalization of the arts (*The Archive and the Repertoire*, 26).

29. Bigenho, *Sounding Indigenous*.

30. Ibid., 88–96.

31. Tsing, "Indigenous Voice," 41.

32. Conklin, "The Shifting Middle Ground"; Ramos, *Indigenism*.

33. Luz del Ande, *Suite ecológico ser*.

34. Liner notes of Piazzolla y su quinteto tango nuevo, *The Vienna Concert*.

35. Listen to Música de Maestros, *Supay*.

36. Harrison, *Signs, Songs, and Memory in the Andes*.

37. Listen to Música de Maestros, *Sexteto Mayor*.

38. Listen to Música de Maestros, *Volumen XI. Surimana*.

39. Listen to Música de Maestros, *Septeto Mayor*.

40. On the life of musicians in La Paz, see my previous work, *Sounding Indigenous*, 103–9.

41. Stanley, *Being Ourselves for You*, 182.

4. A Hobby, a Sojourn, and a Job

1. Indigenous subjects, rather than mestizos, are the point of admiration in many tourist equations. Laurie Kroshus Medina finds tourists more interested in Maya than in mestizo Others; this interest inverts but also maintains the local hierarchy that places mestizos above Mayas ("Commoditizing Culture," 362). In the Andean context, Elayne Zorn similarly discusses this double bind of indigeneity as a locally negative reference and as a source of tourism successes (*Weaving a Future*, 152).

2. Henry Stobart has studied a wide variety of charango tunings, fingerings, and strumming styles in this region—specificities he refers to as "genre-technique-tuning," and these are presented in detailed form in his book *Music and the Poetics of Production in the Bolivian Andes*, 96–98.

3. The Japanese began hosting a Cosquín festival as early as 1981.

4. Rolando Encinas, personal communication, April 2007.

5. Savigliano, *Tango and the Political Economy of Passion*, 235.

6. Atkins, *Blue Nippon*, 19–22.

7. For similar cases in which Japanese learn different performance practices by traveling to the sources, see Marvin Sterling's work on Japanese involvement

in Jamaican dancehall ("The Symbolic Constitution of Japanese Dancehall"), and Yoko Kurokawa's work on Japanese who learn Hawaiian hula ("Yearning for a Distant Music").

8. Deloria, *Playing Indian*, 156.

9. Ibid., 185.

10. Nelson, *A Finger in the Wound*, 183.

11. Deloria, *Playing Indian*, 175.

12. Boym, *The Future of Nostalgia*, 54.

13. Ibid., 41–55.

14. Povinelli, *The Empire of Love*, 2–4.

15. Ibid., 95–174.

16. Gluck, "The 'End' of the Postwar," 17.

17. Condry, "B-Boys and B-Girls," 33–34.

18. Yano, *Tears of Longing*, 141.

19. Kelly, *Fanning the Flames*, 8.

20. Condry, "B-Boys and B-Girls," 36.

21. Miller, "Consumption and Commodities."

22. Stevens, "Buying Intimacy," 54.

23. McVeigh identifies the roots of this crisis in a postwar structure that links the universities too closely to a corporatized state, economics, and employment (*Japanese Higher Education as Myth*, 4, 9–10).

24. Atkins, *Blue Nippon*, 51.

25. Yano, "Letters from the Heart."

26. In an ethnography of a music conservatory, Henry Kingsbury explains how talent is culturally constructed within contexts where classical musicians are trained (*Music, Talent, and Performance*).

27. Ivy, *Discourses of the Vanishing*.

28. Ibid., 34.

29. Ibid., 47.

30. Allison, *Millennial Monsters*, 69.

31. Mok and Lam, "Travel-Related Behavior of Japanese Leisure Tourists." Also see Karen Kelsky's work on the international travel of Japanese middle-class women in the 1990s (*Women on the Verge*).

32. March, "The Japanese Travel Life Cycle."

33. Allison, *Millennial Monsters*, 70.

34. Povinelli, *The Empire of Love*.

35. Mathews, *What Makes Life Worth Living?*, 14–25.

36. Kinsella, "Japanese Subculture in the 1990s," 311, 293.

37. Condry, *Hip-Hop Japan*, 88–96.

38. Inui, "Why Freeter and NEET are Misunderstood."

39. Tobin, *Re-made in Japan*, 8.

40. Allison, *Millennial Monsters*, 71, 87.

41. Later, he did in fact marry and return to Japan.

42. Portillo and Fukuda recording, *Para no caer al cielo*.

43. For an ethnography about the disciplining of Japanese workers, see Dorinne Kondo's discussion of the ethics school to which confectionery factory workers were sent (*Crafting Selves*, 73–114). Joshua Roth described the exacting work conditions in a Yasumi Motors assembly line during the 1990s in which "a few seconds was an eternity"; his ethnography was set in a recessionary moment in which Japanese no longer could depend on what the employment system used to promise: lifetime employment, seniority wages, and company-based unions (*Brokered Homeland*, 44, 38).

44. Condry, "B-Boys and B-Girls," 32–33; Stevens, "Buying Intimacy," 74.

45. For more details about this artist, see work by Norberto Benjamín Torres, *Mauro Nuñez para el mundo*.

46. In previous work, I detail Bolivian musicians' debates around how to count and feel this genre (Bigenho, *Sounding Indigenous*, 47–54).

47. Yano, *Tears of Longing*, 41.

48. Condry, *Hip-Hop Japan*, 58.

49. Yano, *Tears of Longing*, 15.

50. Céspedes, "'Huayño,' 'Saya,' and Chuntunqui,'" 93–97.

51. Yano, *Tears of Longing*, 80–90.

52. See Tsing, "Indigenous Voice."

53. Feld, "A Sweet Lullaby for World Music," 190–91.

54. Brennan, "World Music Does Not Exist," 47.

55. Erlmann, *Music, Modernity, and the Global Imagination*, 185.

56. Attali, *Noise*.

57. Urry, *The Tourist Gaze*.

58. Bigenho, *Sounding Indigenous*.

5. Intimate Distance

1. Unless otherwise noted, I am using pseudonyms in this chapter.

2. Simmel states that desire "can only arise at a distance from objects, a distance that it attempts to overcome, and yet that it presupposes a closeness between the objects and ourselves in order that the distance should be experienced at all" (*The Philosophy of Money*, 76).

3. Yano, *Tears of Longing*, 16. Carolyn Stevens marked the importance of distance in the fantasy of intimacy as lived by fans of the Japanese rock band, The Alfee ("Buying Intimacy," 74).

4. For example, William Kelly suggests, "Fans seek intimacy with the object of their attention—a personality, a program, a genre, a team" (*Fanning the Flames*, 9).

5. Steven Feld presents a complex view of the "increasingly blurred and contested lines between forms of musical invasion and forms of cultural exchange" ("The Poetics and Politics of Pygmy Pop," 254).

6. Atkins, *Blue Nippon*; Condry, *Hip-Hop Japan*.

7. Atkins, *Blue Nippon*, 221–33.

8. See Dorinne Kondo's study of race and Japanese fashion designers who want to "escape ghettoization" of national identifications (*About Face*, 60–61).

9. Hall, "The West and the Rest."

10. His phrases resonate with Marilyn Ivy's discussions about the "Discover Japan" tourism campaign through which an unknown Japan was promoted as the "strangely familiar" or "the native remote" (*Discourses of the Vanishing*, 47).

11. Savigliano, *Tango and the Political Economy of Passion*, 245.

12. After Olsen, *The Chrysanthemum and the Song*, 68.

13. Weismantel, *Cholas and Pishtacos*, 92.

14. Yoshino, "Discourse on Blood and Racial Identity in Contemporary Japan," 200; Condry, *Hip-Hop Japan*, 26.

15. Olsen, *The Chrysanthemum and the Song*, 23.

16. Yoshino, "Discourse on Blood and Racial Identity in Contemporary Japan," 201.

17. Dikötter, *The Construction of Racial Identities in China and Japan*, 9.

18. TallBear, "Narratives of Race and Indigeneity in the Genographic Project," 413–14.

19. Ibid., 415.

20. Ibid., 419.

21. Hamilton, "Revitalizing Difference in the HapMap."

22. Ossorio and Duster, "Race and Genetics," 116.

23. Shaw, "Telling Stories of Human Connection," 236.

24. Palmié, "Genomics, Divination, 'Racecraft,'" 205. Palmié's article anchors an *American Ethnologist* forum on this subject.

25. TallBear, "Narratives of Race and Indigeneity in the Genographic Project," 422.

26. For example, when Steven Feld asked Herbie Hancock about sampling the Pygmy hindehoo in "Watermelon Man" without direct credit, Hancock replied, "It's a brother kind of thing" (Feld, "The Poetics and Politics of Pygmy Pop, 257–59).

27. Radano and Bohlman, *Music and the Racial Imagination*, 5.

28. Judith Butler takes apart the naturalness of sex in relation to the body (*Gender Trouble*). Peter Wade critiques the assumed naturalness of phenotypical variation ("'Race,' Nature, and Culture," 17). Kamala Visweswaran critiqued Boas's supposed division of race from racism because this division still assumed that the former was a biological realm, rendering it adequate for scientific research; such a framework further legitimated rather than undermined scientific racism ("Race and the Culture of Anthropology," 70–71).

29. Zorn, *Weaving a Future*, 151. See also Desmond, *Staging Tourism*, xxiii.

30. Franco, "Globalization and the Crisis of the Popular"; Pratt, "Modernity and Periphery."

31. Young, *Colonial Desire*, 175.

32. See Radano and Bohlman, *Music and the Racial Imagination*, and Viswes-

waran, "Race and the Culture of Anthropology," for critiques of this maneuver in the fields of ethnomusicology and anthropology, respectively.

33. See Strathern, *Property, Substance, and Effect*, 25.

34. Lie, *Multiethnic Japan*, 102.

35. Ong, *Flexible Citizenship*; Young, *Colonial Desire*.

36. Wade, *Race and Ethnicity in Latin America*; Stoler, *Race and the Education of Desire*.

37. Stoler, *Race and the Education of Desire*, 9.

38. Dikötter, *The Construction of Racial Identities in China and Japan*; Yoshino, "Discourse on Blood and Racial Identity in Contemporary Japan."

39. Ann Stoler's pathbreaking work, *Race and the Education of Desire*, greatly shaped by the periods of Foucault's *History of Sexuality*, draws most heavily on late European colonialism, saying little about how the much earlier Iberian colonialism may have shaped race, desire, and the modern project. I thank Karen Spalding for calling my attention to this point (personal communication 2006).

40. Wade, *Race and Ethnicity in Latin America*, 37.

41. Ching, "Yellow Skin, White Masks," 67–68.

42. On Japan, see Ching, "Yellow Skin, White Masks," 78; on Latin American contexts, see Wade, *Race and Ethnicity in Latin America*.

43. Harris, "Ethnic Identity and Market Relations," 360.

44. Many Latin American states gave eugenics their own twist, not dismissing environmental factors from their equations and developing a kind of neo-Lamarckism that blurred the separation of nature and nurture and "kept a place for purposive social action and moral choice" (Stepan, *"The Hour of Eugenics,"* 40–45, 87).

45. Wade, *Race and Ethnicity in Latin America*, 31.

46. Hylton and Thomson, *Revolutionary Horizons*, 55–56.

47. Ibid., 52; also see Mamani Condori, *Taraqu, 1866–1935*.

48. Authors drew variously from Lamarckian ideas, from hybridity, and from ideas about social illness. While the authors Juan Bautista Saavedra, Manuel Rigoberto Paredes, and Alcides Arguedas fell within this anti-mestizaje discourse, Franz Tamayo left open the possibility of incorporating the indian within the nation—an indian who could be educated and civilized (Larson, "Redeemed Indians, Barbarized Cholos," 231–32, 233, 238, 239, 242).

49. On educational reforms and discussions of hygiene see Larson, "Capturing Indian Bodies, Hearths, and Minds," 50; and Stephenson, *Gender and Modernity in Andean Bolivia*, 122. On the Indigenous Congress, see Gotkowitz, "'Under the Dominion of the Indian.'"

50. Platt, *Estado boliviano y ayllu andino*; Rivera Cusicanqui, *Oprimidos pero no vencidos*.

51. Rivera Cusicanqui, *Oprimidos pero no vencidos*, 52–56; Gustafson, "The Paradoxes of Liberal Indigenism."

52. Nancy Postero develops this point in detail, linking multiculturalism to neoliberal governmentality in Bolivia (*Now We Are Citizens*, 13–15). For a discus-

sion of these issues in relation to Central America, see Hale, "Neoliberal Multi-culturalism."

53. Harrison, "The Persistent Power of Race," 47.

54. Canessa, "'Todos somes indígenas.'"

55. Sanjinés, "Mestizaje Upside Down," 52–53.

56. After Patzi Paco, "Rebelión indígena contra la colonialidad y la transnacio-nalización de la economía," 221.

57. Hylton and Thomson, *Revolutionary Horizons*, 130.

58. For an analysis of elite-backed spectacles as symbols of "autonomy" in eastern Bolivia, see Gustafson, "Spectacles of Autonomy and Crisis."

59. See Wade, "'Race,' Nature, and Culture," 28; see also García Canclini, *Hy-brid Cultures*.

60. See Barragán, "Entre polleras, lliqllas, y ñañacas" and "Identidades indias y mestizas"; Rivera Cusicanqui, "La raíz"; Sanjinés, "Mestizaje Upside Down"; Harris, "Ethnic Identity and Market Relations"; Larson, "Capturing Indian Bodies, Hearths and Minds."

61. Weiner, "The Invention of Identity"; Harden, "The Enterprise of Empire," 179; Morris-Suzuki, "Debating Racial Science in Wartime Japan."

62. Weiner, "The Invention of Identity," 105.

63. Robertson, "Biopower," 329.

64. Morris-Suzuki, "Debating Racial Science in Wartime Japan," 358.

65. Ibid., 362; Robertson, "Biopower," 330.

66. Morris-Suzuki, "Debating Racial Science in Wartime Japan," 362.

67. Tanaka, *Japan's Orient*, 4.

68. Howell, "Making 'Useful Citizens' of Ainu Subjects in Early Twentieth-Century Japan," 5.

69. Howell, *Geographies of Identity in Nineteenth-Century Japan*.

70. Siddle, "The Ainu and the Discourse of 'Race,'" 137.

71. Ohnuki-Tierney, "A Conceptual Model for the Historical Relationship Be-tween the Self and the Internal and External Others."

72. Howell, "Making 'Useful Citizens' of Ainu Subjects in Early Twentieth-Century Japan," 12.

73. Howell, *Geographies of Identity in Nineteenth-Century Japan*, 172.

74. Ohnuki-Tierney, "A Conceptual Model for the Historical Relationship between the Self and the Internal and External Others," 44; Howell, "Making 'Useful Citizens' of Ainu Subjects in Early Twentieth-Century Japan," 24. On the "internal exotic" as a part of Japanese tourism campaigns, see Ivy, *Discourses of the Vanishing*, 48.

75. Kelly, "Directions in the Anthropology of Contemporary Japan," 413; Mas-den, "The Impact of Ministry of Education Policy on Pluralism in Japanese Edu-cation," 56.

76. Lie, *Multiethnic Japan*, 121–25.

77. Diane Nelson drew out this metaphor for the case of Guatemala, telling the allegory of the man who had to contort his body in order to fit into a camel hair

suit; in spite of the man's tortured body underneath the clothes, someone still remarked about his beautiful camel hair suit (*A Finger in the Wound*, 179).

78. Lie, *Multiethnic Japan*, 131.

79. Atkins, *Blue Nippon*, 29. E. Taylor Atkins argued that the Japanese view jazz as belonging to black Americans, and therefore Japanese jazz musicians experience difficulties feeling their own music as authentic. As one strategy to authenticate jazz in Japan, Japanese musicians will claim an affinity with African Americans by referencing a parallel international experience of racial discrimination (*Blue Nippon*, 12).

80. Yoshino, "Discourse on Blood and Racial Identity in Contemporary Japan," 204.

81. Dale, *The Myth of Japanese Uniqueness*; also see Yoshino, "Discourse on Blood and Racial Identity in Contemporary Japan," 200.

82. Murphy-Shigematsu, "Identities of Multiethnic People in Japan," 215; Yoshino, "Discourse on Blood and Racial Identity in Contemporary Japan"; Lie, *Multiethnic Japan*.

83. Yoshino, "Discourse on Blood and Racial Identity in Contemporary Japan"; Roth, *Brokered Homeland*.

84. Yoshino, "Culturalism, Racialism, and Internationalism in the Discourse on Japanese Identity," 15.

85. See Atkins, *Blue Nippon*; Hosokawa, "Salsa no tiene fronteras"; Mitsui, "The Reception of the Music of American Southern Whites in Japan"; Savigliano, *Tango and the Political Economy of Passion*.

86. Condry, *Hip-Hop Japan*, 52.

87. Atkins, *Blue Nippon*, 33.

88. Among Japanese followers of Irish music, Sean Williams encountered the same nostalgic reference to childhood remembrance ("Irish Music and the Experience of Nostalgia in Japan," 102).

89. This contrasts with the absence of exotification that Marta Savigliano noted in her study of tangueros in Japan ("Tango in Japan and the World Economy of Passion," 243).

90. On the incarceration of the native, see Appadurai, "Putting Hierarchy in Its Place," 37.

91. Povinelli, *The Empire of Love*, 4–6.

92. Povinelli discussed the intimate event in relation to the autological subject; the intimate event refers to liberal love built on the nuclear family and constructed through the heterosexual reproductive couple (*The Empire of Love*, 182–85).

93. Povinelli, *The Empire of Love*, 199–200.

94. Ibid., 5–6.

95. Hylton and Thomson give a detailed analysis of how Bolivia's recent revolutionary moment depended on long-standing forms of non-liberal governance—ones that were at times incomprehensible to more traditional political organizations (*Revolutionary Horizons*, 9, 25–26, 115).

96. The Bolivians' view here can be likened to the Brazilian idealization of the hypermodern and hyper-traditional aspects that were associated with Japanese culture and the Brazilian Nikkei (Lesser, *A Discontented Diaspora*, xxvii).

97. Borneman, "State, Territory, and Identity Formation in the Postwar Berlins, 1945–1989."

6. Gringa in Japan

1. Nelson, *A Finger in the Wound*, 41–73; also see Adams, "Los cosechadores de órganos y Harbury."

2. Through his analysis of "Oriental studies," and the work of Edward Said, Timothy Mitchell argues that area studies emerged not after World War II but in the interwar period when Europe and the United States were experiencing "civilizational anxiety" ("Deterritorialization and the Crisis of Social Science," 149). This may not point to a definitive discrepancy in arguments about the birth of area studies. Rather it provides evidence that not all "area studies" have the same historical trajectories.

3. Lewis and Wigen, *The Myth of Continents*, 169.

4. For excellent discussions of the area studies debates, see Ali Mirsepassi, Amrita Basu, and Frederick Weaver's edited volume, *Localizing Knowledge in a Globalizing World*. For a discussion of the disciplines of social science in relation to area studies, see Mitchell's work, "Deterritorialization and the Crisis of Social Science." For discussions of area studies in relation to anthropological traditions of "culture areas," see Lederman, "Globalization and the Future of Culture Areas," and Fardon, *Localizing Strategies*.

5. Yoneyama, *Hiroshima Traces*, 5.

6. Ong, *Flexible Citizenship*, 197, 74.

7. Ishihara, *The Japan That Can Say No*.

8. Yoneyama, *Hiroshima Traces*, 6–7.

9. Nathan, *Japan Unbound*, 141–56.

10. Gershon, "Reflexivity in Others' Contexts," 446–47. Bill Maurer also writes of the anthropological "there" that went unquestioned in the reflexive turn (*Mutual Life, Limited*, 12).

11. See Spedding, "Cocataki, Taki-Coca."

12. Anderson encountered this idea in the reading of a "nationalist novel," José Rizal's *Noli Me Tangere*, in which the nineteenth-century protagonist returns home to Manila after a tour of Europe and sees in the local gardens their striking imitation of the gardens he had just visited abroad (*The Spectre of Comparisons*, 2–3).

13. See Marcus and Fischer, *Anthropology as Cultural Critique*; Rosaldo, *Culture and Truth*.

14. Starn, *Nightwatch*, 6.

15. Nicholas Thomas calls for a return of the comparative project, not in the positivist sense but rather as "a regional frame to argue about processes of social

change and diversity" that is self-aware and that proposes arguments "strategi-cally and provisionally rather than universally" ("Against Ethnography," 315–17). Also see Herzfeld, *Anthropology*, 41.

16. Diane Nelson tells a horrific story of a gringa in Guatemala who was ac-cused of child snatching (*A Finger in the Wound*, 64–67). Also see the work of Abigail E. Adams; she analyzes media representations of gringas and stories of organ harvesters in Guatemala, reading these representations in relation to state authorities ("Los cosechdores de órganos y Harbury"). On the symbolics of fat-sucking beings in the Andean region (*pishtacos, kharisiris*), see Weismantel, *Cho-las and Pishtacos*.

17. Malinowski, *Argonauts of the Western Pacific*.

18. Michael Dutton suggested that language training and translation formed core elements of area studies traditions; in the case of Asian studies, these language projects were rooted in philology and in Asian studies' precursor—Oriental studies ("Lead Us Not into Translation," 504). Harry Harootunian, re-sponding to Dutton's piece, called for a crucial distinction between philology's unreflexive and passive approach to language training and the language train-ing for "active understanding" that most area studies actually teach ("Lost in the Translation," 541).

19. Marcus, "Ethnography in/of the World System."

20. Gupta and Ferguson, "Discipline and Practice."

21. Starn, *Nightwatch*, 15; Clifford, *Routes*, 57; Marcus and Fischer, *Anthro-pology as Cultural Critique*, 77–110.

22. Bigenho, *Sounding Indigenous*, 6–16.

23. Clifford, *Routes*.

24. Gluck, "The 'End' of the Postwar," 5.

25. Gupta and Ferguson, "Discipline and Practice," 4–5, 35–39.

26. Haraway, *Simians, Cyborgs, and Women*, 190–92.

27. Roth, "Responsibility and the Limits of Identification," 345–46.

28. Kelsky, *Women on the Verge*, 32.

29. Strathern, *Property, Substance, and Effect*, 25.

30. Nelson, *A Finger in the Wound*, 183.

31. I further develop this point in the article "Inter-Area Ethnography."

32. Arguedas, *El zorro de arriba y el zorro de abajo*.

33. On the racialization of culture that surrounds both the division of labor between musicology and ethnomusicology, see Radano and Bohlman, *Music and the Racial Imagination*.

34. Dirlik, "Culture Against History?"

35. Allison, *Permitted and Prohibited Desires*, 8; also see Kelsky, *Women on the Verge*, 29.

36. Ivy, "Mourning the Japanese Thing," 96.

37. Kelly, "Directions in the Anthropology of Contemporary Japan," 396. One can trace both the study of Japan by Japanese scholars and the study of Japan by US-trained scholars. For example, the Institute of Ethnology, founded in Tokyo in 1943 and linked to government imperial projects, aimed to study the peoples

of Asia, and its workers conducted research in Korea, Mongolia, northern China, Formosa, and Micronesia (Sofue, "Anthropology in Japan," 174; Nakane, "Cultural Anthropology in Japan," 68). According to Takao Sofue's review article of 1961, the end of World War II freed the different fields of anthropology from "the doctrine of the divine origin of the Emperor," and "archaeologists took the lead in studying the real origins and development of the Japanese nation" ("Anthropology in Japan," 175). Folklore studies made rural Japan the place of nostalgic longing for what Japan was losing in the process of modernization (Tamanoi, "Women's Voices," 24; see Ivy, "Mourning the Japanese Thing," 97). But postwar US scholarship on Japan, following American politics of the time, upheld the idea of the Japanese emperor as foundational (see Harootunian and Sakai, "Dialogue," 604).

38. Kelly writes: "a singular, valorized Japan is set against the mirage of an equally unitary but radically different and devalued West" ("Directions in the Anthropology of Contemporary Japan," 396).

39. An exception to this might be found in the argument that Andeanism is something like Orientalism (Starn, "Missing the Revolution"), but the parallels are far from straightforward.

40. Rena Lederman unpacks the anthropological traditions behind "culture areas" (i.e., Melanesian, Mediterranean) and points to the advantages of these constructs because of their conceptualization beyond the nation-state frame that always filters "area studies" approaches ("Globalization and the Future of Culture Areas," 430). Within this project, the "Andean" culture area has proven itself to have a global currency, although not without its commodifying baggage and presently waning value.

41. See Condry's description of these nocturnal rhythms in relation to clubbing (Hip-Hop Japan).

42. Nelson, A Finger in the Wound, 41–48.

43. Bestor, "Inquisitive Observation," 331.

44. Herzfeld, Anthropology Through the Looking Glass; Lassiter, The Power of Kiowa Song; Narayan, "How Native Is a 'Native' Anthropologist?"; Tedlock, "Ethnography and Ethnographic Representation."

45. Yano, Tears of Longing, 14.

46. Harden, "The Enterprise of Empire," 174.

47. Russell, "Race and Reflexivity," 22.

48. Field, In the Realm of a Dying Emperor, 63.

49. Lonely Planet, Lonely Planet Japan.

50. Field, In the Realm of a Dying Emperor, 67.

51. Harootunian and Sakai, "Dialogue," 599.

52. Rivera Cusicanqui, Oprimidos pero no vencidos; Turino, Nationalists, Cosmopolitans, and Popular Music in Zimbabwe.

53. Anderson, The Spectre of Comparisons; Dirlik, "Culture against History?"; Harootunian and Sakai, "Dialogue," 600; Lewis and Wigen, The Myth of Continents.

7. Conclusion

1. The use of American Indian references for team sports has long been cause for Native American protest, but Gironda did not demonstrate knowledge of these thorny issues. I reference the photo and story to point to what I suggested much earlier in relation to the capitalization of the word "indian." North and South American experiences of indigeneity have similarities, but their contrasting histories still need to be more fully understood.

2. See Alborada performing "Ananau," YouTube video, 5:03, posted by belle-megers, viewed September 20, 2008, at http://www.youtube.com/watch?v=z YaXRgNp2Wk.

3. See Fernando José Wayra, YouTube video, 4:05, posted by yurajanka, viewed September 20, 2008, at http://www.youtube.com/watch?v=RFE7SXSbbNc.

4. Stephen, *Transborder Lives*, 19–27.

5. Hylton and Thomson, *Revolutionary Horizons*, 127–28.

6. See Journeyman Pictures's "Dancing with Evo Morales—Bolivia," YouTube video, 28:58, posted by Journeyman Pictures, viewed March 30, 2008, at http://www.youtube.com/watch?v=r-JA7IgatqE.

7. I'm thinking here of Paul Gilroy's discussions of anti-antiessentialism (*The Black Atlantic*, 99–103), and Gayatri Spivak's strategic essentialism ("Subaltern Studies," 13). An uncritical antiessentialist position overlooks historical and political reasons why groups might put forward essentialist positions.

8. Michaels, "Race into Culture."

9. Wade, *Music, Race, and Nation*; Radano and Bohlman, *Music and the Racial Imagination*.

10. Stoler, "Imperial Debris," 193, 200.

11. Marcus, "Ethnography in/of the World System."

12. Rena Lederman's analysis of anthropology's culture areas in the age of globalization speaks directly to these issues ("Globalization and the Future of Culture Areas").

13. Geertz, *The Interpretation of Cultures*.

14. Povinelli, *The Empire of Love*, 7.

15. For example, Andrew Shryock sets up mass media as both requiring and obscuring "zones of intimacy" ("Other Conscious/Self Aware," 3).

16. Miller, "Consumption and Commodities."

17. Condry, *Hip-Hop Japan*.

18. For examples of such critical takes on "authenticity," see Atkins, *Blue Nippon*; and Bigenho, *Sounding Indigenous*, 16–23.

Bibliography

Published Sources

Abercrombie, Thomas. *Pathways of Memory and Power: Ethnography and History among an Andean People*. Madison: University of Wisconsin Press, 1998.

———. "To Be Indian, to Be Bolivian: 'Ethnic' and 'National' Discourses of Identity." In *Nation-States and Indians in Latin America*, edited by Greg Urban and Joel Sherzer, 95–130. Austin: University of Texas Press, 1991.

Abram, Simone, and Jacqueline Waldren. "Introduction: Tourists and Tourism—Identifying with People and Places." In *Tourists and Tourism: Identifying with People and Places*, edited by Simone Abram, Jacqueline Waldren, and Donald V. L. Macleod, 1–11. Oxford: Berg, 1997.

Adams, Abigail E. "Los cosechadores de órganos y Harbury: Relatos transnacionales de impunidad y responsabilidad en Guatemala después de la guerra." *Mesoamérica* 34 (diciembre 1997): 595–632.

Albó, Xavier. "From MNRistas to Kataristas to Katari." In *Resistance, Rebellion, and Consciousness in the Andean Peasant World: 18th to 20th Centuries*, edited by Steve Stern, 379–419. Madison: University of Wisconsin Press, 1987.

———. *Iguales aunque diferentes: Hacia unas políticas interculturales y lingüísticas para Bolivia*. La Paz: Ministerio de Educación, UNICEF, CIPCA, 1999.

Albó, Xavier, and Matías Preiswerk. *Los señores del Gran Poder*. La Paz: Centro de Teología Popular/Taller de Observaciones Culturales, 1986.

Allison, Anne. *Millennial Monsters: Japanese Toys and the Global Imagination*. Berkeley: University of California Press, 2006.

———. *Permitted and Prohibited Desires: Mothers, Comics, and Censorship in Japan*. Berkeley: University of California Press, 2000.

Amin, Ash. "Post-Fordism: Models, Fantasies and Phantoms of Transition." In *Post-Fordism: A Reader*, edited by Ash Amin, 1–40. Oxford: Blackwell, 1994.

Anderson, Benedict. *The Spectre of Comparisons: Nationalism, Southeast Asia, and the World*. London: Verso, 1998.

Appadurai, Arjun. "Putting Hierarchy in Its Place." *Cultural Anthropology* 3, no. 1 (1988): 36–49.

Arguedas, José María. *El zorro de arriba y el zorro de abajo*. Lima: Editorial Horizonte, 1969.

Atkins, E. Taylor. *Blue Nippon: Authenticating Jazz in Japan*. Durham: Duke University Press, 2001.

Attali, Jacques. *Noise: The Political Economy of Music*. Translated by Brian Massumi. Minneapolis: University of Minnesota Press, 1985.

Barragán, Rossana. "Entre polleras, lliqllas, y ñañacas: Los mestizos y la emergencia de la tercera república." In *Etnicidad, economía y simbolismo en los Andes*, edited by Silvia Arze, Rossana Barragán, Laura Escobari, Ximena Medinaceli, 85–117. La Paz: HISBOL, IFEA, SBH-ASUR, 1992.

———. "Identidades indias y mestizas: una intervención al debate." *Autodeterminación: análisis histórico-político y teoría social* 10 (1992): 17–44.

Barragán, Rossana (with Johnny Guerreros, Nancy Maldonado, Carmen Tito, Lía Tito, Mitsuko Shimose, Irineo Uturunco, and Solange Zalles) and Cleverth Cárdenas (with Soledad Ardaya). *Gran poder: La morenada*. La Paz: IEB, Asdi/Sarec, Archivo de La Paz, 2009.

Beasley, William G. *Japan Encounters the Barbarian: Japanese Travelers in America and Europe*. New Haven: Yale University Press, 1995.

Berlant, Lauren, and Michael Warner. "Sex in Public." *Critical Inquiry* 24, no. 2 (1998): 547–66.

Bestor, Theodore C. "Inquisitive Observation: Following Networks in Urban Fieldwork." In *Doing Fieldwork in Japan*, edited by Theodore C. Bestor, Patricia G. Steinhoff, Victoria Lyon Bestor, 315–34. Honolulu: University of Hawai'i Press, 2003.

Bigenho, Michelle. "Embodied Matters: *Bolivian Fantasy* and Indigenismo." *Journal of Latin American Anthropology* 11, no. 2 (2006): 267–93.

———. "Inter-area Ethnography: A Latin Americanist in Japan." *Anthropological Quarterly* 79, no. 4 (2006): 667–90.

———. "Making Music Safe for the Nation: Folklore Pioneers in Bolivian Indigenism." In *Natives Making Nation: Gender, Indigeneity, and the State in the Andes*, edited by Andrew Canessa, 60–80. Tucson: University of Arizona Press, 2005.

———. *Sounding Indigenous: Authenticity in Bolivian Music Performance*. New York: Palgrave Macmillan, 2002.

Borneman, John. "State, Territory, and Identity Formation in the Postwar Berlins, 1945–1989." *Cultural Anthropology* 7, no. 1 (1992): 45–62.

Boym, Svetlana. *The Future of Nostalgia*. New York: Basic Books, 2001.

———. "On Diasporic Intimacy: Ilya Kabakov's Installations and Immigrant Homes." *Critical Inquiry* 24, no. 2 (1998): 498–524.

Brennan, Timothy. "World Music Does Not Exist." *Discourse* 23, no. 1 (2001): 44–62.

Butler, Judith. *Bodies That Matter: On the Discursive Limits of "Sex."* New York: Routledge, 1993.

———. *Gender Trouble: Feminism and the Subversion of Identity*. New York: Routledge, 1990.

Canessa, Andrew. "Introduction: Making the Nation on the Margins." In *Natives Making Nation: Gender, Indigeneity, and the State in the Andes*, edited by Andrew Canessa, 1–31. Tucson: University of Arizona Press, 2005.

———. "'Todos somos indígenas': Towards a New Language of National and Political Identity." *Bulletin of Latin American Research* 25, no. 2 (2006): 241–63.

———. "Who Is Indigenous? Self-Identification, Indigeneity, and Claims to Justice in Contemporary Bolivia." *Urban Anthropology* 36, no. 3 (2007): 195–237.

Cavour Aramayo, Ernesto. *Diccionario enciclopédico de los instrumentos musicales de Bolivia*. La Paz: Producciones Cima, 2003.

Céspedes, Gilka Wara. "'Huayño,' 'Saya,' and 'Chuntunqui': Bolivian Identity in the Music of 'Los Kjarkas.'" *Latin American Music Review* 14, no. 1 (1993): 52–101.

———. "New Currents in Música Folklórica in La Paz, Bolivia." *Latin American Music Review* 5 (1984): 217–42.

Ching, Leo. "Globalizing the Regional, Regionalizing the Global: Mass Culture and Asianism in the Age of Late Capital." In *Globalization*, edited by Arjun Appadurai, 279–306. Durham: Duke University Press, 2001.

———. "Yellow Skin, White Masks: Race, Class, and Identification in Japanese Colonial Discourse." In *Trajectories: Inter-Asia Cultural Studies*, edited by Kuan-Hsing Chen, 65–86. New York: Routledge, 1998.

Chow, Rey. "Where Have All the Natives Gone?" In *Displacements: Cultural Identities in Question*, edited by Angelika Bammer, 125–51. Bloomington: Indiana University Press, 1994.

Clifford, James. "Indigenous Articulations." *Contemporary Pacific* 13, no. 2 (2001): 468–90.

———. *The Predicament of Culture: Twentieth-Century Ethnography, Literature, and Art*. Cambridge: Harvard University Press, 1988.

———. *Routes: Travel and Translation in the Late Twentieth Century*. Cambridge: Harvard University Press, 1997.

———. "Varieties of Indigenous Experience: Diasporas, Homelands, Sovereignties." In *Indigenous Experience Today*, edited by Marisol de la Cadena and Orin Starn, 197–245. Oxford: Berg, 2007.

Comaroff, Jean, and John L. Comaroff. *Ethnicity Inc.* Chicago: University of Chicago Press, 2009.

———. "Millennial Capitalism: First Thoughts on a Second Coming." *Public Culture* 12, no. 2 (2000): 291–343.

Condry, Ian. "B-Boys and B-Girls: Rap Fandom and Consumer Culture in Japan." In *Fanning the Flames: Fans and Consumer Culture in Contemporary Japan*, edited by William W. Kelly, 17–39. Albany: State University of New York Press, 2004.

———. *Hip-Hop Japan: Rap and the Paths of Cultural Globalization*. Durham: Duke University Press, 2006.

Conklin, Beth A. "The Shifting Middle Ground: Amazonian Indians and Eco-Politics." *American Anthropologist* 97, no. 4 (1995): 695–710.

Coronil, Fernando. "Beyond Occidentalism: Toward Nonimperial Geohistorical Categories." *Cultural Anthropology* 11, no. 1 (1996): 51–87.

Dale, Peter N. *The Myth of Japanese Uniqueness*. New York: Routledge, 1986.

De Carvalho, José Jorge. "La etnomusicología en tiempos de canibalismo musical. Una reflexión a partir de las tradiciones musicales afroamericanas." *TRANS-Revista Transcultural de Música* 7, article 5 (2003), http://www.sibetrans.com/trans/.

De la Cadena, Marisol. *Indigenous Mestizos: The Politics of Race and Culture in Cuzco, Peru, 1919–1991*. Durham: Duke University Press, 2000.

De la Cadena, Marisol, and Orin Starn, eds. *Indigenous Experience Today*. Oxford: Berg, 2007.

Deloria, Philip J. *Playing Indian*. New Haven: Yale University Press, 1998.

Desmond, Jane. *Staging Tourism: Bodies on Display from Waikiki to Sea World*. Chicago: Chicago University Press, 1999.

Dikötter, Frank, ed. *The Construction of Racial Identities in China and Japan: Historical and Contemporary Perspectives*. London: Hurst and Company, 1997.

Dirlik, Arif. "Culture against History? The Politics of East Asian Identity." In *Localizing Knowledge in a Globalizing World: Recasting the Area Studies Debate*, edited by Ali Mirsepassi, Amrita Basu, and Frederick Weaver, 193–215. Syracuse: Syracuse University Press, 2003.

Dutton, Michael. 2002. "Lead Us Not into Translation: Notes toward a Theoretical Foundation for Asian Studies." *Nepantla: Views from South* 3, no. 3 (2002): 495–537.

Ellmeier, Andrea. "Cultural Entrepreneurialism: On the Changing Relationship between the Arts, Culture and Employment." *International Journal of Cultural Policy* 9, no. 1 (2003): 3–16.

Erlmann, Veit. *Music, Modernity, and the Global Imagination: South Africa and the West*. Oxford: Oxford University Press, 1999.

Errington, Shelly. *The Death of Authentic Primitive Art and Other Tales of Progress*. Berkeley: University of California Press, 1998.

Escobar, Arturo. "Culture Sits in Places: Reflections on Globalism and Subaltern Strategies of Localization." *Political Geography* 20, no. 2 (2001): 139–74.

Fairley, Jan. "La nueva canción latinoamericana." *Bulletin of Latin American Research* 3, no. 2 (1984): 107–15.

Fardon, Richard. "Localizing Strategies: The Regionalization of Ethnographic Accounts: General Introduction." In *Localizing Strategies: Regional Traditions of Ethnographic Writing*, edited by Richard Fardon, 1–35. Edinburgh and Washington: Scottish Academic Press and Smithsonian Institution Press, 1990.

Faulkner, Robert R. *Hollywood Studio Musicians: Their Work and Careers in the Recording Industry*. Chicago: Aldine Atherton, 1971.

Favre, Henri. *El indigenismo*. México: Fondo de Cultura Económica, 1998.

Feld, Steven. "The Poetics and Politics of Pygmy Pop." In *Western Music and Its Others: Difference, Representation, and Appropriation in Music*, edited by Georgina Born and David Hesmondhalgh, 254–79. Berkeley: University of California Press, 2000.

———. "A Sweet Lullaby for World Music." In *Globalization*, edited by Arjun Appadurai, 189–216. Durham: Duke University Press, 2001.

Field, Norma. *In the Realm of a Dying Emperor: Japan at Century's End.* New York: Vintage Books, 1991.

Flores, Juan. *From Bomba to Hip-Hop: Puerto Rican Culture and Latino Identity.* New York: Columbia University Press, 2000.

Franco, Jean. "Globalization and the Crisis of the Popular." In *Critical Passions: Selected Essays*, edited by Jean Franco, with Mary Louise Pratt and Kathleen Newman, 208–20. Durham: Duke University Press, 1999.

Fujikane, Hiroko. "Approaches to Global Education in the United States, the United Kingdom and Japan." *International Review of Education* 49, nos. 1–2 (2003): 133–52.

Fuss, Diana. *Identification Papers: Readings on Psychoanalysis, Sexuality, and Culture.* New York: Routledge, 1995.

García Canclini, Néstor. "Cultural Reconversion." In *On Edge: The Crisis of Contemporary Latin American Culture*, edited by George Yúdice, Jean Franco, and Juan Flores, 29–43. Minneapolis: University of Minnesota Press, 1992.

———. *Hybrid Cultures: Strategies for Entering and Leaving Modernity.* Translated by C. L. Chippari and S. L. López. Minneapolis: University of Minnesota Press, 1995.

Geertz, Clifford. *The Interpretation of Cultures.* New York: Basic Books, 1973.

Gershon, Ilana. "Reflexivity in Others' Contexts: An Introduction." *Ethnos* 71, no. 4 (2006): 445–52.

Geschiere, Peter, and Francis Nyamnjoh. "Capitalism and Autochthony: The Seesaw of Mobility and Belonging." *Public Culture* 12, no. 2 (2000): 423–52.

Gilroy, Paul. *The Black Atlantic: Modernity and Double Consciousness.* Cambridge: Harvard University Press, 1993.

Gluck, Carol. "The 'End' of the Postwar: Japan at the Turn of the Millennium." *Public Culture* 10, no. 1 (1997): 1–23.

Goodman, Jane E. *Berber Culture on the World Stage: From Village to Video.* Bloomington: Indiana University Press, 2005.

Goodwin, Andrew, and Joe Gore. "World Beat and the Cultural Imperialism Debate." *Socialist Review* 20, no. 3 (1990): 63–80.

Gotkowitz, Laura. "'Under the Dominion of the Indian': Rural Mobilization, the Law, and Revolutionary Nationalism in Bolivia in the 1940s." In *Political Cultures in the Andes 1750–1950*, edited by Nils Jacobsen and Cristóbal Aljovín de Losada, 137–55. Durham: Duke University Press, 2005.

Graburn, Nelson. "Tourism: The Sacred Journey." In *Hosts and Guests: The Anthropology of Tourism*, 2nd ed., edited by Valene L. Smith, 21–36. Philadelphia: University of Pennsylvania Press, 1989.

Graham, Laura R. "Image and Instrumentality in a Xavante Politics of Existential Recognition: The Public Outreach Work of EtÉnhiritipa Pimentel Barbosa." *American Ethnologist* 32, no. 4 (2005): 622–41.

Greenwood, Davydd J. "Culture by the Pound: An Anthropological Perspective on Tourism as Cultural Commoditization." In *Hosts and Guests: The Anthropology of Tourism*, 2nd ed., edited by Valene L. Smith, 171–85. Philadelphia: University of Pennsylvania Press, 1989.

Gupta, Akhil, and James Ferguson. "Discipline and Practice: 'The Field' as Site, Method, and Location in Anthropology." In *Anthropological Locations: Boundaries and Grounds of a Field Science*, edited by Akhil Gupta and James Ferguson, 1–46. Berkeley: University of California Press, 1997.

Guss, David. "The Gran Poder and the Reconquest of La Paz." *Journal of Latin American Anthropology* 11, no. 2 (2006): 294–328.

Gustafson, Bret. "The Paradoxes of Liberal Indigenism: Indigenous Movements, State Processes, and Intercultural Reform in Bolivia." In *The Politics of Ethnicity: Indigenous Peoples in Latin American States*, edited by David Maybury-Lewis, 267–306. Cambridge: Harvard University Press, 2002.

———. "Spectacles of Autonomy and Crisis: Or, What Bulls and Beauty Queens Have to Do with Regionalism in Eastern Bolivia." *Journal of Latin American Anthropology* 11, no. 2 (2006): 351–79.

Hale, Charles R. "Between Che Guevara and the Pachamama: Mestizos, Indians, and Identity Politics in the Anti-quincentenary Campaign." *Critique of Anthropology* 14, no. 1 (1994): 9–39.

———. "Neoliberal Multiculturalism: The Remaking of Cultural Rights and Racial Dominance in Central America." *Political and Legal Anthropology Review* 28, no. 1 (2005): 10–28.

Hall, Stuart. "The West and the Rest: Discourse and Power." In *Race and Racialization: Essential Readings*, edited by Tania Das Gupta, Carl E. James, Rojer C. A. Maaka, Grace-Edward Galabuzi, and Chris Andersen, 56–60. Toronto: Canadian Scholars Press, 2007.

Hamilton, Jennifer A. "Revitalizing Difference in the HapMap: Race and Contemporary Human Genetic Variation Research." *Journal of Law, Medicine, and Ethics* 36, no. 3 (2008): 471–77.

Haraway, Donna J. *Simians, Cyborgs, and Women: The Reinvention of Nature.* New York: Routledge, 1991.

Harden, Jacalyn D. "The Enterprise of Empire: Race, Class, Gender, and Japanese National Identity." *Identities: Global Studies of Culture and Power* 1 nos. 2–3 (1994): 173–99.

Harootunian, Harry. "Lost in the Translation." *Nepantla: Views from South* 3, no. 3 (2002): 539–42.

Harootunian, Harry, and Naoki Sakai. "Dialogue: Japan Studies and Cultural Studies." *Positions: East Asia Cultures Critique* 7, no. 2 (1999): 593–647.

Harris, Olivia. "Ethnic Identity and Market Relations: Indians and Mestizos in the Andes." In *Ethnicity, Markets, and Migration in the Andes: At the Crossroads of History and Anthropology*, edited by Brooke Larson and Olivia Harris, with Enrique Tandeter, 351–90. Durham: Duke University Press, 1995.

Harrison, Faye V. "The Persistent Power of 'Race' in the Cultural and Political Economy of Racism." *Annual Review of Anthropology* 24 (1995): 47–74.

Harrison, Regina. *Signs, Songs, and Memory of the Andes: Translating Quichua Language and Culture.* Austin: University of Texas Press, 1989.

Harvey, David. *The Condition of Postmodernity: An Enquiry into the Origins of Cultural Change.* Oxford: Basil Blackwell, 1989.

Hebdige, Dick. *Subculture: The Meaning of Style*. London: Methuen, 1979.

Herzfeld, Michael. *Anthropology: Theoretical Practice in Culture and Society*. Oxford: Blackwell, 2001.

———. *Anthropology through the Looking Glass: Critical Ethnography in the Margins of Europe*. Cambridge, UK: Cambridge University Press, 1987.

———. *Cultural Intimacy: Social Poetics in the Nation-State*. New York: Routledge, 1997.

Higashide, Seiichi. *Adios to Tears: The Memoirs of a Japanese-Peruvian Internee in U.S. Concentration Camps*. Foreword by C. Harvey Gardiner. Preface by Elsa H. Kudo. Epilogue by Julie Small. Seattle: University of Washington Press, 2000.

Himpele, Jeff D. "The Gran Poder Parade and the Local Movement of the Aymara Middle Class: A Video Essay." *Visual Anthropology* 16 (2003): 207–43.

Hochschild, Arlie Russell. 1983. *The Managed Heart: Commercialization of Human Feeling*. Twentieth anniversary edition with new afterword. Berkeley: University of California Press, 2003.

hooks, bell. *Black Looks: Race and Representation*. Boston: South End Press, 1992.

Hosokawa, Shuhei. "Salsa no tiene fronteras: Orquesta de la Luz and the Globalization of Popular Music." In *Situating Salsa: Global Markets and Local Meanings in Latin Popular Music*, edited by Lise Waxer, 289–311. New York and London: Routledge, 2002.

Howell, David L. *Geographies of Identity in Nineteenth-Century Japan*. Berkeley: University of California Press, 2005.

———. "Making 'Useful Citizens' of Ainu Subjects in Early Twentieth-Century Japan." *Journal of Asian Studies* 63, no. 1 (2004): 5–29.

Hylton, Forrest, and Sinclair Thomson. *Revolutionary Horizons: Past and Present in Bolivian Politics*. London: Verso, 2007.

Inui, Akio. "Why Freeter and NEET Are Misunderstood: Recognizing the New Precarious Conditions of Japanese Youth." *Social Work and Society* 3, no. 2 (2005): 244–51.

Ishihara, Shintaro. *The Japan That Can Say No*. Frank Baldwin, trans. New York: Simon and Schuster, 1991.

Ivy, Marilyn. *Discourses of the Vanishing: Modernity, Phantasm, Japan*. Chicago: University of Chicago Press, 1995.

———. "Mourning the Japanese Thing." In *In Near Ruins: Cultural Theory at the End of the Century*, edited by Nicholas Dirks, 93–111. Minneapolis: University of Minnesota Press, 1998.

Iwabuchi, Koichi. 2002. "Nostalgia for a (Different) Asian Modernity: Media, Consumption of 'Asia' in Japan." *Positions: East Asia Cultures Critique* 10, no. 3 (2002): 547–73.

Jameson, Fredric. *Postmodernism, or, the Cultural Logic of Late Capitalism*. Durham: Duke University Press, 1991.

Jansen, Marius B. *The Making of Modern Japan*. Cambridge: Belknap Press of Harvard University Press, 2000.

Kapchan, Deborah A. "The Promise of Sonic Translation: Performing the Festive Sacred in Morocco." *American Anthropologist* 110, no. 4 (2008): 467–83.

Kelly, William W. "Directions in the Anthropology of Contemporary Japan." *Annual Review of Anthropology* 20 (1991): 395–431.

———, ed. *Fanning the Flames: Fans and Consumer Culture in Contemporary Japan*. Albany: State University of New York Press, 2004.

Kelsky, Karen. *Women on the Verge: Japanese Women, Western Dreams*. Durham: Duke University Press, 2001.

Kingsbury, Henry. *Music, Talent, and Performance: A Conservatory Cultural System*. Philadelphia: Temple University Press, 1988.

Kinsella, Sharon. "Japanese Subculture in the 1990s: Otaku and the Amateur Manga Movement." *Journal of Japanese Studies* 24, no. 2 (1998): 289–316.

Kirshenblatt-Gimblett, Barbara. *Destination Culture: Tourism, Museums, and Heritage*. Berkeley: University of California Press, 1998.

Kondo, Dorinne. *About Face: Performing Race in Fashion and Theater*. New York: Routledge, 1997.

———. *Crafting Selves: Power, Gender, and Discourses of Identity in a Japanese Workplace*. Chicago: University of Chicago Press, 1990.

Kurokawa, Yoko. "Yearning for a Distant Music: Consumption of Hawaiian Music and Dance in Japan." PhD diss., University of Hawai'i, 2004.

Larson, Brooke. "Capturing Indian Bodies, Hearths, and Minds: The Gendered Politics of Rural School Reform in Bolivia, 1920s–1940s." In *Natives Making Nation: Gender, Indigeneity, and the State in the Andes*, edited by Andrew Canessa, 32–59. Tucson: University of Arizona Press, 2005.

———. "Redeemed Indians, Barbarized Cholos: Crafting Neocolonial Modernity in Liberal Bolivia, 1900–1910." In *Political Cultures in the Andes 1750–1950*, edited by Nils Jacobsen and Cristóbal Aljovín de Losada, 230–52. Durham: Duke University Press, 2005.

Lassiter, Luke E. *The Power of Kiowa Song: A Collaborative Ethnography*. Tucson: University of Arizona Press, 1998.

Lazar, Sian. *El Alto: Rebel City*. Durham: Duke University Press, 2008.

Lederman, Rena. "Globalization and the Future of Culture Areas: Melanesianist Anthropology in Transition." *Annual Review of Anthropology* 27 (1998): 427–49.

Lesser, Jeffrey. *A Discontented Diaspora: Japanese Brazilians and the Meanings of Ethnic Militancy, 1960–1980*. Durham: Duke University Press, 2007.

Lewis, Martin W., and Kären E. Wigen. *The Myth of Continents: A Critique of Metageography*. Berkeley: University of California Press, 1997.

Lie, John. *Multiethnic Japan*. Cambridge: Harvard University Press, 2001.

Llórens Amico, José Antonio. *Música popular en Lima: criollos y andinos*. Lima: Instituto de Estudios Peruanos/Instituto Indigenista Interamericano, 1983.

Lonely Planet. *Lonely Planet Japan*, 7th ed. Oakland: Lonely Planet Publications, 2000.

Lott, Eric. *Love and Theft: Blackface Minstrelsy and the American Working Class*. Oxford: Oxford University Press, 1993.

Malinowski, Bronislaw. 1922. *Argonauts of the Western Pacific*. Illinois: Waveland Press, 1984.

Mamani Condori, Carlos B. *Taraqu, 1866–1935: Masacre, guerra y "renovación" en la biografía de Eduardo L. Nina Qhispi.* La Paz: Ediciones Aruwiyiri, 1991.

March, Roger. "The Japanese Travel Life Cycle." *Journal of Travel and Tourism Marketing* 9, nos. 1–2 (2000): 185–200.

Marcus, George E. "Ethnography in/of the World System: The Emergence of Multi-Sited Ethnography." *Annual Review of Anthropology* 24 (1995): 95–117.

Marcus, George E., and Michael M. J. Fischer. *Anthropology as Cultural Critique: An Experimental Moment in the Human Sciences.* Chicago: University of Chicago Press, 1986.

Masden, Kirk. "The Impact of Ministry of Education Policy on Pluralism in Japanese Education: An Examination of Recent Issues." In *Emerging Pluralism in Asia and the Pacific,* edited by David Y. H. Wu, Humphrey McQueen, and Yamamoto Yasushi, 29–63. Hong Kong: Hong Kong Institute of Asia-Pacific Studies/Chinese University of Hong Kong, 1997.

Masterson, Daniel, and Sayaka Funada-Classen. *The Japanese in Latin America.* Urbana: University of Illinois Press, 2004.

Mathews, Gordon. *What Makes Life Worth Living? How Japanese and Americans Make Sense of Their Worlds.* Berkeley: University of California Press, 1996.

Maurer, Bill. *Mutual Life, Limited: Islamic Banking, Alternative Currencies, and Lateral Reason.* Princeton: Princeton University Press, 2005.

McClintock, Anne. *Imperial Leather: Race, Gender and Sexuality in the Colonial Contest.* New York: Routledge, 1995.

McVeigh, Brian J. *Japanese Higher Education as Myth.* Armonk, NY: M.E. Sharpe, 2002.

Medina, Laurie Kroshus. "Commoditizing Culture: Tourism and Maya Identity." *Annals of Tourism Research* 30, no. 2 (2003): 353–68.

Meintjes, Louise. "Paul Simon's Graceland, South Africa, and the Mediation of Musical Meaning." *Ethnomusicology* 34, no. 1 (1990): 37–73.

Meisch, Lynn A. *Andean Entrepreneurs: Otavalo Merchants and Musicians in the Global Arena.* Austin: University of Texas Press, 2002.

Mendoza, Zoila. "Crear y sentir lo nuestro: La Misión Peruana de Arte Incaico y el impulso de la producción artístico-folklórica en Cusco." *Latin American Music Review* 25, no. 1 (2004): 57–77.

Michaels, Walter Benn. "Race into Culture: A Critical Genealogy of Cultural Identity." *Critical Inquiry* 18, no. 4 (1992): 655–85.

Miller, Daniel. "Consumption and Commodities." *Annual Review of Anthropology* 24 (1995): 141–61.

Mirsepassi, Ali, Amrita Basu, and Frederick Weaver, eds. *Localizing Knowledge in a Globalizing World: Recasting the Area Studies Debate.* Syracuse: Syracuse University Press, 2003.

Mitchell, Timothy. "Deterritorialization and the Crisis of Social Science." In *Localizing Knowledge in a Globalizing World: Recasting the Area Studies Debate,* edited by Ali Mirsepassi, Amrita Basu, and Frederick Weaver, 148–70. Syracuse: Syracuse University Press, 2003.

———. "The World as Exhibition." *Comparative Studies in Society and History* 31, no. 2 (1989): 217–36.

Mitsui, Toru. "The Reception of the Music of American Southern Whites in Japan." In *Transforming Tradition: Folk Music Revivals Examined*, edited by Neil V. Rosenberg, 275–93. Chicago: University of Illinois Press, 1993.

Mok, Connie, and Terry Lam. "Travel-Related Behavior of Japanese Leisure Tourists: A Review and Discussion." *Journal of Travel and Tourism Marketing* 9, nos. 1–2 (2000): 171–84.

Monroy Chazarreta, Manuel. "De la protesta a la proyección." In *Historia de la cultura boliviana en el siglo XX: I. La música*, edited by Gabriel Chávez Casazola, 85–112. Sucre: Fundación "La Plata," 2005.

Moreno Cha, Ercilia. "Alternativas del proceso de cambio de un repertorio tradicional argentino." *Latin American Music Review* 8, no. 1 (1987): 94–111.

Morris-Suzuki, Tessa. "Debating Racial Science in Wartime Japan." *Osiris*, 2nd series, 13 (1998): 354–75.

Muratorio, Blanca. "Nación, identidad y etnicidad: Imágenes de los indios ecuatorianos y sus imagineros a fines del siglo XIX." In *Imágenes y imagineros: Representaciones de los indígenas ecuatorianos, Siglos XIX y XX*, edited by Blanca Muratorio, 109–96. Quito: FLACSO-Sede Ecuador, 1994.

Murphy-Shigematsu, Stephen. 2003. "Challenges for Multicultural Education in Japan." *New Horizons for Learning* 9, no. 2 (2003). http://home.blarg.net/~building/strategies/multicultural/murphy-shigematsu.htm.

———. "Identities of Multiethnic People in Japan." In *Japan and Global Migration: Foreign Workers and the Advent of a Multicultural Society*, edited by Mike Douglass and Glenda S. Roberts, 196–216. New York: Routledge, 2000.

Nakane, Chie. "Cultural Anthropology in Japan." *Annual Review of Anthropology* 3 (1974): 57–72.

Narayan, Kirin. "How Native Is a 'Native' Anthropologist?" In *Situated Lives: Gender and Culture in Everyday Life*, edited by Louise Lamphere, Helena Ragoné, and Patricia Zavella, 23–41. New York: Routledge, 1997.

Nathan, John. *Japan Unbound: A Volatile Nation's Quest for Pride and Purpose*. Boston: Houghton Mifflin Company, 2004.

Nelson, Diane. *A Finger in the Wound: Body Politics in Quincentennial Guatemala*. Berkeley: University of California Press, 1999.

Ohnuki-Tierney, Emiko. "A Conceptual Model for the Historical Relationship between the Self and the Internal and External Others: The Agrarian Japanese, the Ainu, and the Special-Status People." In *Making Majorities: Constituting the Nation in Japan, Korea, China, Malaysia, Fiji, Turkey, and the United States*, edited by Dru C. Gladney, 31–51. Stanford: Stanford University Press, 1998.

Olsen, Dale A. *The Chrysanthemum and the Song: Music, Memory, and Identity in the South American Japanese Diaspora*. Gainesville: University Press of Florida, 2004.

Ong, Aihwa. *Flexible Citizenship: The Cultural Logics of Transnationality*. Durham: Duke University Press, 1999.

Ossorio, Pilar, and Troy Duster. "Race and Genetics: Controversies in Biomedical, Behavioral, and Forensic Sciences." *American Psychologist* 60, no. 1 (2005): 115–28.

Palmié, Stephan. "Genomics, Divination, 'Racecraft.'" *American Ethnologist* 34, no. 2 (2007): 205–22.

Patzi Paco, Felix. "Rebelión indígena contra la colonialidad y la transnacionalización de la economía: Triunfos y vicisitudes del movimiento indígena desde 2000 a 2003." In *Ya es otro tiempo el presente: Cuatro momentos de insurgencia indígena*, edited by Forrest Hylton, Felix Patzi, Sergio Serulnikov, and Sinclair Thomson, 199–279. La Paz: Muela del Diablo Editores, 2003.

Platt, Tristan. *Estado boliviano y ayllu andino: Tierra y tributo en el norte de Potosí*. Lima: IEP, 1982.

Poole, Deborah. *Vision, Race, and Modernity: A Visual Economy of the Andean Image World*. Princeton: Princeton University Press, 1997.

Postero, Nancy Grey. "Andean Utopias in Evo Morales's Bolivia." *Latin American and Caribbean Ethnic Studies* 2, no. 1 (2007): 1–28.

———. *Now We Are Citizens: Indigenous Politics in Postmulticultural Bolivia*. Stanford: Stanford University Press, 2006.

Povinelli, Elizabeth A. *The Empire of Love: Toward a Theory of Intimacy, Genealogy, and Carnality*. Durham: Duke University Press, 2006.

Pratt, Mary Louise. "Arts of the Contact Zone." *Profession* 91 (1991): 33–40.

———. "Globalización, desmodernización y el retorno de los monstrous." Lecture given at Tercer Encuentro de Performance y Política, Universidad Católica, Lima, Perú, 2002.

———. "Modernity and Periphery: Toward a Global Relational Analysis." In *Beyond Dichotomies: Histories, Identities, Cultures, and the Challenge of Globalization*, edited by Elisabeth Mudimbe-Boyi, 21–48. Albany: State University of New York Press, 2002.

Radano, Ronald, and Philip V. Bohlman, eds. *Music and the Racial Imagination*. With foreword by Houston A. Baker Jr. Chicago: University of Chicago Press, 2000.

Ramos, Alcida Rita. *Indigenism: Ethnic Politics in Brazil*. Madison: University of Wisconsin Press, 1998.

Rappaport, Joanne. *Intercultural Utopias: Public Intellectuals, Cultural Experimentation, and Ethnic Pluralism in Colombia*. Durham: Duke University Press, 2005.

Ringmar, Erik. "Nationalism: The Idiocy of Intimacy." *British Journal of Sociology* 49, no. 4 (1998): 534–49.

Rios, Fernando. "*La Flûte Indienne*: The Early History of Andean Folkloric-Popular Music in France and Its Impact on *Nueva Canción*." *Latin American Music Review* 29, no. 2 (2008): 145–89.

Rivera Cusicanqui, Silvia. *Oprimidos pero no vencidos: Luchas del campesinado aymara y qhechwa de Bolivia, 1900–1980*. Con prefacio de la autora. La Paz: Aruwiyiri/Yachaywasi, 2003.

———. "La raíz: colonizadores y colonizados." In *Violencias encubiertas en Bolivia I*, edited by Xavier Albó and Raúl Barrios, 27–139. La Paz: CIPCA/ Aruwiyiri, 1993.

Roberts, Martin. "'World Music' and the Global Cultural Economy." *Diaspora* 2, no. 2 (1992): 229–42.

Robertson, Jennifer. "Biopower: Blood, Kinship, and Eugenic Marriage." In *A Companion to the Anthropology of Japan*, edited by Jennifer Robertson, 329–54. Oxford: Blackwell, 2005.

———. *Takarazuka: Sexual Politics and Popular Culture in Modern Japan*. Berkeley: University of California Press, 1998.

Rodríguez Ostria, Gustavo. *Sin tiempo para las palabras: Teoponte, la otra guerrilla guevarista en Bolivia*. Cochabamba: Editorial Kipus, 2006.

Rosaldo, Renato. *Culture and Truth: The Remaking of Social Analysis*. Boston: Beacon Press, 1989.

Roth, Joshua Hotaka. *Brokered Homeland: Japanese Brazilian Migrants in Japan*. Ithaca, NY: Cornell University Press, 2002.

———. "Responsibility and the Limits of Identification: Fieldwork among Japanese and Japanese Brazilian Workers in Japan." In *Doing Fieldwork in Japan*, edited by Theodore C. Bestor, Patricia G. Steinhoff, and Victoria Lyon Bestor, 335–51. Honolulu: University of Hawai'i Press, 2003.

Russell, John. "Race and Reflexivity: The Black Other in Contemporary Japanese Mass Culture." *Cultural Anthropology* 6, no. 1 (1991): 3–25.

Said, Edward. *Orientalism*. New York: Pantheon, 1978.

Salmón, Josefa. *El espejo indígena: El discurso indigenista en Bolivia 1900–1956*. La Paz: Plural Editores/UMSA, 1997.

Sánchez Patzy, Mauricio. "La música popular en Bolivia desde mediados del siglo XX y la identidad social." In *La música en Bolivia: De la prehistoria a la actualidad*, edited by C. Wálter Sánchez, 269–307. Cochabamba: Fundación Simón I. Patiño, 2002.

Sanjek, Rojer. "The Enduring Inequalities of Race." In *Race*, edited by Steven Gregory and Roger Sanjek, 1–17. New Brunswick, NJ: Rutgers University Press, 1994.

Sanjinés, Javier. "Mestizaje Upside Down: Subaltern Knowledges and the Known." *Nepantla: Views from South* 3, no. 1 (2002): 39–60.

Sassen, Saskia. *Globalization and Its Discontents: Essays on the Mobility of People and Money*. New York: The New Press, 1998.

Savigliano, Marta E. *Tango and the Political Economy of Passion*. Boulder: Westview Press, 1995.

———. "Tango in Japan and the World Economy of Passion." In *Re-Made in Japan: Everyday Life and Consumer Taste in a Changing Society*, edited by Joseph J. Tobin, 235–52. New Haven: Yale University Press, 1992.

Schein, Louisa. "Importing Miao Brethren to Hmong America: A Not-So-Stateless Transnationalism." In *Cosmopolitics: Thinking and Feeling beyond the Nation*, edited by Pheng Cheah and Bruce Robbins, 163–91. Minneapolis: University of Minnesota Press, 1998.

Seeger, Anthony. *Why Suyá Sing: A Musical Anthropology of an Amazonian People.* Cambridge, UK: Cambridge University Press, 1987.

Shaw, Carolyn Martin. "Telling Stories of Human Connection: Comments on Stephan Palmié's Genomics, Divination, 'Racecraft.'" *American Ethnologist* 34, no. 2 (2007): 236–37.

Shryock, Andrew. "Other Conscious/Self Aware: First Thoughts on Cultural Intimacy and Mass Mediation." In *Off Stage/On Display: Intimacy and Ethnography in the Age of Public Culture*, edited by Andrew Shryock, 3–28. Stanford: Stanford University Press, 2004.

Siddle, Richard. "The Ainu and the Discourse of 'Race.'" In *The Construction of Racial Identities in China and Japan: Historical and Contemporary Perspectives*, edited by Frank Dikötter, 136–57. London: Hurst and Company, 1997.

Simmel, Georg. *On Individuality and Social Forms: Selected Writings.* Edited by Donald N. Levine. Chicago: University of Chicago Press, 1971.

———. *The Philosophy of Money.* Edited by David Frisby. Translated by Tom Bottomore and David Frisby. London and New York: Routledge, 1990.

Smith, Valene L., ed. *Hosts and Guests: The Anthropology of Tourism*, 2nd ed. Philadelphia: University of Pennsylvania Press, 1989.

Sofue, Takao. "Anthropology in Japan: Historical Review and Modern Trends." *Biennial Review of Anthropology* 2 (1961): 173–214.

Spedding, Alison L. "Cocataki, Taki-Coca: Trade, Traffic, and Organized Peasant Resistance in the Yungas of La Paz." In *Coca, Cocaine, and the Bolivian Reality*, edited by Madeline Barbara Léons and Harry Sanabria, 117–37. Albany: State University of New York Press, 1997.

Spivak, Gayatri Chakravorty. "Subaltern Studies: Deconstructing Historiography." In *Selected Subaltern Studies*, edited by Ranajit Guha and Gayatri C. Spivak, 3–32. Oxford: Oxford University Press, 1988.

Stanley, Nick. *Being Ourselves for You: The Global Display of Cultures.* London: Middlesex University Press, 1998.

Starn, Orin. "Missing the Revolution: Anthropologists and the War in Peru." *Cultural Anthropology* 6 (1991): 63–91.

———. *Nightwatch: The Politics of Protest in the Andes.* Durham: Duke University Press, 1999.

Steinhardt, Arnold. *Violin Dreams.* Boston: Houghton Mifflin Company, 2006.

Stepan, Nancy Leys. *"The Hour of Eugenics": Race, Gender, and Nation in Latin America.* Ithaca, NY: Cornell University Press, 1991.

Stephen, Lynn. *Transborder Lives: Indigenous Oaxacans in Mexico, California, and Oregon.* Durham: Duke University Press, 2007.

Stephenson, Marcia. *Gender and Modernity in Andean Bolivia.* Austin: University of Texas Press, 1999.

Sterling, Marvin D. "The Symbolic Constitution of Japanese Dancehall." *Social and Economic Studies* 55, nos. 1–2 (2006): 1–24.

Stern, Steve J. "The Tragedy of Success." In *The Peru Reader: History, Culture, Politics*, edited by Orin Starn, Carlos Iván Degregori, and Robin Kirk, 112–36. Durham: Duke University Press, 1995.

Stevens, Carolyn S. "Buying Intimacy: Proximity and Exchange at a Japanese Rock Concert." In *Fanning the Flames: Fans and Consumer Culture in Contemporary Japan,* edited by William W. Kelly, 59–77. Albany: State University of New York Press, 2004.

Stobart, Henry. *Music and the Poetics of Production in the Bolivian Andes.* Hants, UK: Ashgate, 2006.

Stoler, Ann Laura. "Imperial Debris: Reflections on Ruins and Ruination." *Cultural Anthropology* 23, no. 2 (2008): 191–219.

———. *Race and the Education of Desire: Foucault's* History of Sexuality *and the Colonial Order of Things.* Durham: Duke University Press, 1995.

Strathern, Marilyn. *Property, Substance, and Effect: Anthropological Essays on Persons and Things.* London: Athlone Press, 1999.

Stronza, Amanda. "Anthropology of Tourism: Forging New Ground for Ecotourism and Other Alternatives." *Annual Review of Anthropology* 30 (2001): 261–83.

Suzuki, Taku. "Becoming 'Japanese' in Bolivia: Okinawan-Bolivian Trans-(national) Formations in Colonia Okinawa." *Identities: Global Studies in Culture and Power* 13 (2006): 455–81.

———. "Viewing Nations, Narrating Hybridity: Okinawan Diasporic Subjectivity and Japanese Satellite Telecasts in Colonia Okinawa, Bolivia." *Diaspora: A Journal of Transnational Studies* 14, no. 1 (2005): 75–107.

Tai, Eika. "Multicultural Education in Japan." *Japan Focus* (2007), online journal: ID# 2618.

TallBear, Kim. "Narratives of Race and Indigeneity in the Genographic Project." *Journal of Law, Medicine, and Ethics* 35, no. 3 (2007): 412–24.

Tamanoi, Mariko Asano. "Women's Voices: Their Critique of the Anthropology of Japan." *Annual Review of Anthropology* 19 (1990): 17–37.

Tanaka, Stefan. *Japan's Orient: Rendering Pasts into History.* Berkeley: University of California Press, 1993.

Taylor, Diana. *The Archive and the Repertoire: Performing Cultural Memory in the Americas.* Durham: Duke University Press, 2003.

Tedlock, Barbara. "Ethnography and Ethnographic Representation." In *Handbook of Qualitative Research,* 2nd ed., edited by Norman K. Denzin and Yvonna S. Lincoln, 455–86. Thousand Oaks, CA: Sage Publications, 2000.

Thomas, Nicholas. "Against Ethnography." *Cultural Anthropology* 6, no. 3 (1991): 306–22.

Thomson, Sinclair. *We Alone Will Rule: Native Andean Politics in the Age of Insurgency.* Madison: University of Wisconsin Press, 2002.

Tobin, Joseph J., ed. *Re-Made in Japan: Everyday Life and Consumer Taste in a Changing Society.* New Haven: Yale University Press, 1992.

Torgovnick, Marianna. *Gone Primitive: Savage Intellects, Modern Lives.* Chicago: University of Chicago Press, 1990.

Torres, Norberto Benjamín. *Mauro Nuñez para el mundo.* Sucre: Editorial "Tupac Katari," 2006.

Tsing, Anna Lowenhaupt. *Friction: An Ethnography of Global Connection*. Princeton: Princeton University Press, 2005.

———. "Indigenous Voice." In *Indigenous Experience Today*, edited by Marisol de la Cadena and Orin Starn, 33–67. Oxford: Berg, 2007.

Turino, Thomas. *Moving Away from Silence: Music of the Peruvian Altiplano and the Experience of Urban Migration*. Chicago: University of Chicago Press, 1993.

———. *Nationalists, Cosmopolitans, and Popular Music in Zimbabwe*. Chicago: University of Chicago Press, 2000.

Turner, Terence. "The Social Dynamics of Video Media in an Indigenous Society: The Cultural Meaning and the Personal Politics of Video-making in Kayapó Communities." *Visual Anthropology Review* 7, no. 2 (1991): 68–76.

Urry, John. *The Tourist Gaze: Leisure and Travel in Contemporary Societies*. London: Sage Publications, 1990.

Visweswaran, Kamala. "Race and the Culture of Anthropology." *American Anthropologist* 100, no. 1 (1998): 70–83.

Wade, Peter. *Music, Race, and Nation: Música Tropical in Colombia*. Chicago: University of Chicago Press, 2000.

———. *Race and Ethnicity in Latin America*. London: Pluto Press, 1997.

———. " 'Race,' Nature and Culture," *Man* 28, no. 1 (1993): 17–34.

———. "Working Culture: Making Cultural Identities in Cali, Colombia." *Current Anthropology* 40, no. 4 (1999): 449–71.

Warner, Michael. "Publics and Counterpublics." *Public Culture* 14, no. 1 (2002): 49–90.

Weiner, Michael. "The Invention of Identity: Race and Nation in Pre-War Japan." In *The Construction of Racial Identities in China and Japan: Historical and Contemporary Perspectives*, edited by Frank Dikötter, 96–117. London: Hurst and Company, 1997.

Weismantel, Mary. *Cholas and Pishtacos: Stories of Race and Sex in the Andes*. Foreword by Catherine R. Stimpson. Chicago: University of Chicago Press, 2001.

Williams, Sean. "Irish Music and the Experience of Nostalgia in Japan." *Asian Music* 37, no. 1 (2006): 101–19.

Wolf, Eric. "Perilous Ideas: Race, Culture, People." *Current Anthropology* 35, no. 1 (1994): 1–12.

Wood, Joe. "The Yellow Negro." In *Giant Steps: The New Generation of African American Writers*, edited by Kevin Young, 310–33. New York: Perennial, 2000.

Yano, Christine R. "Letters from the Heart: Negotiating Fan-Star Relationships in Japanese Popular Music." In *Fanning the Flames: Fans and Consumer Culture in Contemporary Japan*, edited by William W. Kelly, 41–58. Albany: State University of New York Press, 2004.

———. *Tears of Longing: Nostalgia and the Nation in Japanese Popular Song*. Cambridge: Harvard University Asia Center and Harvard University Press, 2002.

Yoneyama, Lisa. *Hiroshima Traces: Time, Space, and the Dialectics of Memory*. Berkeley: University of California Press, 1999.

Yoshino, Kosaku. "Culturalism, Racialism, and Internationalism in the Discourse on Japanese Identity." In *Making Majorities: Constituting the Nation in Japan, Korea, China, Malaysia, Fiji, Turkey, and the United States*, edited by Dru C. Gladney, 13–30. Stanford: Stanford University Press, 1998.

———. "Discourse on Blood and Racial Identity in Contemporary Japan." In *The Construction of Racial Identities in China and Japan: Historical and Contemporary Perspectives*, edited by F. Dikötter, 199–211. London: Hurst and Company, 1997.

Young, Robert J. C. *Colonial Desire: Hybridity in Theory, Culture and Race*. London and New York: Routledge, 1995.

Zorn, Elayne. "From Political Prison to Tourist Village: Tourism, Gender, Indigeneity, and the State on Taquile Island, Peru." In *Natives Making Nation: Gender, Indigeneity, and the State in the Andes*, edited by Andrew Canessa, 156–80. Tucson: University of Arizona Press, 2005.

———. *Weaving a Future: Tourism, Cloth and Culture on an Andean Island*. Iowa City: University of Iowa Press, 2004.

Recordings

Caballeros del Folklore, Los. 1973. *Memories of the Tour around the World to Japan, USA, and Latin American Countries*. N.p.: No label of production listed, 1998.

Cavour, Ernesto. 1972, 1975, and 1977. *Ernesto Cavour: "De Colección."* La Paz: Discolandia, 1993.

Grupo Aymara. *Live in Japan*. Japan: Disco Amigo, 1995.

Jairas, Los. 1969 and 1974. *Lo Mejor de Los Jairas: "De Colección."* La Paz: Discolandia, 1993.

Kallawaya. *Shaman*. Bath, UK: Tumi (Music), 2001.

Khantati. *Charla del Viento*. La Paz: Lauro Records, 2002.

Luz del Ande. *Suite ecológico ser*. La Paz: Eponeo Records, 1998.

Música de Maestros. *Septeto Mayor de Música de Maestros*. La Paz: Roli Producciones, 2003.

———. *Sexteto Mayor de Música de Maestros*. La Paz: Roli Producciones, 2001.

———. *Volumen I y II*. La Paz: Roli Producciones (re-release), 1996.

———. *Volumen VI. Supay*. La Paz: Roli Producciones, 1999.

———. *Volumen XI. Surimana*. La Paz. Roli Producciones, 2006.

Piazzolla, Astor, y su quinteto tango nuevo. 1984. *The Vienna Concert*. Frankfurt: Messidor, 1991.

Portillo, David, and Daiji Fukuda. *Para no caer al cielo*. La Paz: Serpiente Alada Producciones, 2002.

Segi, Takamasa. *Forest Rain*. Sapporo: Polystar, 1998.

———. *Luna*. Tokyo: Polystar, 1997.

———. *Nieve*. Tokyo: Polystar, 1996.

————. *Silencio*. Sapporo: Polystar, 1999.
————. *Songs of the Wind*. Tokyo: Polystar, 2000.
————. *Tree of Life*. Tokyo Polystar, 2002.
————. *Una zampoña para el mundo*. La Paz: Discolandia, 1990.
Simon, Paul, and Art Garfunkel. *Simon and Garfunkel's Greatest Hits*. New York: Columbia CBS, 1972.

Interviews
All interviews conducted by Michelle Bigenho.

Abe, Hisao. La Paz, Bolivia. June 2003.
Akimoto, Hiroyuki. La Paz, Bolivia. June 2003.
Aldana, Favio. La Paz, Bolivia. June 2004.
Arias, Gerardo. La Paz, Bolivia. June 2004.
Benavides, Virginia. La Paz, Bolivia. July 2007.
Bustillo, Edgar. La Paz, Bolivia. June 2003.
Cámara, Alejandro. Cochabamba, Bolivia. June 2004.
Castro, Oscar. La Paz, Bolivia. June 2004.
Cavour, Ernesto. La Paz, Bolivia. May 2003 and June 2004.
Cavour, Ernesto, with Rolando Encinas. La Paz, Bolivia. August 2007.
Cordero, Juan Carlos. La Paz, Bolivia. June 2003.
Daza, Carlos. La Paz, Bolivia. May 2003.
Encinas, Yuliano. On ferry to Okinawa, Japan. November 2002.
Espinoza, Donato. La Paz, Bolivia. June 2003.
Fukuda, Daiji. La Paz, Bolivia. June 2003.
Fukuda, Kyotaro. La Paz, Bolivia. May 2003.
Gironda, Victor Hugo. Osaka, Japan. October 2002.
Guillén, Luis. La Paz, Bolivia. June 2003.
Gutiérrez, Efraín. Tokyo, Japan. August 2003.
Hamada, Jiro, with Takaatsu Kinoshita and Koji Hishimoto present. Tokyo, Japan. August 2003.
Hashimoto, Hitoshi, with Koji Hishimoto translating Japanese into Spanish. Tokyo, Japan. August 2003.
Hirayama, Masato, and Los Borrachos (Katsuji Kobayashi, Yoko Fukuyo, Tomo-kazu Kawahira, Ryuta Mori, and Hirota Hisaki), with Mariko Kobayashi translating Japanese into English. Tokyo, Japan. August 2003.
Hishimoto, Koji. Prefecture Okeyama, City of Cuse, Japan. November 2002.
Inazawa, Kenichi. La Paz, Bolivia. May 2003.
Ito, Suyoku, with David Mareño, Tsuya Noguchi, Miguel Angel Tórres Súarez, and Yasuko Condo. Nara, Japan. August 2003.
Jiménez, Fernando. La Paz, Bolivia. June 2004.
Kaiya, Yoshihiro. Tokyo, Japan. August 2003.
Kawamoto, Ernesto, and Shizue Shimada. Tokyo, Japan. July 2003.

Kinoshita, Takaatsu. Tokyo, Japan. July 2003.

Kokobun, Yoko, and Genzo Otsuka. Tokyo, Japan. July 2003.

Kusanagi, Toyo, and María Luisa Kusanagi. Tokyo, Japan. July 2003.

Los Vientos: Yanagi, Kazuo; Miyamoto, Mariko; Shibata, Keiichi; Nohara, Hiro-
    fumi; Tsuchiya, Masayuki. Tokyo, Japan. August 2003.

Magne, Javier. La Paz, Bolivia. June 2003.

Mamani, Zenobia. Tokyo, Japan. August 2003.

Mimura, Hidejiro. Tokyo, Japan. August 2003.

Miyahara, Hiroaki. La Paz, Bolivia. June 2004.

Molina, Jorge, and Reynaldo Peñarrieta. La Paz, Bolivia. June 2004.

Molina, Wilson. La Paz, Bolivia. June 2003.

Monroy Chazarreta, Manuel. La Paz, Bolivia. June 2004.

Nishida, Makoto. Kyoto, Japan. August 2003.

Nishiyama, Kenji, Kayoko, and Niki, with Koji Hishimoto translating Japanese
    into Spanish. Tokyo, Japan. August 2003.

Nishiyama, Rica. Tokyo, Japan. August 2003.

Noda Masao, René, and Edgar Patiño. La Paz, Bolivia. June 2003.

Okada, Hiroyasu, with Masato Condo, Hisashi Maeda, and Yasuhisu Yumi. Nara,
    Japan. August 2003.

Orosco, Clarken. La Paz, Bolivia. June 2004.

Osada, Takeshi. Gamagori, Japan. August 2003.

Pantoja, Edwing. On ferry to Okinawa, Japan. November 2002.

Paredes, Julio César. La Paz, Bolivia. June 2004.

Peña, Marcelo. La Paz, Bolivia. June 2003.

Ponce, Carlos. La Paz, Bolivia. June 2004.

Ponce, Hernán. La Paz, Bolivia. June 2004.

Porco Herrera, Rubén (director of Grupo Norte Potosí). La Paz, Bolivia. June
    2004.

Rokusawa, Takako. Tokyo, Japan. August 2003.

Salas, Gilka. La Paz, Bolivia. August 2005.

Sartor, Luis. Tokyo, Japan. August 2003.

Segi, Takamasa. Tokyo, Japan. August 2003.

Severich, Luis Carlos. Tokyo, Japan. July 2003.

Shishido, Makoto. Cochabamba, Bolivia. June 2004.

Sugiyama, Takashi. La Paz, Bolivia. June 2004.

Taller de Cueca, Zenobia Mamani translating Japanese into Spanish, with twelve
    Japanese students of Bolivian cueca dance. Tokyo, Japan. August 2003.

Torrico, Fernando. Hamamatsu, Japan. August 2003.

Vega, Reynaldo. La Paz, Bolivia. June 2004.

Villanueva, Adrian. La Paz, Bolivia. July 2007.

Villarroel, Edgar. El Alto, Bolivia. June 2004.

Yanagawa, Ken, and Miho, with Zenobia Mamani translating Japanese into
    Spanish. Tokyo, Japan. August 2003.

Index

Note: page numbers in *italics* refer to illustrations; those followed by "n" indicate endnotes.

Michelle Bigenho is associate professor of anthropology
in the School of Critical Social Inquiry at Hampshire College.

Library of Congress Cataloging-in-Publication Data

Bigenho, Michelle
Intimate distance : Andean music in Japan /
Michelle Bigenho.
p. cm.
Includes bibliographical references and index.
ISBN 978-0-8223-5220-4 (cloth : alk. paper)
ISBN 978-0-8223-5235-8 (pbk. : alk. paper)
1. Bolivians—Japan—Music—History and criticism.
2. Bolivians—Music—History and criticism.
3. Ethnomusicology—Bolivia—History and criticism.
I. Title.
ML239.B6B54 2012
781.62'6884052—dc23   2011041896